THE GRIM SLEEPER

TALKING WITH AMERICA'S MOST NOTORIOUS SERIAL KILLER, LONNIE FRANKLIN

VICTORIA REDSTALL

JOHN BLAKE

Published by John Blake Publishing,
2.25, The Plaza,
535 Kings Road,
Chelsea Harbour
London, SW10 0SZ

www.johnblakebooks.com

www.facebook.com/johnblakebooks 🄵
twitter.com/jblakebooks 🄴

First published in paperback in 2018

ISBN: 978 1 78606 866 8

British Library Cataloguing-in-Publication Data:

A catalogue record for this book is available from the British Library.

Design by www.envydesign.co.uk

Printed and bound in Great Britain by Clays Ltd, Elcograf S.p.A.

1 3 5 7 9 10 8 6 4 2

Papers used by John Blake Publishing are natural, recyclable products made from
wood grown in sustainable forests. The manufacturing processes conform to the
environmental regulations of the country of origin.

Every attempt has been made to contact the relevant copyright-holders, but some
were unobtainable. We would be grateful if the appropriate people could contact us.

John Blake Publishing is an imprint of Bonnier Publishing
www.bonnierpublishing.com

ACKNOWLEDGEMENTS

I would like to thank so many of my friends in the Los Angeles County Sheriff's Department, who have helped and supported me over the years, throughout my career, which also includes the writing of this book and giving me extra time in the jail to conduct my interviews.

I would also like to give a huge thank you to Homicide Detective Cliff Shepard, who gave me so much insight into how they caught The Grim Sleeper, along with Detective Dennis Kilcoyne and Detective Paul Coulter. Without these dedicated individuals' hard work, The Grim Sleeper would still be killing today.

I would also like to thank my father, John Redstall, who came with me on a number of the interviews I had with Lonnie David Franklin Jr at the Men's Central Jail in Los Angeles.

CONTENTS

PROLOGUE

I undertook to write about the then alleged Grim Sleeper using the very words from the man himself who stood accused – Lonnie David Franklin Jr. This does not mean that all he said is true, I am simply repeating and often transcribing what he said to me. After the initial trial ended on 5 May 2016 and before the final trial, known as the Penalty Phase, got underway, I was told by two detectives that some of what Franklin told me in instances regarding his relationships (or lack of them) with women was embellishment. I trust their word over an accused serial killer any day.

Unlike most authors who write books on serial killers, I go straight to the horse's mouth to get the full story. Most authors often gather research for their books from outside sources but not their main subject. This is due to not being able to gain access to the jail and/or gain any communication with the accused. I, however, have been fortunate to be able to gain access to many killers and alleged killers with my contacts in law enforcement, and have done my best to make sure that the subject responds to me. Therefore I am able to bring the reader a more personal picture of the subjects themselves. This has been the cause of a great deal of resentment and jealousy from those unable to gain exclusivity with the subjects themselves, and I have had writers accuse me of 'befriending serial killers'. I do not 'befriend' any kind of killer, nor would I. Simply put, my analogy is this: I am a cook/home chef. When I make a beef casserole, I start with the beef before adding the stock, spices, vegetables, etc. However, if I didn't start cooking with the beef from the outset, I wouldn't make a 'beef' casserole: the beef is the main part of the dish; everything else is added afterwards. Hence the serial killer is the main focus of this book, and afterwards I will go to the trial and interview other inside sources pertinent to the case to build an even bigger picture and complete a full book.

This book is my journey into the mind of Lonnie David Franklin Jr from his own words. I gathered my information through weekly extensive jail interviews with him sitting across from me, face to face, with only a piece of Plexiglas between us. There was also written correspondence between us and regular phone calls throughout the years after his arrest in July 2010. I have transcribed some of these phone calls and visits I had, for a number of hours every week, with Franklin over the years since his arrest.

Franklin has given me exclusive rights to tell his story from his own words. He has not spoken to anyone else besides me outside of his family members since his arrest. He is allowed only two visits per week; I interviewed him every Thursday and his wife Sylvia and other family members visited him

PROLOGUE

every Saturday. Franklin never said to me whether he was guilty or innocent of the crimes of which he stands accused. Rarely do serial killers admit guilt before they go to trial. In fact, most of them proclaim their innocence. However, because we covered so much of his innermost life and in such great detail, I felt it necessary to write this book using these interviews, along with his upcoming trial.

This book is simply his life, from what he said to me in his own words, verbatim. Here, I will lead you to understanding the reason why he committed these heinous crimes. I will explain in depth, from his own words, his life as a child and the excessive ridicule he received from his peers and his older brother, Christopher, together with his environment and upbringing.

The victims of these odious crimes had families and friends who loved them, yet their young lives were so tragically wiped out by this monster, who believed he could play God. The Grim Sleeper destroyed the lives of multitudes of families for his own selfish satisfaction, however his victims will never be forgotten.

THE ARREST AND MURDERS

LONNIE DAVID FRANKLIN JR
DOB: 08.30.1952
Booking No: #2394548

At 9.20 a.m. on Wednesday, 7 July 2010, police visited a home at 1722 W 81st Street, South Los Angeles, 90047, where a 57-year-old African-American, LAPD mechanic Lonnie David Franklin Jr, lived. They arrested him on suspicion of multiple murders.

At the time I wrote this section, Franklin had been held in jail for almost four years and charged with some of the worst crimes in the United States. His DNA had been linked to ten victims and some say he brutally murdered dozens more. When he was convicted, he was thought to have been the longest-operating serial killer in Los Angeles history.

To give you a little history on what was going on at LAPD in the eighties regarding DNA... At that time, we didn't even know what DNA was. All we could test for was ABO (blood typing). If we had a biological sample of something (spit, sperm, etc), we *might* be able to determine the blood type of the donor. About 80 per cent of the population secretes their blood with their other bodily fluids. That is good to include someone or exclude someone as a donor to a sample. However, it is not specific. But in the eighties that was all we had. If we developed a person as a possible suspect, we could collect a blood sample and see if it was a match. So the first six victims, Debra Jackson, Henrietta Wright, Barbara Ware, Bernita Sparks, Mary Lowe and Alicia Alexander, were murdered between 1985 and 1988. By the third victim, homicide detectives from 77th, Newton and RHD (Robbery Homicide Division) knew that they had a serial murderer working, because of bullet comparisons. Those from Debra Jackson, Henrietta Wright and Barbara Ware were shot with the same gun. RHD detectives assumed the responsibility for those murders and the continuing investigation. Much of it was done by Detectives Bill Gailey and Rich Haro. Any murder of a woman whose body was left in an alley, dumpster, street, etc, they looked at. Now, most of the victims had a problem with cocaine so, as you can imagine, the killer had no problem luring them into his car, then doing what he wanted.

When Enietra Washington was shot and dumped, she provided a description of the attacker and his car

THE ARREST AND MURDERS

AND a location where she was taken. A great deal of manpower was put into this. Stakeouts, vehicle stops, etc. But our guy was not identified.

Then the murders seemed to have stopped. The aforementioned murders stopped receiving attention. In November 2001, the LAPD started a Cold Case Unit, thanks in large part to Detective David Lambkin.

There were six detectives, plus Dave Lambkin, who was the OIC [Officer In Charge]. We reviewed hundreds, if not thousands, of murders. DNA and the DNA database were new to us. We had to learn what we could do with it, and what we needed. When reviewing the cases, about 6,000 unsolved murders between 1960 and 1997, we were looking for those cases that could have biological evidence. It took time. Our first big success was with Chester Turner (ten adult victims and a foetus). With that, the Captain of RHD asked if we had any other serial cases that we could look at. I told him we would check.

I was aware of a few cases – the aforementioned was one series. I went through them, looking for those that had biological evidence that was still in our evidence room. Of course, we had incompetent detectives who looked at these cases over the years, and even though the detectives were not officially responsible for them, they had the evidence destroyed. In 2004 I requested the evidence in the Barbara Ware, Bernita Sparks and Mary Lowe cases to be examined. That led to a match with a 2003 murder, victim Valerie McCorvey, then to Princess Berthomieux. It wasn't until April 2007 when we were notified of a match to Janecia Peters that the Task Force was started.

Homicide Detective Cliff Shepard

The first murder committed by Lonnie David Franklin Jr was during the height of the crack epidemic in Los Angeles in the 1980s. His first known victim was an African-American woman named Debra Jackson, who was twenty-nine at the time. According to the TV show *America's Most Wanted*, she was last seen alive when she had left her friend's apartment in Lynwood and was walking to the bus stop when she disappeared. On 10 August 1985, Debra was found dead, in an advanced state of decomposition, fully clothed and under an old carpet, in an alleyway in the West Gage Avenue/South Vermont Avenue (1000) block, LA. She had been sexually assaulted, then shot three times in the chest with a .25 calibre handgun. Bullets were recovered from her body, DNA swabs were taken and an attempt was made to match this trace evidence with a profile in California's DNA profile database. The DNA results were only able to prove her blood type.

Almost a year to the day later, Henrietta Wright, thirty-five, was found dead on 12 August 1986, in the 2500 block of West Vernon Avenue, LA – only a few miles away from where Debra Jackson's body had been dumped. Henrietta had been shot twice in the chest, wrapped in a blanket, covered by a mattress, and a man's long-sleeved shirt was stuffed in her mouth. Like the previous victim, she was fully clothed, with the exception of her shoes, and ballistic tests proved the murder weapon to be the same as the one used to snuff out the life of her predecessor. When I questioned investigator Cliff Shepard about this victim, he was eager to tell me more.

> Strangely enough, most of the evidence collected was authorised to be destroyed by senior homicide detectives from the 77th Division. What is most surprising was RHD had the investigative responsibility, not 77th Division. Why did they do this? Why they didn't look at their control books to see what the status of the case was, I don't know. Fortunately, they didn't destroy the bullets.
>
> Cliff Shepard

Once again, DNA swabs were taken and sent off for comparison, returning from the database negative, but a positive match to the previous killing.

Only days later, on 14 August 1986, Thomas Steele, thirty-six, was found shot dead in the middle of the intersection of 71st Street and Halldale Avenue. This man was originally thought to be one of the victims of The Grim Sleeper, however, it was later found he was murdered during a robbery by an unknown assailant.

The corpse of Barbara Ware, twenty-three, was found, covered in trash, on 10 January 1987, in the 1300 block of East 56th Street, LA. Cause of death was a single .25 calibre bullet discharged into the chest. She was fully clothed, with a plastic bag draped over her upper torso and head. DNA comparison at the lab proved negative for a match with a known offender, but again bodily fluids matched the previous cases – the killer of all of these women was the same man.

A 911 tape from an 'anonymous' caller was also collected for evidence.

Twenty-three-year-old Bernita Sparks had gone out to buy some cigarettes and never returned. She was found the following day, on 16 April 1987, again in a dumpster and in an alleyway – this time in the 9400 block of South Western Avenue, LA. A single .25 calibre bullet to her chest had brought her life to a premature end. However, it was determined that she had been beaten and also strangled beforehand. She had trash dumped all over her. Once again it was the same old story with regard to DNA; the lab came back with a 'no-match', yet DNA proved it was the same offender – a serial killer was on the loose.

Mary Lowe was an African-American, happy 26-year-old who loved to party. On 31 October 1987, she told her mother, Betty, she was going to a Halloween party at the Love Trap Bar. It was pouring down with rain and Betty tried to dissuade her from venturing out. Shortly thereafter, Mary was seen climbing into a rust/orange coloured Ford Pinto car, which appeared to have been driven by a young, black male. Mary's body was found in an alleyway on Western Avenue on 1 November. She had been shot dead and her body dumped just as if it was garbage. The DNA and ballistic evidence still exists.

Lachrica Jefferson, twenty-two, was found shot dead on 30 January 1988. A mattress covered her fully-clothed body in the 2000 block of West 1022nd Street, in Lennox, LA. A napkin with 'AIDS' written on it had been placed over her face. Two .25 calibre bullets were recovered; there was no DNA match on record, but bodily fluids confirmed our serial killer had struck again.

Alicia 'Monique' Alexander was just eighteen. Her body, like all of the previous victims, was found in an alleyway, on 11 September 1988. The location: the 1700 block of West 43rd Street and Western Avenue. There was a single .25 calibre gunshot to the chest. She was naked and covered by a mattress. There is no DNA evidence to connect her to the other victims, however the ballistic evidence still exists.

All of these young women had been sexually assaulted. Most had been shot with a .25 calibre handgun, and all were dumped, as if they were garbage, in alleyways within close proximity to each other. All of these victims were young African-American females and were out on the streets due to having their share of problems, usually drugs-related. Irrespective of whether they had drug addictions and/or other forms of dangerous and high-risk lifestyles, they had all been unwillingly taken from the streets, mostly after accepting a ride from a stranger. Each and every one of these women had families who loved them, and these people will continue to feel the pain of their loss until the day when they can join their loved ones in heaven.

A serial killer profiler might have deduced that the killer had a vendetta against the type of women who engage in high-risk activities or who might have mouthed off to him or been feisty. There were some prostitutes that The Grim Sleeper was nice to and didn't kill, but others met their fate at the hands of this monster. This is echoed in his past murderous behaviour when he would leave his victims so cold-bloodedly, disposing them like garbage and placing them in and around garbage. He would use and abuse these young women for whatever he could, then callously kill and discard them as if they were trash. It was as simple as that.

After a short while, he then struck again.

On 20 November 1988 Enietra Washington (age unknown) was attacked in South Los Angeles by a black man, aged around thirty, driving an orange Ford Pinto. She was on her way to a party when she was stopped by, according to her eyewitness testimony, a well-dressed African-American man wearing a lot of 'bling' and driving a rather snazzy-looking car. It had been decked out with white racing stripes, making it look almost like a toy car.

The man asked Enietra if she wanted him to give her a ride to the party. At first she rebuffed him in a playful way, yet she was still intrigued by him and his car and he knew it. With a playful smile she continued talking to the man and eventually invited him to accompany her to the party. Seeing that he was a very clean-cut man, driving a nice car and wearing lots of expensive-looking jewellery, she felt safe and climbed into his car. 'How bad could he be?' she thought.

As they drove, the man said he needed to make a stop at his uncle's house. When he returned to the car a few minutes later, his mood had completely changed. He slammed the door and got right up in her face, shouting, 'Why'd you dog me out [insult me]?' He had mistaken her for a well-known neighbourhood prostitute. Enietra protested and said she hadn't a clue what he was talking about. With that, the man pulled out a .25 calibre handgun and shot her in the chest at point-blank range. Immediately she blacked out, but she didn't die.

THE ARREST AND MURDERS

When she came to, a Polaroid camera was flashing in her face and the man was raping her at the same time. She pleaded with him to take her to the hospital, but he refused as he insisted he 'couldn't get caught'. 'What the heck was that supposed to mean?' she wondered. So instead he decided to push her out of his moving vehicle, assuming that would finish her off.

By the grace of God, Enietra survived and would go on to give the police a description of her assailant. There will be more on Enietra and her attack, along with others, later on in this book, with the events in the trial.

The bullet recovered matched those used in the previous 'strawberry killings', as did the DNA of the man police were hunting. Women who traded sex for drugs instead of money are known as 'strawberries', hence the name 'strawberry killings'. It is apparent that this man hated prostitutes and would therefore kill any and all that he could get his hands on. I prefer to say that they were women who had their share of problems and not label them so harshly.

According to police reports, the murders apparently stopped for thirteen years until 2002. Or did they?

Soon after the arrest of Lonnie David Franklin Jr on 7 July 2010, more bodies were tied to the same killer using DNA. The killer had now gained the nickname The Grim Sleeper, due to the number of years he supposedly lay dormant from his killings. Later, it was found that our boy wasn't 'sleeping' at all, as his DNA was found on more bodies in the so-called 'silent/sleeping years'. With this knowledge I would prefer to call him The Grim Sleepwalker. But it's a name not for me to change as it was so cleverly given to him by *LA Weekly* reporter Christine Pelisek.

THE GRIM SLEEPER

By now the still-unknown sociopath had become hooked on the thrill of stalking and enticing his prey into his killing ground. Obviously mobile, he knew his territory intimately. A 'homeboy' and comfortable in his own community, he appeared to be a non-threatening character. Described by the surviving victim, Enietra Washington, as 'neat, tidy, slim, short and even kinda geeky', he wore a black polo shirt tucked into khaki trousers. He was 'polite, well groomed, a decent African-American guy'.

But there is a little more about this man that begs closer scrutiny. The orange Pinto supposedly had a white racing stripe on the hood; the upholstery was all-white, diamond-patterned. Enietra was impressed with the gear-shift handle topped with a ping-pong-sized marble ball. This man was certainly neat and tidy and perhaps even a well-organised blue-collar worker. In fact, one of his many jobs was working as a vehicle mechanic for the local LAPD. However, Enietra's favourable impression of this man soon evaporated after she mentioned that she was on her way to a party. The murderous 'Mr Bling' made a stop outside a mustard-coloured house in a quiet residential area and told her to stay put – he wouldn't be long.

While she waited in the car, the man went inside the house and seemed to have an argument with someone. Then he came back to the car, moving rather quickly, and started to drive away. After a short time in the car, he pulled out his gun and shot her: it was as simple and callous as that.

Slipping in and out of consciousness, Enietra remembers that her assailant drove at a high rate of speed along the streets. After he slowed the car down to shoot her, he then

THE ARREST AND MURDERS

started taking Polaroids of her. She pleaded with him to be taken to hospital, but this suave, now out-of-control monster resumed his typical serial killer behaviour by saying, 'No, I may get caught.' Then he pushed her out of the car, with great difficulty. She lay on the side of the road where she fell, on her way to dying a slow death. However, thankfully, she lived. She dragged herself along the road, touching parked cars as she moved slowly, still with blood pouring out from her chest. Finally she made it to her friend's porch; when her friend arrived home, she immediately called 911 and an ambulance showed up minutes later to take Enietra to hospital.

The killer did not surface again until 19 March 2002, when Princess Berthomieux, aged fifteen, was found in an alleyway in the 8100 block of South Van Ness Avenue, Inglewood. She had been in and out of foster homes for most of her short life and had also been mixing with the wrong crowd on the streets. Three months after her disappearance on 21 December 2001, she was found on 19 March 2002. She was the first victim who showed signs of strangulation as well as having been shot.

Just over a year after Princess's body was found, another young woman lay dead in an alleyway. On 11 July 2003 Valerie McCorvey, an African-American who was known to take drugs, was discovered. Aged thirty-five, she had also been strangled and shot. The corpse lay discarded between 108th and 109th Streets, near Denver Avenue. DNA tied McCorvey, Princess Berthomieux and Mary Lowe together.

On New Year's Day, 2007, the body of Janecia Peters, twenty-five, was found by a homeless man in a dumpster

11

near 9500 Western Avenue. She had been shot in the back, strangled and then dumped in a garbage bag. As with all of the previous murders, there was no DNA match on the police database, but bodily fluids matched those attributed to the as-yet-unidentified serial killer. Janecia had been shot with the same handgun.

Years went by and the streets of South LA seemed to get worse and worse by the day. The safe city where Lonnie David Franklin Jr grew up was now home to some of the worst crack addicts, drug dealers and gang members of anywhere in sunny Southern California. Now known as South Central, the city was becoming increasingly littered with the dead and forgotten members of society. Such people were used to either being ignored or arrested by the police, but now they were living with the two worst enemies of all: the crack epidemic and an active serial killer on the loose.

Murders seemed to blend into one another in South Central, Los Angeles, and in 1985 alone, nearly 800 killings took place in this City of Angels. I was told by Cliff Shepard that fifty-two prostitutes were brutally murdered over a four-year period. Sadly, thirty-four of these fifty-two murders remain unsolved. Was it because people simply didn't care about the wellbeing of prostitutes and drug addicts? Or was there insufficient manpower to deal with all the crime in South Central Los Angeles around then?

At the time, the police told ABC News that they believed the murders to be the work of up to five different men. Some were accused and looked at for the Grim Sleeper killings, however they were let go due to their DNA not being a match. A few of these men have since been caught and are mentioned in this book, however, the Grim Sleeper killings were all down to one man.

After arrests had been made of the Southside Slayer – Chester Turner, who killed fourteen prostitutes between 1987 and 1988, and Michael Hughes, who killed seven prostitutes between 1986 and 1993 – the LAPD realised there was still a serial killer in action on the streets of Los Angeles and he might be the person responsible for the Grim Sleeper murders. Throughout the investigation, only two suspects had appeared on the law enforcement's radar: one was Roger Hausmann, on whom the *LA Weekly* wrote an extensive profile. However, Hausmann was an unlikely suspect for various reasons. For one thing he certainly didn't match the profile of a middle-aged black man.

According to the *LA Weekly*, in 1979 Hausmann was arrested for having sex with a minor in Fresno (a city 220 miles north of Los Angeles), but to avoid prosecution, he then (unwillingly) married her. Unquestionably an unsavoury character, throughout the years, among other petty crimes, he had been picked up for assault, pimping, lewd acts against a child, and carrying loaded and concealed weapons, according to the *LA Weekly* profile. It didn't help that he had allegedly mouthed off to Fresno police about killing prostitutes, according to another *LA Weekly* story. But when his DNA was tested, he was off the hook: he wasn't the killer the cops were looking for.

Shockingly, the other suspect pursued seriously by police was one of their own. He was a Los Angeles County Sheriff's Department deputy by the name of Rickey Ross.

In 1989, Ross was arrested in connection with a string of crimes that are now believed to be those of The Grim Sleeper. He was arrested and found with a 9mm gun in his possession in

THE GRIM SLEEPER

February 1989, but after several months, and an independent investigation, it was discovered that the LAPD crime lab's ballistics tests were inaccurate and all the charges were dropped.

At first glance, Ross seemed like a good fit, especially considering the eyewitness details of Enietra Washington. He was black and well dressed, but didn't remotely resemble the picture the victim had conjured up with a police sketch artist. Ross allegedly had personal problems and was picked up by police while he was with a prostitute. He was fired from the force and later sued the department for $400 million. The case was settled out of court.

By now, and almost at their wits' end, the police had started looking at DNA profiles that even partly matched using a technique called Familial DNA Analysis. This then pointed to someone who would be a close relative of a man by the name of Christopher Franklin, previously arrested on firearms charges.

At the time, Franklin was in his late twenties so he couldn't possibly have committed these murders while in diapers. Soon after this hit, law enforcement first looked at his uncle who lived in Rancho Cucamonga, almost 100 miles away. This seemed a little far, as the killings were all based in Los Angeles, so they also looked at Franklin's father, Lonnie David Franklin Jr, who lived directly in the area where the killings all took place.

After surveilling Franklin for days, they finally managed to obtain a slice of pizza from a restaurant in Buena Park by the name of John's Incredible Pizza, where the suspect was attending a children's birthday party. The DNA came back as a perfect match to that of the Grim Sleeper.

THE BEGINNING

I had anxiously waited for Lonnie David Franklin Jr to be classified by the Men's Central Jail in Los Angeles since his arrest on 7 July 2010. Being classified meant that he would be put in the housing facility that suited the crimes of which he had been accused and then he would be allowed visitors.

Alleged serial killers and other high-profile inmates are usually classified as 'Ad Seg', which means they are administratively segregated from the GP, the general population. At the Men's Central Jail they are usually housed in the 1750 or 1700 block and considered to be K10s. K10 inmates are also known as 'special handle inmates'. This is a name that is added to their security level depending on their crime and prior criminal history. Security levels range from 1–9. Special handles like these are assigned by the need of the inmate and safety of other inmates and staff. Lonnie Franklin was made a K10 more to protect himself than the other inmates from him. K10s are constantly monitored and escorted by deputies to ensure everybody's safety.

THE GRIM SLEEPER

Since Franklin's arrest on 7 July 2010, I had called the jail on a weekly basis to see when he would be allowed his first visit. Finally, after months of waiting, on 15 October I was told that he had just been classified that week.

On 28 October 2010 I made my trip to the Men's Central Jail to line up for my very first interview. I had written Franklin a letter a week or so prior to my visit, introducing myself as an author and giving him a heads up that I planned to visit him in order to possibly write a book on his life using his own words. I went on to explain in my letter that I also write and produce shows about incarcerated individuals, those who are guilty of murder and others who have been wrongly convicted. I enclosed a picture of myself so that he knew who I was and explained that I wanted to see if he was interested to tell his story to me in his own words. This usually works when I am pursuing subjects for my books and/or TV shows, especially as incarcerated individuals always feel that their words have never been heard and the truth has not yet come out.

The pages that follow explain what Franklin said to me in his own words. Often the facts are all over the place and repeated again later on, as they were in all my interviews with him. In my opinion he has a chronic case of attention deficit disorder (ADD). When I quote words that I transcribed from him, I have put those words in italics. It will become clearer once the dates of these interviews appear before each interview.

★ ★ ★

On 30 August 1952, in the Methodist Hospital of California, located in a suburb south of Los Angeles at 1401 Hope Street,

THE BEGINNING

a pretty petite African-American woman by the name of Ruby Franklin gave birth to a bouncing baby boy. Her husband, Lonnie David Franklin Sr, a man she adored, was over the moon at the birth of his first son, Ruby's second. This was a wonderful addition to the young couple's life, their first son together. They decided to name him Lonnie David Franklin Jr. Franklin arrived in this world at well over a whopping 8lb and he had a larger-than-normal sized head. Not something Ruby or Lonnie Sr was expecting as Ruby had such a small stature. She herself was so excited at the arrival of her second baby boy that this didn't bother her one jot.

Ruby's first-born son, Chris, was already fourteen at the time and was living with her parents out in Texas. Chris's father was a man named Otis Cooley but it isn't known if Ruby and Otis were ever married. He also lived in Texas so was able to see his son on a regular basis. When Ruby left him, she fled to California to start a new life and that was where she met Mr Lonnie Franklin Sr.

Ruby's parents hailed from Houston and they were a good old church-going family, producing five healthy children. The sixth died as a toddler. Ruby was the eldest of the five and she had two sisters and two brothers. She was the cutest of them all and was looked up to as the matriarch of the family.

Lonnie Jr was brought home from the hospital and was immediately the apple of his father's eye, especially being his first-born. Ruby's heritage was black mixed with Native American. Lonnie Sr was African-American from Louisiana and he had a substantial amount of French in him due to the French settlement in Louisiana. At least this is what he told me.

THE GRIM SLEEPER

The new parents doted on baby Lonnie, especially as he was the only child they had to take care of at the time. Little did they know that this beautiful chubby child would be known, fifty-eight years later, as The Grim Sleeper, accused of being the most prolific serial killer ever to walk the streets of Los Angeles, killing dozens of innocent women in his wake.

Meanwhile the new arrival of a baby brother in California didn't faze his elder sibling, Chris, one bit. He was happy living in Texas and growing up as a Southern boy.

Lonnie Sr and Ruby began married life living at 1705 W. 85th Street in Los Angeles 90047. It was where they raised Lonnie Jr alone for the first five years of his life until Ruby got the 'baby bug' again just like her mother before her. Ruby was always holding out for a girl and then, five years later, little Patricia came along. Patricia, Franklin's sister, currently lives in Fresno, California... from his recollection. She had a child out of wedlock a number of years ago so their parents adopted Patricia's son as their own.

From the age of eleven to eighteen Franklin lived in this house on West 85th Street, with his parents and Patricia. Throughout his childhood and into his teenage years he was chubby, which caused him to be the target of much taunting, harassment and ridicule among his peers. I will get to this later on in the book. Despite this, he knew a number of people and was very friendly to most people in the neighbourhood. Ronald Battle lived on 87th Street and would be about fifty-eight now. Reynolds Maurice lived in the only two-storey house on 83rd Street. Reynolds's mother was German and his father was black.

Unlike most serial killers, who often have abusive

childhoods, Franklin's upbringing was quite the reverse: his memories were happy and playful. As a child he was never beaten by his parents outside of a slap every now and then from his mother or a light whooping (an African-American term for smacking or hitting) from his father on the rare occasion when he acted up. However, there was certainly nothing that would be considered abuse. In fact, Franklin always got along very well with both his parents during the five years that he was an only child and even after that time when he had a baby sister. He had always longed for a little sister, which is perhaps unusual for a boy. Most boys crave a little brother, but no, he had always wanted a sister, and five years later, his wish came true when Patricia was born.

Although Franklin had a lot of acquaintances when he was growing up, there was none he looked up to more than his older brother Chris. He remembers vividly two of the most humiliating moments of his young life, both involving his big brother, and they happened when he was under the age of sixteen. Lonnie had always felt that Chris had always protected him, however there was one incident that proved to him, in his eyes, that this was not the case. Every year his Texan half-brother would come to LA to visit him and their mother in the summertime, and he planned to move out to LA for good only six months before his seventeenth birthday, just before he joined the Marines. Franklin was only three at the time and a late developer who couldn't yet speak. At seventeen, Chris joined the Marines for two years and when he returned, he moved back in with his mother, stepsister Patricia, stepfather Lonnie Sr and stepbrother Lonnie Jr. They all lived either on 78th Street between Avalon and Century or it might still have been 1705 West 85th Street – even Franklin himself is confused about this one.

On the day that Franklin remembers, he met up with his half-brother soon after his return home from the Marines – Lonnie must have been about five or six at the time. This particular day stands out in his mind because Chris had decided to take him ice-skating for the very first time. There was a rink down the road from where they lived and Chris loved skating. Lonnie was so excited that his big brother was going to take him out.

Franklin often felt self-conscious due to his size, but on this particular day being with his hero brother made him feel secure and pretty confident in himself. He certainly wasn't thinking that anyone would try to pick on him at the ice rink. However, walking towards them at the rink was a group of older boys, giggling and pointing as they passed by. Sadly, Chris did nothing to protect his little brother from the onset of these older boys, who were taunting him and leaving him feeling threatened and unprotected all over again. Chris did absolutely nothing to frighten these boys off and almost brushed the incident aside as though it was nothing. Understandably, Lonnie was deeply hurt, particularly as his brother had been a Marine, someone who was eager to protect his own country. In his eyes this was truly unforgivable and unforgettable and confirmed to him that his older brother didn't really care for him at all.

Franklin remembers that his dad taught him to drive at the age of seven and then let him drive solo for the very first time.

THE BEGINNING

Lonnie Sr would follow him down the road and let him drive all the way to the mechanics by himself.

While Chris was living in Los Angeles, he owned a Chevrolet Corvair. Lonnie was envious of his brother's car and always dreamt of driving it one day. Chris treasured his Chevy but eventually decided to sell it as he needed the extra money. Lonnie was a little upset – from a young age he'd had a fascination with cars and how they worked and now his older brother was going to get rid of the very car he'd fantasised about driving since he'd first sat behind a wheel. Being nice, Chris decided to offer the car to his stepfather first and sold it to Lonnie Sr for just $300. It was Lonnie Sr's plan to buy this dream car for Lonnie Jr to drive so that his first ever car would be a Chevrolet Corvair. Even at the tender age of fourteen, Franklin was so proud to be driving the very car that once belonged to his elder brother, who he still looked up to despite everything.

During this time Chris had been dating a woman by the name of Sandra. He was even planning on marrying her. However, Sandra already had three daughters of her own and ruled the roost when it came to decision making between herself and Chris. Chris knew exactly what he was taking on when he asked to marry young Sandra, but he loved her so much, it didn't matter. With these enormous responsibilities about to impact his life, he changed his mind and decided not to sell the car to his father for a measly $300 but to sell it elsewhere at a higher price – he needed to buy a much bigger car to fit his new family. It was yet another disappointment in young Franklin's life that involved his beloved brother. After a short time Chris sold the Chevy Corvair for a great deal more than he would have made by selling it to his father, in order to buy a station wagon for his new family of five.

Soon after Chris and Sandra were married, they adopted a boy by the name of Eric. They had always wanted a son and adoption seemed the best option at the time. Not long after Eric joined his three sisters, Sandra became pregnant with the couple's first girl. They named her Michelle – Michelle Cooley. So, Franklin had three step-nieces, a nephew and another one on the way. Chris and Sandra were now living nearby in Compton and supposedly enjoying their married life and huge family. However, Sandra certainly wasn't holding back when it came to her attraction for Chris's young brother Lonnie. Wearing the sexiest clothes she could find, she would then drive her 'new car' around to Franklin's house. She would jump out of the car, sauntering up to the Franklin family's front door to innocently ask if Lonnie would like to come out and go for a ride with her. This, I'm sure, is a story fabricated by Franklin when he had a delusional teenager's mind.

Young Lonnie was only twelve or thirteen at the time, and like most other males of that age, all he could think of was sex, though he was still a virgin. He had no interest in Sandra whatsoever and not because she was his brother's wife. When it came to women, from a young age Franklin had a certain type and Sandra just didn't fit the bill. A bit of a moocher, she would use Lonnie and Chris's mother Ruby for money the whole time. It was widely assumed that she also used her husband in this way as well. After all, Chris agreed to support her three daughters as his own, and soon after came the arrival of two more children.

Indeed Franklin found Sandra so distasteful that he used to call her 'Ela' meaning elephant. As much as he loved his older brother, he never really got along with him and as soon as he became a teen, he realised that Chris had less and less time for him. My guess is that as Chris began to like girls, he wanted to spend a lot more time with them than with his younger and very impressionable brother. Franklin secretly nicknamed his older brother 'Roach'. Therefore in his eyes 'Roach' and 'Ela' belonged together and he could do just as well without either of them living in the neighbourhood.

As time went by, Franklin and his brother continued to drift apart. Thankfully, Chris never found out about his wife's wandering eye – at least as far as Lonnie was concerned. The last time Franklin spoke to his brother was on the phone in 2008. They never had a close relationship so it's unlikely he will be receiving a visit from him any time soon. Chris divorced Sandra in the eighties and remarried. He might be married for the second time or the third time, Franklin cannot be sure on that one as these days they are not in touch at all.

MY FIRST INTERVIEW WITH THE GRIM SLEEPER

28 OCTOBER 2010

It was a cold brisk morning in Los Angeles on the morning of Thursday, 28 October 2010, when I made the journey down to the Men's Central Jail in Los Angeles to visit the alleged Grim Sleeper for the very first time. Having parked my car right by the main entrance in the covered parking lot for $8.00, I then walked across the open area where all the official Los Angeles County Sheriff's Department (LASD) vehicles were parked. I followed the arrows pointing to the High Power line, where about twenty-five people stood chatting. High Power is the area in the jail which is designated for inmates who are segregated from the general population either due to being 'infamous', a gang member or gang member dropout, or a highly dangerous inmate. I felt extremely uncomfortable as I had never been to the Men's Central Jail as a visitor before – I had only ever been on walk throughs, also known as 'jail tours', on the inside of the jails with Sheriff's officials. I'm planning to go into law enforcement when (or if) my on-camera career ever subsides, so going on various official tours of jails has been something I have done a number of times over the past two decades I've lived in America.

There were mainly women standing in the High Power line, all chatting about the family members they were there to see: brothers, husbands, cousins, boyfriends, etc. I was careful to keep my mouth shut as I was certainly not there to see a friend or family member!

After about an hour and a half, we gave our IDs to the deputy who had come outside to start the line moving forward. We were each handed a slip of paper to fill out, asking for our name, address, the inmate we were visiting, the inmate's booking number and our 'relationship to the inmate'. Well, I was stuck on the last one, so when I made it to the counter on the inside of the building, another deputy took my paperwork and asked me how I knew Mr Franklin as I'd left that box blank.

'Well, you see I don't really know him, he's more of an acquaintance…' I explained to the deputy. 'I used to live near where he lived in South Central when I first came to America and well, I…' The deputy put Franklin's name in and I could see the following numbers written 10 times by his name – 187, 187, 187, etc. This meant he had been charged with 10 counts of murder so far. The deputy then looked back at me and said, 'Really? You know this guy?' He stumbled and almost laughed at the difficulty I was having in trying to explain how I knew him. Maybe he could see just based on what I looked like and how I was dressed that I was probably a writer, but he knew at least I wasn't going in with a camera, which is forbidden in the LA County jails. So after a short while he said: 'I heard he was a good mechanic,' with a wink, 'isn't that how you know him?' To which I responded with a smile, 'Yes, that's it! He was my mechanic.' The deputy filled in the box and from then on I put the word 'acquaintance' in the part where it asked for 'relationship to inmate'. I wrote this each and every time I visited him.

I was then ushered to sit on the cold metal seats where everyone else was sitting and chatting as if they'd known each other for years. However, I felt very out of place and was also being stared at as if I didn't belong there, so I sat with my head down and hands in my lap. Maybe my fellow visitors were only staring because I was new to the visiting room, but I have no idea. The atmosphere was happy in an ironic sort of way and the smell was that of a jail, which is very hard to describe. All jails and prisons have the same smell: a mixture of processed food, disinfectant, cheap perfume and sweaty bodies.

As I glanced up from my hands for a moment, there were three Hispanic girls smiling at me. They moved up a seat and gestured for me to sit down with them. I smiled back, and obviously sensing my discomfort, they opened up a conversation with me. They chatted to me and volunteered that they were all there to see their 'homeboy' (their best friend) as he'd got himself in trouble of sorts. 'Again,' they said in unison. They were all his best friends. Lucky guy, I thought, having these really nice girls all come to see him here in jail. Then it came to their question for me, as to why I was there and who I was there to see. I dreaded what I would say in response but they seemed sweet enough so I told them, 'I'm here to visit the alleged Grim Sleeper.' I used the word 'alleged' to protect myself just in case he was found 'not guilty'. I told them I'd written to him so he knew who I was and that he would be expecting a visit from me. They were all shocked, having heard of the most prolific serial killer in LA history, who had recently been caught.

'How long ago did you write to him?' one of the girls asked me. To which I replied, 'Some time last week.' All three laughed again in unison before one of them told me: 'He's a K10 High Power Ad Seg inmate, he won't get that letter until at least a month from now!'

Realising how potentially awkward and embarrassing this encounter could be, I immediately went up to the counter to borrow a pencil from one of the deputies, then visited the ladies' room, where I quietly broke open a toilet roll and removed the inner cardboard part. I stayed quietly in the stall and wrote these words on it: 'I told them that you were my mechanic and we go way back! Please go with that.'

I hid it in my waistband and went back to sit with the three girls who had been so kind to me. I showed them what I had done and hoped it would be enough for Franklin to talk to me, at least for the duration of the visit.

The deputy started reading the last names from the list he had: 'Lopez, Castro, Johnson, Gonzalez, Henderson, Gomez...' Once he read the last names twice, the visitors were then able to get up from their seats and stand in line to collect their visiting slips and walk to the area where their loved one or homeboy sat awaiting their arrival behind the glass. Again, another list of names was read and Franklin was still not mentioned. I thought they had forgotten about me.

MY FIRST INTERVIEW WITH THE GRIM SLEEPER

Even my new friends had rushed off twenty minutes before, and I was still just sitting there with my hands in my lap, staring at them as I didn't want to make eye contact with anyone else.

Finally, the deputy came up and read out just one name – 'Franklin'. With my head down I walked to the counter, feeling everyone's eyes on me again. I was handed a slip of paper and it had 'A15' written on it, so I asked where I should go. The deputy pointed to a room to the right, not where everyone else had gone, and told me that he'd be sitting in that area. Slowly, I walked into this cold, cramped area of the jail, the smell of disinfectant reeking from every corner.

In the first cubicle to my right sat a white male behind the glass, holding the phone in his hand resting under his chin. He was obviously waiting for his visitor. In the next cubicle was a small, petite-looking African-American, and above the glass was the number 'A15'. It couldn't possibly be The Grim Sleeper, I thought, as he looked very large in the newspapers and from what I'd seen on television. In the next cubicle was a Hispanic male, then on the other side there were three more Hispanic males. They all kept their heads in their hands and would just raise their eyes upwards to see who was walking by the glass. Very eerie... He's got to be in this area, I thought, so I then turned back to the small-looking black man sitting there with his hands under his chin, and when I leaned down to look more closely, I saw a name band around his left wrist. Written on the band was 'Lonnie David Franklin Jr'. I slowly sat down and he immediately leaned back in his chair on the other side of the glass, shaking his head as if to say, 'No, you're not here to visit me, I've never even seen you before.'

THE GRIM SLEEPER

To put it frankly, when I sat down opposite him, he looked like he'd seen a ghost and couldn't have pushed his chair any further away from the glass. I almost thought he was going to call for security!

I picked up the jail phone and said: 'Hi, Lonnie, can you hear me?' The phones weren't turned on yet and I was sitting there with this man who was clearly very uncomfortable not knowing who in God's name I was. So, yet again, I too was feeling rather uncomfortable, an understatement considering I was most likely sitting across from one of the worst serial killers in American history. I then looked to my right and left and all the other visitors were patiently waiting for their phone lines to be switched on as well. So, I just sat there awkwardly, smiling. I then remembered the message I had scribbled in the loo that was still in my waistband, so I pulled it out and placed it on the glass for him to read. He leant forward, read the note, wrinkled his nose and sheepishly nodded that he kind of got it.

Then, suddenly, I heard chattering from my side of the glass from the other visitors. The phone lines were now working, so again I said: 'Hi, Lonnie, how are you? It's really good to see you again after such a long time. I heard you got locked up for something and I was in the area today so I thought I'd stop by and see you to say hi.' I was winking very obviously the entire time. 'My car has never been the same since I left the LA area and moved the other side of the hill.'

'Yeah, yeah, yeah,' was his confused response. 'I remember you… Yeah, how you doin'? You had always had that transmission problem, right? Yeah, yeah, I remember you. Is it still bad?' As he spoke I could see that one of his teeth was chipped quite badly, but I didn't feel right about mentioning it and asking him how it happened, especially since it was our first meeting.

Our conversation progressed from there and our banter was spot on for any officials who would have been listening in at the time, and they were. I was quite impressed that he was able to pick up so quickly on my elaborate story of him being my mechanic.

'Did you get my letter?' I asked. He said that he hadn't and then reiterated what the girls in the visiting room had told me, that all letters take months to get through if they are written to K10 inmates. I told him that recently, in my journalism career, I had started writing books on both the wrongly convicted and the guilty, just as long as they had been charged with first-degree murder.

'Somewhere, Lonnie, you must fit in to one of those two demographics,' I said, smiling sweetly so as not to offend him.

He went on to tell me that he had pleaded not guilty on the advice of his lawyers and was now awaiting trial. He said that his vehicle was seen by witnesses, which he didn't understand as he had sold it long before (I think he was talking about the orange Pinto but he wasn't clear on that). He spoke of his family, of his wife Sylvia, who he loves very much, his son Christopher as well as his granddaughter. Christopher was the name he chose for his son, in my opinion, because of his deep-rooted respect and love for his older brother.

Although Franklin is close to his wife, he said they both attended different churches on a Sunday morning. His wife was consistent and went every Sunday without fail whereas he himself went often but not every week. He went to a different church close to their home that focused on helping gang members get off the streets.

Franklin's sister, Patricia, sometimes visited him, but only when she came to LA to get her hair done and that wasn't very often. She lives up in Northern California. However, his wife visits like clockwork every Saturday morning.

After my first few visits with Franklin, I stressed how important it was that if I was to put all my time and energy into writing a book, from his own words, he gave me exclusivity and didn't talk to anyone else about his story. He agreed to this and made that promise to me both verbally and in writing.

Franklin is a Type A personality (a personality type characterised by a tendency to be impatient, anxious and proactive) and has an abundance of energy. Even though he was firmly seated across from me he was bouncing around like he was on a bouncy castle – I could hardly keep up with him. It made me wonder if he was on any medication, so I asked him and he happily listed them off:

> Yeah, yeah, I have to take Omeprazole CR for my acid reflux, Metoprolol Tartrate and Benazepril for my blood pressure and hypertension, Aspirin for my heart, Hydrochlorothiazide for fluid retention and one for my hernia which I forgot the name, that's all I can think of right now.

Excitably erratic with his conversation, he was jumping all over the place. He started by telling me how he was stationed in Germany when he was in the Army and also moonlighting as a DJ on the side. He proudly stated that he had been married for over thirty years and his parents were married for over fifty years. As a side job, he secretly told me, he would sell lingerie to people in Belize, where his wife Sylvia is from, and mark up the price six times or more, making a huge profit. After that slew of information he went on to share with me that he doesn't have a single hair on his chest, nor does he have any tattoos. I certainly didn't wish to see the proof!

The visit lasted way more than the allocated time of thirty minutes, which was invaluable for my writing. What really nice deputies, I thought. They didn't have to do that, especially as these deputies aren't the ones I have any connection with. Later on I found out it was the lieutenant who ran the jail, who I had known since he was a deputy in West Hollywood when I was only nineteen, whom I had to thank: he had seen my name on the visiting list and made sure the deputies gave me more than the permitted time whenever I was there. I had no idea of this until years later. That first time, I left over an hour later when I was only supposed to have had a twenty-minute visit.

From that day forward I went to visit and interview Franklin in the Men's Central Jail every Thursday morning without fail. He was allowed two twenty-minute visits a week: one on a Thursday and the other on a Saturday due to him being an Ad Seg inmate and High Power too. Therefore I visited him every Thursday and never on a Saturday, as I knew that was his day for his wife or any other family members, who believe it or not, all firmly believed in his innocence and continue to do so.

SCHOOL YEARS, GIRLS AND SEX

Franklin attended 87th Street Elementary School in South LA, where his favourite teacher was Miss Moss. At first he seemed to be the target of ridicule due to his size and weight. From age five to eleven he was bullied and tormented by his peers for being too short and too fat for his age. He was bullied not only because he was shorter than the rest of his peers but because he was also quite podgy. His mother, Ruby, was a Southern lass and always cooked fried foods, hence his weight gain and stunted growth. So with all this bullying from peers in his formative years, like so many of his killer brethren, he felt abused and worthless at a young and impressionable age.

After Elementary school, he then went on to attend Horace Mann Junior High School, and for some strange reason, the bullying stopped even though he was still a little chunky for his age. However, the scarring was already there and forever ingrained on his soul. So, while in Junior High, he deliberately started to eat far fewer fried foods and instead switched to junk food from age twelve or thirteen. He still hadn't slimmed down completely, but he had certainly decreased a lot in size. From eighteen onwards, he started to eat really healthily and that was when he was at his 'fighting weight'.

When Franklin turned fourteen he lost his virginity to Elaine Washington, who was a year or two his junior. She was 5ft 6in and very proud to be bisexual. Even back in those days when sex between boys and girls was even more taboo than it is today, she made no qualms about the fact that she enjoyed it with boys and girls equally.

As you can imagine, Elaine was known to be a little 'easy' to get into bed by the boys in the neighbourhood, but this didn't faze Franklin at all. Elaine's father – Booker T. Washington – and her mother lived on the 1800 block of W. 76th Street in South Central Los Angeles at the time, not too far from the Franklin household. However, Booker didn't like Franklin much because at the time he rode a motorcycle.

Years went by and although Franklin and Elaine were no longer lovers, they still remained friends. He had never fallen in love with her so it was easy for him to stay friends with her. They were at the same school but usually had separate classes. There was a time when Elaine was on crutches for a long while, due to having bad knees, and another girl picked a fight with her because she was jealous of her friendship with Franklin, although the jury's out as to whether this was really the case or one of Franklin's fabrications. Although Elaine's bisexuality didn't bother Franklin at all, it was during this fight that he stepped into the middle. It was obvious that the girl who had started the fight had a crush on Elaine and he felt threatened by this. He was eighteen at the time and this particular girl had tried to get him out of the way, so she started swinging Elaine's crutch at him. Not being one to back down, Franklin snatched the crutch from her and hit her over the head with it in self-defence. Soon after, he ended up in jail for this assault, because he certainly wasn't going to stand for some girl trying to take a swing at him.

After Horace Mann Junior High, Franklin then went on to Washington High School, and at the ripe old age of sixteen he got his first job working as a bagger at Market Max, a local supermarket, which was also known as Market Basket. He worked there for almost a year and then went on to work at Lucky's, another popular store.

At sixteen and a half Franklin finally fell in love, for the first time, with Audrey Johnson. Only three months his junior, she was very mature for her age. She was his first true love.

It was a well-known fact that Audrey's stepfather – a 6ft 4in, 300lb strapping man – was crazy in love with his stepdaughter Audrey. He made no bones about it either. He would even write love letters to her, stating in one of them that he had 'failed his real estate exam because all he could do was think of her'. It was presumed that she was also being molested by the stepfather but this was never proven.

Franklin loved to skip school and usually averaged C grades. On one of the days when he played hooky, he met a girl he thought was 'kind of cute': her name was Mary. Within a day of meeting her, they both decided to play hooky and wandered over to the Health building, which was quite near to the school. They wanted to make it to the top floor, and after they got in the elevator, Franklin planted a wet sloppy kiss on Mary just for the fun of it to see what she'd do. In fact she writhed in pure ecstasy and he was completely taken aback by her reaction to what he had done so many times before. He felt that she would have stripped right then and there with all the noises she was making just from a simple kiss.

Not one to hold back, Franklin hit the button for the top floor and they both got out at the attic floor. Sparing me some of the details, he told me that he had sex with Mary on the top floor of the Health building, standing up to boot! This sounds like a fabricated story, as I found out later that Lonnie didn't have the best luck getting women, hence the need he felt to seek out prostitutes. However, I am writing it verbatim so it is up to the readers' discretion.

'*It was a good screw,*' he said. On one occasion, he would take Mary to the drive-through and they would have sex there too. She seemed to be very open to making love in all sorts of public places and this didn't bother Franklin one jot. However, Mary was a Catholic, hence the name, so contraception was out of the question.

According to him, in Los Angeles in the 1960s black girls would often get pregnant. When they did, the boyfriend's parents would always dish out the money for the child until he or she was eighteen. Some parents would ship their promiscuous sons out of state to avoid the payments and some young boys would disappear of their own accord. But this was not in Franklin's nature: he would stick around whether the girl was pregnant or not, but he wasn't always informed when they were.

It was common among this community that when a girl

became pregnant, she wouldn't tell her man for the mere fact that he would most likely have to leave her, one way or another. So, in Mary's case, she kept it secret. As she had always carried a little extra padding, just the way Franklin liked his women, she certainly didn't look any different in his eyes. She was tall, very well built and a little on the heavier side, and carried herself well, so a small bump in her mid-section might have gone unnoticed by anyone at the time. Mary liked Franklin a lot, maybe even loved him, certainly quite a bit more than he liked her. So the last thing she would have done was tell him she was carrying his child for fear of him leaving her. The concern that he would bolt out of state or disappear from her life completely was too depressing, so she kept her mouth firmly shut.

Although Mary adored Franklin, the feeling wasn't mutual. He always had an eye for other women and that never changed throughout adulthood. When he was eighteen Mary introduced him to her 'sister' (in this case, I believe 'sister' was used more as a slang version of best friend) Denise, who went to Crenshaw High School. Assuming they were the same age, Franklin was taken aback by Denise's exquisite looks and immediately fell for her. In fact she was only fourteen years old and a virgin.

He and Denise started dating for a while but she was not about to 'put out' to anyone, least of all to an 18-year-old. Franklin had no idea of this and tried to woo her with everything he could, including his beloved car. Their relationship ended almost as soon as it had begun, while he and Mary continued being 'friends with benefits' as they always had been before.

THE GRIM SLEEPER

Mary had now secretly given birth to Franklin's baby boy, yet it never dawned on him that it might be his. Why would it? He knew her to be on the looser side, like most of the women he was with, and she never said anything about who the father was. Therefore he never asked. She'd always go by his place with the baby and Franklin always offered to go for a drive and feed them all.

Franklin went on to Trade Tech College BCI in Los Angeles and studied Business. Then, in 1971, he decided to enlist in the Army whereupon he was immediately shipped off to Germany. He was stationed there for five years, although never went into combat. He stayed at the lower rank of Corporal. In 1976, Franklin returned to the States. Thanks to the Army he was able to attend the University State of Washington for one and a half years, his studies being paid for by the service, but as always, he came out with C grades overall.

THE ARMY

When Franklin was in the Army he had only a few friends, with two of his closest friends being James and Larry. In August 1971 when he went in person to be accepted by the Army, the day played out as follows:

At 6 a.m. on a weekday morning on Wilshire, west of Crenshaw, Franklin went to a recruitment agency to apply for the Air Force. The recruiters attending that day were the Army, the Navy, the Air Force and the Marines. The Air Force didn't have any openings for young Franklin so he was '*s*** out of luck there*' in his words. He knew full well that he didn't want to be stuck out on a boat with the Navy. The Marines were far too strict and would instill a lot more discipline. So his only other choice would be the Army, in which his father had served. Lonnie Sr was only 5ft 2in and a little chunky too when he joined the Army in the 1940s. He, Franklin Sr, served only nine months, and it was all he could do to keep up with the other taller and fitter guys. Following this he then left of his own accord, or so Lonnie says.

Luckily for Franklin, the Army had immediate openings so he thought, why not enlist voluntarily? He chose not to get enlisted at once as he wanted to take the tests first. Being enlisted meant he would be drafted immediately, which was not what he wanted, so he enlisted voluntarily instead.

Franklin performed well in his tests, especially communications and also electronics, where he scored 120. He took his medical and physical tests and passed these too with flying colours. Then he became fully enlisted and was drafted soon afterwards to Germany.

On that very first day, the bus came at 3 p.m. and young Franklin was taken to Fort Ord, near Monterey in California. The bus drove the back route through Salinas, which is right by Fort Ord. He was dressed only in his civvies – his street clothes. The jeans and shirt that he wore on the bus were sent home to his family and he was given the traditional Army garb to wear. Being only eighteen, he was still living at home with his parents and sister Patricia in Los Angeles.

The following day he was woken at about 4 or 5 a.m. by soldiers screaming at the new recruits to all 'Get up you SOBs, get up, you lazy mother f***ers, wake up, you pieces of shit!' Not the way he was accustomed to being woken by his adoring mother at home in Los Angeles, but now he had joined the big boys and was certainly given a loud wake-up call that morning.

According to Franklin, at the beginning the black guys would stick around and make friends with other black guys, the whites with the whites, but after a while there were no colour lines and everyone mingled.

He stayed for ten months at Fort Ord before being drafted to Germany. On the way there he had a layover in New Jersey for one week. He finished the basic training, but was then badly injured after falling off a telecommunications pole at the base and it took four months for him to recover.

Soon after this incident he was accused of going AWOL as he disappeared for over fifteen days and was further than one hundred miles away from Frankfurt. Later, it was confirmed that he had returned to the US, with a woman no less. He wasn't charged with being AWOL, however. It was the crucial time for him to have been promoted to the full-time position of acting sergeant – the buck sergeant, also known as E5. He was given the position temporarily but he wasn't able to take the tests, being too busy getting up to mischief with this woman in Frankfurt and then in America. On his return he went back to his rank of E1, which is the lowest rank and title a person is given when they begin an Army career.

Close to the base in Germany, there was a club by the name of The Revolution in a nearby town that Franklin and his friends would frequent at every chance they could get. According to him, the German woman just swooned over him. Franklin told me that one night he had met two female orphans from the nearby orphanage: one blonde, the other brunette. They were both German. The brunette was '*wild and as loose as hell*', he said. One night she not only had sex with him but then with three of his friends immediately afterwards. Franklin was disgusted, especially when she thought he would have sex with her again after being with the other men – he was only thankful to have been the first.

I was never quite sure whether Franklin was telling me the truth during any of our interviews, and whilst he was telling me this particular story, I instinctively knew that he was lying to me, although I didn't know which details were untrue at the time. Sure enough, this story of a supposedly wild night was later proven to have been totally fabricated. In reality, a brutal gang rape took place. It was in Stuttgart in April 1974 that Ingrid W. was waiting at the train station for the train to take her home late one night. Three men, one of them being Franklin, drove up, threw her in their car and took her out into the middle of nowhere, where each raped her with one of the men holding a knife to her throat. Over forty years later, she would be flown to the US to testify against Franklin at his trial.

Always on the lookout to make a quick buck, Franklin would also buy cocaine in Amsterdam and sell it in Germany at all the discos he would frequent. He'd make $200 every time and would buy the drugs for $100. Nowadays that would be the equivalent of making $500 (or £340) and only buying the drugs for less than half of that. He never took drugs himself though, nor did he ever experiment with them. However, when he'd have time off on the occasional evening, he would drive over to Amsterdam for a few days, buy the drugs and then pop right back to Germany to sell them.

He finally left the Army in 1975 due to being discharged for this gang rape, and came out as a Corporal E4, which is one rank below a buck sergeant, known as an E5 – the rank he really wanted to have. He left the Army because he knew he wouldn't have the opportunity to be promoted to a higher rank. For example, a man could join up and become an officer if he had had a college education, something Franklin never had.

To be accepted for the Officer Candidate School was something else that would be virtually impossible for him – he would have had to have some kind of degree for that door to be opened. He didn't see a way in and certainly no way to move up so he saw his salary remaining the same from that point on and into the future.

Even as an enlisted man, Franklin was always at the bottom of the totem pole so he chose not to sign up for the draft because he wanted to go to school first. He completed four months of training: two months of basic training and two months of more intense training.

And now to recap on Franklin's possible children and girlfriends… Before he went into the Army he had a girlfriend by the name of Denise in 1971. Mary was his girlfriend in high school, who he now knows he had a child with (who would be forty-eight or forty-nine by now, but he hasn't a clue about the child's name).

MEETING SYLVIA,
MARRIED LIFE AND JAIL

After five years in the US Army, Franklin was twenty-four years old. He returned to California in the September of 1976. For the second time in his life, and soon after returning to Los Angeles, he fell in love with the one true love of his life: Sylvia. This time he knew this woman would become his wife.

Sylvia, like Lonnie's mother Ruby, was also one of five children. She was the eldest child, just as Ruby was, and she had three brothers and one sister. (Lonnie Sr was an only child.) She was quickly swept off her feet by the charismatic and charming Lonnie David Franklin Jr and by April 1977, they were married in South Los Angeles.

Sylvia Franklin was an attractive woman, petite but curvaceous, who was born and raised in Belize. The couple's thirty-nine-year marriage has so far survived Franklin's three-plus affairs, one of them producing a daughter some nineteen years ago (two of these affairs were long-term). Sylvia sounds like one hell of a strong, yet very insecure, woman; most would have walked at the inkling of affair number one, let alone the supposed illegitimate children and numerous arrests that followed.

Over the course of Franklin's life, he spent about five separate instances being arrested and serving time in jail. The first time was when he had just turned eighteen and was found with a concealed weapon in his car. A loaded gun, no less! He was standing quite a few feet away from his car at the time and for some reason the cops stopped him and walked him back to his car, which they subsequently proceeded to search. After they found the loaded weapon in his Dodge Challenger RT, he was taken to jail for a few days, which was a shock for him as it was his first brush with the law. He said he had the weapon for his own protection – but why? Who did he need to be protected from? All the women who were apparently '*swooning*' over him? I found this hard to believe.

Another time he was arrested was when he was in his late twenties to early thirties. It was in the eighties and he went away for GTA (Grand Theft Auto). However, he only spent two days in jail for this. I'm sure the reason was because nothing was stolen out of the car, nor had it been wrecked. He just found it fun to steal a car and drive from point A to point B, and according to him, '*the rush*' was incredible! He wasn't stealing the car or even stealing parts from it, so, at the time, he didn't think he was doing much wrong. However, this didn't correspond with the next time he was incarcerated.

The next time Franklin went to jail, he was the owner of a pick-up truck. He had previously bought a radio for this truck from a guy who had sold it to him cheaply. My guess is that it was stolen. Whether he knew it or not, the radio had indeed been stolen from a BMW. Another day previously, he had worked on fixing a car and the guy paid him in weed. Franklin doesn't smoke weed nor does he use any other kind of drug, but he did however accept it as just payment. Consequently he put the weed in the ashtray of his truck.

A few evenings later, he was hanging out with a girl and they were driving around for a while listening to the radio, before they drove to a park to sit and chat, so he says. For some reason the Sheriff car drove up on his truck with the two of them sitting inside and they were instructed to exit the vehicle. Franklin was searched thoroughly and was cleared of anything untoward, yet the cops continued on and searched the inside of the pick-up truck, where they stumbled across the radio and also the marijuana in the ashtray.

After a more thorough search they surmised that the radio did not belong to the vehicle. The serial number showed that it had been stolen from a BMW. Ultimately, Franklin and his companion were both taken to jail for 'receiving stolen property' and 'possession of marijuana'. The owner of the BMW had seen the guy steal the radio and confirmed it wasn't Franklin: the description did not match him. In fact the suspect was a white male, which is why Franklin wasn't charged with theft. He was about thirty-four years old at the time and spent only a few days in jail, however law enforcement told me it was much longer than that.

Soon after this episode, Franklin spent a longer period of time in the slammer for... yes, you've guessed it... receiving stolen property. This time he spent four months in jail. Again it was the same white guy that he knew who stole cars and parts from the cars. This guy would see someone in a nice car get out and go into a shop, then he would manage to get in the car, call for a tow truck and pretend that 'his' car didn't start. Therefore he got it towed to wherever he wanted it towed. After the cars were stolen, Franklin would then take out items of value from the vehicles and sell them. Due to his previous convictions, he was given four months in jail. I would guess that he may have stolen a number of cars in his lifetime but he mainly dealt and made money in selling the parts from them.

Overall, Sylvia and Franklin lived a very good life together and rarely exchanged a cross word. He rarely raised his voice to her and if he did so, he would say things like, '*She'd throw kitchen knives at me.*' (More on this later) Overall, it was a loving and smooth relationship outside of his short stints in jail, yet Sylvia seemed to work a lot more hours than her husband. Personally I feel that they were like two ships passing in the night in their married life. Lonnie said that five months was the longest he spent in jail out of the six times he had been on the inside prior to his arrest in 2010. Personally, I believe their marriage was very disconnected and Sylvia was never home due to work, and when she came home to sleep, Franklin was off driving around the neighbourhood.

Sylvia would always turn a blind eye to her husband's antics as he was a good man to her and their son Christopher, who was born in 1977. She kept herself busy working all the hours that God gave and doing all she could to bring home the bacon. In return, Franklin loved to cook and was the main cook in the family, making a home-cooked meal for Sylvia and the rest of the family – Christopher and Crystal – on a daily basis. He wasn't really a house husband, although his jobs weren't quite as regular as his wife's work and were always varied, some of them being against the law. But he always wanted to provide for his family and be the man of the house.

Lonnie was raised a Methodist but as an adult preferred going to churches that were Baptist, although he and his wife went to separate churches only a block or so away from each other. I have no idea why they did this, but I would think it was because Sylvia was far more devout than Lonnie, who hardly ever went. Sylvia went every week without fail to the church on Martin Luther King Blvd and San Pedro Street.

In the early eighties, Franklin answered an ad in the *Wave* paper: the Los Angeles Police Department (LAPD) were looking for GAs – garage attendants, also known as mechanics. He got the job and was based at the Central Facility Station, which was on 6th and Wall Street. He then was upgraded to mechanic helper (MH). For this he would ship parts and equipment for police vehicles to nearly all the stations in LA and the surrounding areas. After this job, he became a tow truck driver working specifically for the LAPD. Although he was only a civilian employee, he worked for the LAPD for about three years in total. He became friends with a rookie female LAPD officer, who in his eyes was really cute, but the LAPD weren't really allowed to fraternise with civilian employees so as soon as anyone came around the corner, they would immediately stop talking. From there, he went on to become a sanitation worker for fifteen years from 1983 until about 1995.

Between 2008 and 2010 and up until he was arrested, Franklin owned and ran a domestic cleaning business called

Blessed Cleaning (previously Just Clean). He cleaned carpets with a lady who lived close by in the city of Watts. She was forty-two years old at the time and they would go and clean people's houses together.

★★★

22 DECEMBER 2010: PHONE CALL FROM FRANKLIN

The generic pre-recorded operator's voice came on the line and said, 'I have a prepaid call from…'

'*Lonnie,*' came Franklin's gravelly voice on the line.

'An inmate in Men's Central Jail. Your balance is twenty-three dollars,' said the operator again and then the conversation started.

'Hi Lonnie.'

'*What's goin' on wich you?*'

'I'm good, how are you doing?'

'*They just let me take a shower and…*'

'But Lonnie, you've been in all the papers.'

'*Again?*'

'Yeah, they said the body count's gone up to a hundred and eighty.'

'*A hundred and what?*'

'A hundred and eighty.'

'*Yeah, but you know all those pictures they got…*'

'Well, did you take those pictures or what?'

'*OK, let me give you the 411… Where you gonna be tomorrow?*'

'I'm going to come and see you tomorrow.'

'*Oh, OK, I'll be here. Yeah, but those pictures… Well, they…*'

I can tell you more tomorrow, but it's like… every one of those pictures, like, um, they got pictures from 19… 1971.'

'Unbelievable, but were they in your house? Weren't some of them your relatives?'

'Yeah, yeah, yeah, it was a trip on that… It's like, er, you know… Yeah, it was like some of the people were like, you know… Well, like, one of my… er… neighbours. I can't be on this phone too long… But, like, one of my neighbours, erm, graduated from high school even. So, erm… they erm… they took those pictures too.'

'Oh.'

'See what they did, see, like some of those pictures, like say you were in a picture with a guy, and er, they would then single you out and cut out the people on both sides and…'

'Oh, I see what you're saying. But Lonnie, it's unbelievable! They've put you on the front page of the *LA Times*. Did you see the paper? It's a picture of you, you look awful… You look like a serial killer in that picture! It's ridiculous.' No matter who I'm interviewing, I'm always aware that I need to phrase things in a sympathetic-sounding way in order to get my subject to open up, and I knew then that this show of sympathy would help me create the bond I needed in order to gain Franklin's trust.

'Yeah, yeah, that's what they do.'

'This call is being recorded and monitored,' interrupted the pre-recorded operator.

'Part of it… of what I got on the news… you can't hear no sound, they don't give us any sound, but you can just see the pictures and then they got the mayor on there… er… Villaraigosa… and they had all these pictures, you know, and they had that one lady in a nurse uniform, you see that one?'

'Yes, I think I did.'

'*And did you see that one white girl on there? She looks kind of like you? Well, she… That's my brother-in-law's wife.*'

'Oh, I see what you're saying.'

'*And he said she's in excellent health at this time.*'

'Well, good! I know the papers as I too have been written about in the papers and they make up stuff just for shock value and sensationalistic purposes.'

'*So the way they put it out there was: every one of those pictures that they showed… this is the way I perceived it… when I saw it on TV the way they presented it and I'm lookin' at all these pictures and I'm like, you know. OK, all these pictures were killed by him… me… and that's the way I perceived it coz that's the way they put it out there.*'

'But they're saying that you did it, that they're all your victims.'

'*Yeah, that's the way they put it out there.*'

'Right, I understand. Well, I just have to write a book on you, whether you're innocent or not. I already have started to write… We have to do this together.'

'*Well, see, I was… like… trying to get in touch with my attorney but I didn't have her 800 number.*'

'You want me to call her for you?'

'*Er, well, I don't have her number on me.*'

'I hope the media aren't trying to come in to talk to you. I don't want them to see or speak to you.'

'*Nah, nah, I wouldn't talk to them anyway. I told you I'm only talking to you and they don't come in where you come in anyway. They're also not even allowed.*'

'How come?'

'*Because you put that you are "not media" and that we are "acquaintances" on the visiting form.*'

'Oh yes, I forgot… We go way back, don't we, Lonnie?'

'*Yeah, yeah, it's like somebody asking me something about you and I tell 'em. Like, you know, you don't know who anybody is round here. Like the guy next to me, Ron Wood, he… he… His sister works in the jail here, she's a deputy. And the reason he's in High Power is not that he's a bad criminal or nothing, it's just his sister works across the street at Twin Towers. So he's just in here for protective custody (PC). So, it's like you can't just talk to anybody coz you don't know who's who. They got, like, K1s and K10s… Those are all cops that went bad, or brothers of cops. Like O.J. Simpson, he was housed on the same block and he was the only one on that row. They cleared out the whole row just for him.*'

'Right, I get it. But when people ask you about me, do you tell them how you used to always fix my car and you never charged me a dime?'

'*No, no, no! Like I said, it's like, I go like this… When I look back, I had a lot of ads running in the Recycler and, like, it was your brother ended up buying some stuff for me from the Valley and bought stuff and we ended up becoming friends and I would, ya know, you'd come up and talk to us while me and him were together. We were best friends…*'

'You mean my brother?' (I don't even have a brother.)

'*Yeah, yeah… So I keep it kind of neutral, you know… We just became friends, I tell them, and so on and so forth like that.*'

'I'm sorry we lost touch for all of those years.'

He laughed.

'*I've gotta go now coz our time's up. Bye for now, see ya soon!*'

'OK then, Lonnie… Probably next week then… Bye.'

'*Hey, you remember those little cars, the MR2s? Well, I used to build those, rebuild them, bottom stripped and then put 'em back together. Anyway, back to those pictures... So, it's such a trip, you know. I was tryin' to remember... It was a trip and one lady, her... er, she was a diabetic and she ended up living in Inglewood and, er, her name was Diane. Diane... it was one of those funny last names. Anyway, when she got sick her daughter came back home to look after her and then she died and she was only about seventy-five pounds. Yeah, yeah, she got in bad shape and she was only, like, two years older than me... and...*'

'Wait a second, so you're saying she was in one of those pictures in the paper, Lonnie?'

'*Yeah, she was and she died, like, five years ago. She was the one in the burgundy dress.*

And you know some of those pictures was when I was in Germany and some were from when I was in Belize. The cops took all my pictures and cut me out of the shot to make me look real bad.'

'Wait a second, when they searched your home in July, why didn't they find these pictures then?'

'*Oh, they did. They're just bringing this stuff out little by little. When they did the initial search, that was the only search they did.*'

'OK, then how many of those people were people who have been murdered?'

Silence.

'*Er, five or six, I don't know.*'

'They're trying to make it look like you killed them all.'

'*They had about a hundred and eighty pictures that they took from my home.*'

'I forgot to tell you that you made the front page of the English newspapers too – you know that? I've got friends calling me up, saying you're all over Europe too!'

'Ah, man! That's coz of all those pictures, like, I mean… when did they start showing them?'

'Last Wednesday was when they started showing the pictures, then you were front page of the *LA Times*.'

'OK, OK… You know I found out that…'

'Your call is being recorded and monitored,' interrupted the pre-recorded operator.

'I found out that they informed my people Friday, I believe, that Friday before, and I talked to my people that Monday, and because my people didn't react so they just put them up on TV?'

'Who's your "people"? Your attorneys?'

'Nah, nah, my wife, my sister… Hey, they got my sister on there too. She's in one of those pictures… Yeah, yeah, my sister and her two daughters.'

'Oh God, that's ridiculous!'

'So… er…. I can go into more detail when I see you tomorrow. It's hard to remember that name… You know, the girl that l ives down the street from you. You know, 1548 West… 15 something…'

'You need to get more pills, Lonnie, for your memory. You've got enough pills that you take, but now you really need something for your memory because you're not good with that. You're getting Alzheimer's, I think.'

At this he laughed.

'Yeah, well, that's why I never went nowhere without a camera. Like, everywhere I went, I had a camera. I was taking pictures everywhere I went… so… Oh, what?' He shouted to another

inmate who needed the phone. *'Hey, I gotta go now, they're taking the phone... See you tomorrow.'*

'Yes, see you tomorrow, Lonnie.'

After nineteen minutes and fifteen seconds the line went dead.

★★★

Now back to the subject at hand. It might seem as though I am jumping around but that's because I am following Franklin's words in the order he says everything and that is very out of order. I will give some more background on this very complex character as I continue.

It seems to me that not only does Franklin end up being accused of scores more murders each time I interview him, but also he ends up with two or three more kids from his various extra-marital activities each time I see him as well. Three visits ago, his body count had risen from eight victims to possibly thirty. Two visits ago, it had gone from thirty to the crazy number of up to 180 possible victims. I was getting quite used to this increase. However, during my last visit, he had told me that one of his three affairs had produced a daughter, who is now seventeen. She would be the third child along with his two children, Crystal and Chris (Christopher), from his marriage to Sylvia. Today, however, he thinks he has a son in his late forties – actually he is almost positive of it – and he has another daughter, also called Crystal, who is thirty-five years old. This daughter was specifically named Crystal by her mother after his 'planned' daughter Crystal, who was about six years older – she would be about forty-one now.

MEETING SYLVIA, MARRIED LIFE AND JAIL

The plot grows from here. Crystal and Crystal – the half-sisters – are friends but they don't know they are sisters. Yes, they go way back and have always thought it was a mere coincidence that their names happen to be the same and also their mothers are friends. However, we are not in Arkansas now, we are talking South Central Los Angeles in the eighties. Franklin had always kept his lips firmly sealed, knowing that both girls were not only his daughters and also very close friends, but they were half-sisters too.

Sylvia still had no idea this 35-year-old buxom beauty was her husband's biological daughter. In the eighties Franklin had an affair with another Catholic girl named Gloria, also with firm anti-birth control beliefs. They were together just four or five months and then she too became pregnant and gave birth to a boy. David would be in his late forties now and this is the child who Franklin believes is his flesh and blood. Gloria had hazel eyes and olive skin but he cannot remember much more about her than that.

Gloria already had one little girl and they had been living in Long Beach with her boyfriend, a large African-American whose name Franklin doesn't recall. When Gloria became pregnant, she led her other half to believe it was his. However, as the child grew, it was obvious that little David was looking less and less like his so-called father. So before too long, Gloria and her daughter moved back to LA from Long Beach and moved close to Franklin and his 'real' family. She made sure that she rented a home only one block from where he lived with his wife Sylvia and two children. Franklin knew she was close by and it became increasingly uncomfortable for him because he didn't want to rock the boat.

One day he bumped into Gloria and was forced to acknowledge her as they were passing on the same side of the street. She was with both of her children, one of them most likely his. He mumbled a flippant hello as if she might have been a stranger. However, once he started thinking with his private parts again, having an easy piece of ass around the corner was something he wasn't going to ignore. It became regular that he would stop by Gloria's for a quickie on his way to and from work.

After a short time, Gloria started to feel used, so she played games, making Franklin stay longer so he would get in trouble with his wife. Once he even fell asleep at hers and she didn't wake him up, hoping she might be the cause of a break-up with Sylvia. But that never happened and to this day Sylvia remains the number one love of his life.

Ultimately he started to get annoyed with Gloria's obvious games and decided to pull back from her. He stopped calling her and she gradually got the message: he loved his wife and wasn't going anywhere with anyone else any time soon. After a short time, rumours had spread that this strikingly large man from Long Beach, who had spent years with Gloria, was not the father of young David. So this man came storming up to LA to track Gloria down and confront her at her home. Understandably, she was very afraid and told Franklin that they should try and kill him before he created some serious harm to either of them or their son, David. But Franklin wanted nothing to do with this and tried to disengage, breaking all ties as best he could, despite the fact they shared a son together.

To this day Sylvia knows little about these affairs, nor does she know about some of the resulting offspring. Franklin says that he is still in touch with one of his daughters, Crystal, who he had with Sandra, even though she left for Panama thirty-three years ago when his daughter would have been about twelve. I don't believe Sylvia is fully aware of her husband's son, who is now in his late forties, whom he had with Mary and I doubt she would know of his most recent family to date either. Therefore I will say no more here.

Back in the early 2000s Franklin and his wife Sylvia hired an 18-year-old nanny for their son Christopher and she became friends with her boss. They had hired her as it was during the short period of time when Franklin actually had a full-time job working nine to five. However, being so unused to a daily routine, he would complain that he suffered with so much traffic on his daily commute. So he decided to pop the nanny in the car with him so that he could use the carpool lane. I was sceptical that this was the only reason as I know that sex was always on his mind. However, in Franklin's opinion, she wasn't an attractive girl by anyone's standards. After sharing many a story together, she wasn't bashful about telling him that she had never been intimate with a man. So, after one too many hints that she was still a virgin at the ripe young age of eighteen, Franklin's ears started to flap even more. It was never mentioned how she got home but I assume that Franklin took her to where she was supposed to end up before he then headed off to work.

Despite not being attracted to her one jot, he said he decided to do her a favour and pop her cherry. This sexual encounter, which he allegedly engaged in along with his multiple homicides, went undetected by his unassuming wife. By this time they had been married for over twenty years. Again, this 'cherry popping' story could very well have been a fabricated one – I never found out.

27 JANUARY 2011: INTERVIEW WITH FRANKLIN

I arrived at the High Power line at 8.40 a.m. to be let in at 10 a.m. After we were let in and had had our IDs checked, I sat in my regular spot next to Mabel, with whom I would sit every Thursday when we came for our visits. The same regular routine went on and inmates' last names were called twice. After thinking they had forgotten about me, they finally called 'Franklin', which was also repeated twice. I went up to the counter to take my white slip and proceeded to booth A15, which seemed to be the same one where he was always stationed.

I sat down on my uncomfortable metal stool and lifted the receiver. Franklin was sitting there, bouncing around as always. The first thing he mentioned was that he was concerned that my letters weren't reaching him, so he asked me to write to the guy in the next cell but one from him: #1062589, who had been charged with the murder of a man by kicking him to death in a fight.

The point behind this would be to see how quickly the letter reached Ward. Franklin had brought down a piece of paper with the words 'Victoria Franklin' on it. I could see it upside down from where I was sitting, so I said, 'What? Are we related now?' He put his finger to his lips, saying '*Shhh,*' as the phone lines were always recorded. He went on to explain subtly that he wanted me to write to this man as a test. I followed his instructions and waited to see what transpired.

Franklin loved to read about black history – it was a subject he really excelled in and also the one he earned the best grades in at school. I learned a lot about it from him and found it to be very interesting. One time, he explained to me all about slavery and how it formed the mixed races.

If a plantation owner accidentally impregnated a slave, the pregnant slave would then be sent to another plantation to work. When she was due to give birth, she would be driven to a black neighbourhood to have the baby and be forced to drop the child off there. Then out of the blue Franklin interjected with: *'You know that my DNA was found on ten bodies so far?'* After I realised he had gone off on yet another tangent, I thought about all of the other dozens of souls who were pictured in the *LA Times* as more of his possible victims and wished he would expand on this subject further. However he closed it down after making that open ended comment. I prayed that most of them would be confirmed to be alive and living a happy and healthy life somewhere. Multiple women pictured in the *LA Times* photo were never found. Some were proven to be family members of his, but most were just Jane Does (women who were never identified by anyone).

As always, my visit lasted just over an hour, thanks to the higher-ups at the LASD, who went out of their way to give me that extra time. This was especially helpful as by now they knew I was writing a book.

★★★

THE GRIM SLEEPER

THE MORNING PAPER

28 January 2011: the very next morning, Franklin was front page of the *LA Times* all over again, with two more bodies found with traces of his DNA on them. This would ultimately mean that The Grim Sleeper was not actually sleeping during the thirteen years he was supposed to have been lying dormant. In fact, he had killed at least two more victims over that period of time. To me this indicated that he should no longer be called The Grim Sleeper as he never seemed to have slept at all.

As my visits with him became more frequent and our phone calls were becoming more in-depth, he opened up to me on almost all levels. Sometimes he would tell me a whole story in great detail, then at the end he would say to me: '*Now, don't go putting that in your book, coz my wife, my sister, my kids, they don't know nothin' 'bout that.*' So, right in front of him, I ripped the page up so that I didn't mix it up with what I was going to be documenting.

One day, Franklin lowered his voice to almost a whisper and in a very calm tone really opened up and started to tell me a very private story that he'd rarely told anyone before. He said that when he was in his mother's womb, she was in a very bad car accident. She was travelling with her husband, Lonnie Sr, and they had a head-on collision with another car. This caused her to receive a lot of body and head trauma.

She suffered a broken ankle and broken ribs so was subsequently put on strong medication and forced to wear a body cast for a substantial period of time. All the while she was pregnant with a future serial killer. After a few months of taking heavy medication, Franklin Jr was born. Rumour has it that he also suffered indirect trauma, possibly cranial damage. Could it be that he followed in the footsteps of some of the other notorious serial killers before him?

From my experience and interviews with many serial killers, including Wayne Adam Ford and Bobby Joe Long, any kind of brain injury, especially to the frontal lobe, can cause a person to change dramatically in the area of violent behaviour. The frontal lobe is the primary area that determines a human being's emotions – good and bad. When this area is damaged there is no telling how a person's behaviour can change; often it is for the worse, as in the case of many serial killers.

Franklin believes that the reason why he suffered a learning disability at school was due to the damage done to his mother with the impact of the car accident and the strong medication that she was given while carrying him. He was always eager to learn at school but couldn't quite grasp it.

Miss Moss took a lot of time with each of her students but she would take extra time with young Franklin. She had a very positive impact on his life, especially with him being so young and impressionable and being the centre of ridicule for much of his childhood.

Miss Moss was still teaching Franklin at the third grade level although the rest of the class was now learning the fifth grade. In each class there were anywhere between thirty-two and thirty-six children so they were clearly over-populated. At the time Franklin attended, the school was predominantly black – the Hispanic community didn't start to move in until the late nineties.

4 April 1968 was a day that went down in history as the day

THE GRIM SLEEPER

Martin Luther King was assassinated in Memphis, Tennessee. Miss Moss always had a soft spot for Franklin and would always turn a blind eye when her pupil would smuggle a radio into the classroom. She knew he would listen to the radio via an earphone in one ear throughout his studies, and with the other ear he listened to her. It helped him stay focused, she considered.

On this particular day, it was announced on Franklin's radio that Martin Luther King, the patriarch of the African-American community, had been assassinated. Miss Moss knew Franklin was the only one with a radio in the classroom so she called him up to stand in front of the class and turn up the volume for everyone to listen.

Through their tears, they listened to Franklin's radio as the whole terrible event was taking place. There was nothing anyone could do but sit there transfixed to the most devastating news ever to hit the black community. It was also a ground-breaking day for the rest of America as well.

Coincidentally, Franklin always loved to protest – he didn't care about the cause, he would just protest whenever and wherever there was an opportunity. In high school he protested to vote: he didn't have any reason to vote and certainly wouldn't have known who to vote for, but nevertheless protesting was one of the things he did best. It made him feel powerful and important, something he rarely felt due to his size and the continuous bullying he endured from his peers. He even protested that there should be a public holiday for Martin Luther King's birthday, something that now exists.

MEETING SYLVIA, MARRIED LIFE AND JAIL

24 FEBRUARY 2011: INTERVIEW WITH FRANKLIN

I took the train as usual to Union Station and arrived very early. Not even 8.30 a.m. and I was already waiting in the High Power line to be let through at 10 a.m. The same women were there again and we chatted for the entire time until we were let through.

This time Franklin's name was called first. It was said with about eight other inmates' names too, which was odd. No sooner had I sat down to wait for his name to be called, I was let through to the visiting area. It was about 10.40 a.m. when I finally walked over to A15, where he had been not so patiently waiting for goodness knows how long. We said our hellos and I saw his eyes were watering heavily. I thought he was crying but he said that all the dust around the cubicle he was sitting in was making his eyes water. It certainly looked as though he'd been crying – they obviously don't do much dusting at the LA County Jail.

Franklin opened up with the news that his wife, Sylvia, had come to see him the previous Saturday and they had expressed how much they loved each other. However, he also told me that his baby's mama was coming the following Saturday. Thankfully, I hadn't bumped into any of them yet! I wanted to reel him in again so that he would focus on telling me more about his home life and his diverse and colourful neighbourhood, but for me that was always a chore for he would bounce off the walls every time he opened his mouth. I'm not sure if this was caused by the medication he was on or because he has ADD (Attention Deficit Disorder), but it was annoying having to always try to reel him in from talking about all and sundry when I was there to talk on only one subject – his life before jail.

As I mentioned before, Franklin lived on 81st Street with his wife and children – Sylvia, Christopher and Crystal. Their house was built in 1928 and is 1,770 square feet and green in colour. After his arrest in 2010, it was repainted grey. I found that out when I was flying on patrol in a certain law enforcement helicopter (I won't say which); it was at night and when we were in the South LA area, the pilot asked if I wanted to fly over the house of the 'alleged' Grim Sleeper, as he knew this was the book I was working on at the time. I gave the address of Franklin's home, which was 1728 81st Street, and told him it was green in colour. They lit up the house with the nightsun and the house they'd lit up was grey. I told them they must be lighting up the wrong house as I knew for a fact it was green. After we orbited a number of times with the nightsun firmly lighting up 1728 81st Street, I realised the house must have been repainted. I later discovered that it had been repainted a grey colour soon after Franklin's arrest as his wife still lived there and didn't like people driving by all the time. Poor Sylvia, that night was certainly more than a drive-by – I hope she wasn't home when we were lighting her home up like that.

Across the street from where Franklin and his family lived, there was a guy called Gerald, who lived with his brother Rick and also his mother, Grace. (Some of these names have been changed for reasons of privacy.) Rick lived in the back house and Gerald lived in the front house. It was a known crack house in the neighbourhood and this really bothered

Franklin because he believed that it made the area dangerous. Personally, I believe it was Franklin himself who made the neighbourhood more dangerous. Gerald was a tall guy, who was not only addicted to crack but a crack dealer too. He certainly liked to deal out of the house all day and all night long. This drove Franklin nuts.

Grace either ignored what was going on with her sons or she simply wasn't aware. Perhaps she just thought they were popular and had a lot of friends. Ah, the innocence and naivety of the older generation! It seemed that when anyone was released from jail, they would inevitably make a beeline for Gerald's house and light up a crack pipe. One time, Franklin threatened the mother by stating firmly that he would call the cops on what they were doing in her house, as it was '*making the neighbourhood dangerous*'. He went on to say that if she didn't stop her sons from behaving like this, he would make sure their home would be levelled to the ground and become a parking lot for the city.

Grace had only paid $10,000 for the property, which consisted of two two-bedroom duplexes, one at the front and the other at the back. It was a steal at that price and she certainly didn't want to lose it because of her sons' bad behaviour.

Franklin's wife, Sylvia, dutifully went to work, as a carer looking after elderly people, bright and early every morning at 6.30 a.m. – she was so punctual that you could set your watch by the time she would leave the house. She never noticed that only steps away from her home were a number of drugged-up guys sloppily lined up by the fence to buy and sell crack directly opposite from where she and her husband lived.

Also, she never ventured into the garage where her husband kept the place like the slum lord of a porn shop. Sylvia never knew that in the garage that was attached to their house were numerous pictures of naked and semi-naked women, some looking as though they were dead or drugged-up. There were pornographic movies, guns, microwaves, televisions and a whole lot more. None of this made sense until the trial, so it was a good thing she never entered the garage. Although Lonnie hadn't expressly forbidden her to go in there, it was to be his space and was overloaded with all of his collections, which is the reason I feel Sylvia never went in there.

Although Franklin had little association with drugs or drug dealers, he did, however, own at least six guns, which were kept in the house. He always kept at least one in the trunk of his car. I asked him why he would keep so many guns when he wasn't a gang member or drug dealer, but he firmly shut me down and proudly said that it was because he was an avid collector.

Of course I knew from what the detectives had already told me that the guns in his possession were all found to be loaded. So, although I already knew the answer, I wanted to challenge him and so I boldly asked if any of the guns in his home were loaded. He responded honestly and told me they all were. I don't know of any gun collectors who keep their guns loaded in their homes, so for me this was a first and also very telling. I naturally pushed further and even though I knew the answer, I asked him if the ballistics from the crimes of which he had been accused matched any of his guns. He openly admitted that yes, the ballistics did in fact go back to at least one of his guns.

MEETING SYLVIA, MARRIED LIFE AND JAIL

A while back, Gerald and Rick had stolen a gun from their mother and sold it to Franklin. Coincidentally, he had one of his guns stolen in 1996 but somehow ended up with the same gun again in 2006, which had originally been the one that was stolen from his driveway. Here's what happened:

It was a typical weekday morning and Lonnie's wife Sylvia was warming up the Cadillac to drive their children to school as she did almost every morning. This particular day was bitterly cold, unusual in Los Angeles, so she had the heater blaring to warm the car up first. She then went back inside to collect Christopher and Crystal and put them both in the car, but by the time she'd come outside again, the vehicle had disappeared from the driveway. It had been stolen. Finally, when the family car was recovered, around five weeks later, it was missing most of the parts and had clearly been stripped. To Franklin's dismay, the gun that he always kept hidden in the trunk had been stolen.

Years later, in 2006, Franklin bought a gun which he seemed to recognise. Coincidentally it was his own gun from years before which had been stolen, along with his car, back on that cold day in 1996. What goes around comes around, even when it comes to buying and selling guns, I guess.

Franklin spoke of a neighbour to the west side of his house on 81st Street. She was an older woman who lived with her son and his girlfriend. He thinks they lived at 1730 81st, next door to his family home. Oliver, the son, along with his girlfriend, had come back from living in Washington State to live with his elderly mother here in South LA. This was in the mid-nineties, about 1994. Oliver was a light-skinned black guy who drove a '91 olive green Toyota

Tercel. He was a very smart guy but he ended up smoking crack within the first three months of moving home. His girlfriend caught on pretty quickly too. His mother lived in the front house and she put Oliver and his girlfriend in the duplex at the back.

Franklin remembers that nearly every night at about 12.30 a.m. there would be the sound of a car screeching into reverse and, like clockwork, it would be Oliver racing out of his driveway. Within four or five minutes he'd be back. Then the whole thing would be repeated half an hour later, with the accelerating out of the driveway, shooting off down the road to a dope house and coming back to chase the next high. Sometimes he would do this three or four times in the same night, which drove Franklin nuts. Although he has never done any kind of drug, he had asked people he knew who used drugs what was going on in his neighbourhood. I do believe Lonnie when he says he never took drugs and I know he also rarely drank. This helped in the control he had in being able to supply them to the prostitutes in the area. He knew the power that drugs had and he took full advantage, yet insisted he never touched them himself.

I know very little about crack outside of those that the LASD would arrest whenever I went out on my weekly patrol with them in West Hollywood. Although Franklin has never tried drugs himself, he seemed to know a lot about them. He would explain to me in great detail the effect crack has and why it is so addictive, and how the very first hit is the ultimate high. After that, crack addicts are always trying to chase that same high but can never quite achieve it again. Each 'rush' is that much weaker than the last so they have to take more and more each time. Franklin knew this, and knew that it gave him power over them.

After enough time goes by and after ingesting so much of this lethal chemical, crack users ultimately spiral down until they completely bottom out or even die. Often when I was riding along with the LASD we'd have some cracked-out individual sitting in the back of the car with us so high that I thought they were going to die. Some of them acted as if they were schizophrenic and maybe they were. In those days I really couldn't tell the difference between a schizophrenic and someone on a heavy drug. Nowadays I think I can. It's always been shocking to me how someone would choose to make themselves act that psychotic by ingesting a controlled and illegal substance, but over the years I have learned that drug addiction truly is a disease and often isn't the person's fault. After all, no one chooses to become addicted to drugs, and when they are, they can sell their soul to the devil to get their next high. We must feel sorry for these people and not judge them so harshly as society seems to do.

Going back to the neighbours on 81st Street... Oliver's girlfriend was kind of nice-looking, but she would always walk up to Western, which was only three or four houses up from where they lived on 81st Street. She was about 5ft 1in and it was apparent to Franklin that she had started to sell herself for crack due to her addiction. Oliver didn't seem concerned about the welfare of his girlfriend, just so long as she got him the crack that he too was addicted to.

Apparently all men that do crack with their 'girlfriends' know full well that the woman is selling herself but will never admit to it. They know that crack doesn't just fall out of the sky so they're likely to be doing something untoward. The boyfriends are often quite happy for their girlfriends to sell themselves for crack because they get to benefit from the transaction.

Oliver's girlfriend was always a very polite woman and would often shout over the fence to their neighbour: 'Hello, Mr Frankie.' ('Frankie' was her name for him.) Franklin knew full well that she was a 'strawberry' and that she would score crack for herself and Oliver. One evening at about 8 p.m., he saw her walking by herself up the road towards 81st and Western. He was driving his red Mazda RX-7 and he told me that he thought she was on her way to Kmart – yeah, right! So he pulled over and asked if she needed a ride. She declined with 'Oh no, thank you, Mr Frankie.' He pressed further and asked her again, but still she refused.

Just as he was about to go on with telling me this very long-winded story, the visit ended abruptly. We weren't even given twenty-five minutes, the scheduled amount of time for a visit, let alone the full hour we usually had. Franklin would get very long-winded with his stories, which got me a little narked. He could have said that story in a quarter of the time but he got side-tracked and distracted very easily. This, I felt, was because he didn't want to answer any of the real questions that he knew I had for him. Suddenly, after about twenty -five minutes, the phones completely shut off, which got him very annoyed. We did our usual and continued to talk by lip-reading through the glass.

Usually the deputies gave us an hour plus and never cut us off at the scheduled time, but this time the session wasn't as long as usual, so I didn't get to write much down.

However, I wasn't about to complain as I was always given way more time than anyone else on all my other interviewing days.

'*I was on a roll*,' he mouthed and I nodded in response. I asked him to try and remember the story for when we talked on the phone on Monday. Like clockwork, he would call me every Monday evening and a few times during the week if he had the phone. So, at about 12.15 p.m. the visit ended. He mouthed the words '*peace out*' and '*goodbye*' and then I left the visiting area.

3 MARCH 2011: INTERVIEW WITH FRANKLIN

I went to one of the regular cubicles this time – A17, not A15, and sat down opposite Franklin. Again, we said our hellos and he put up to the glass the letter that I had written to his 'friend' in the cell close to him.

Over a month ago Franklin had asked me to write to this man and use a fake return address, with my name being Victoria Franklin so that the guy would know it was set up by him. So I did just that, posting the letter on 27 January, and he mouthed through the glass that he had only received it the previous day – 2 March. So, Franklin's question had been answered. They weren't just delaying his mail, but the mail to all High Power K10 individuals. This would have been because mail written to these inmates often contained secret codes in the wording and so required extra scrutiny. He said, '*There's no such street address like this in Compton*.' Well, of course there wasn't – I was just making it up to look real!

He told me how he hated the food in jail so much that he

had refused to eat it that morning and most days, which has caused him to lose a huge amount of weight since his most recent arrest in 2010. Routinely he would always lose a lot of weight on the inside so that by the time he got out, he was skinny.

One time, he said, he was in jail for four months; he went in at 175lb and was released at 131lb. That's exactly my weight, I thought. He didn't feel bad not eating the food because he knew he'd only be in for a short time and could eat all he wanted when he came out. To which I responded in a subtle chastising way with: 'So, how much longer do you think you'll be in for this time?' I put on a serious face to see what he would do. He just breathed in and gave a very slow and calculated laugh. As if to say, 'Very funny, you know as well as I do that I'm not coming out.' But he had to respond and he then said: *'No, this time will probably be longer. Maybe six months, a year or a year and a half. Something like that.'* I gave a knowing smile just so he knew that I knew that I obviously just asked him a trick question. I went on to ask in an almost superficial way: 'But you are planning on coming out, aren't you?' To which he just talked over me before I finished, saying, 'Yeah, yeah, yeah, yeah.' Brushing me off, of course.

He was telling me how frustrated he gets when the deputies seem to get their kicks from intentionally cutting the phone lines off when he's calling his family. He explained that he was on the phone the other day with his wife Sylvia and they cut him off: *'Yeah, yeah, they be pulling that plug on us deliberately on four separate times, just because they din't like somethin' I was saying to her.'* I happen to know that it costs quite a lot for the receiving party to keep calling back, as the first minute is always the most expensive one. I feel that this story of Franklin's is true because I do know of other serial killers who have been picked on by the guards so it could possibly be the case here.

I told Franklin that coincidentally one of the detectives investigating his case also interviewed another serial killer, one whom I wrote a book about called *Serial Killers: Up Close and Very Personal* (John Blake Publishing, 2011). This serial killer, Wayne Adam Ford, is currently living on Death Row and was recently interviewed regarding the same victim who Lonnie Franklin Jr is accused of killing. Calling from Death Row, in the summer of 2011, Wayne Ford told me on the phone that only a few days before, an investigator had flown up to San Quentin from LA to interview him regarding an unsolved case. He wanted to find out if he had anything to do with the murder and dismemberment of a black prostitute in the South Los Angeles area because one of her breasts was cut off. This was Ford's modus operandi when he was out killing; however, he said it wasn't him. Wayne Adam Ford often told me that serial killers nearly always kill within their own race (although I'm not completely sure what he was basing this on), hence he had never killed any black or Asian women. According to the Grim Sleeper case, Franklin wasn't known to have dismembered any of his victims or cut off their breasts, it just wasn't the modus operandi here. So, I compartmentalised, as I always do, and proceeded to ask Franklin: 'The Grim Sleeper didn't chop anyone's breasts off, did he?'

He replied quickly with: '*Nah, nah, nah…. They're even accusing me of having body parts in my backyard.*' I found it very telling that he would answer by bringing the conversation right back to himself – you see, that was my trick. When I asked that question he subconsciously related it to himself, knowing he is The Grim Sleeper. However, he wanted to brush me off and not dwell on that point. But it was too late because he went straight on to something else they were accusing him of: having body parts in his garden. 'Really, I never read that anywhere,' I said. I went on to ask if he had ever owned an orange Pinto because The Grim Sleeper was supposed to have driven one. He firmly responded with a definite no on that one. He'd certainly had a Pinto, but according to him, he had never owned or driven an orange one. Hmm, we'll see about that…

I really wanted to get down and talk business with him, but as always, he wanted to go on about more trivial matters that he could have written about in a letter. Again, he was evading my questions so that he wouldn't slip, like he has done before, by giving me too much information. I found his habit of constantly changing the subject and evading my questions incredibly annoying, but I would usually respond by asking the question again, phrasing it in a different way in order to successfully get an answer out of him. I also knew how much he liked having me come to 'visit' him (yet, for me, it was always an interview) every week, as I too have a bubbly personality like him and I would talk about my life and everything I was up to in order to open him up more. This tactic often worked.

He went on and on about an old case that he firmly believes was a law enforcement cover-up, which happened years ago. It concerned an African-American woman who walked out of the Malibu Lost Hills Sheriff's station a few years ago and was later believed to have been murdered. She had not paid her bill in a restaurant, the cops were called and she was taken to jail. However, she was apparently released to no one and wasn't even driving a car at the time. Franklin said there was never any video of her walking out of the jail yet there was footage of her entering the jail. He is sure that the deputies killed her on the inside.

When they searched for her in the wooded areas near the station they found nothing. They searched twice more. However, the third time they uncovered badly decomposed bones belonging to this woman. He believes there was a big cover-up... but then he also believes O.J. Simpson is innocent! A lot of his conspiracy theories fall on deaf ears with me, especially anything implying such a convoluted and grandiose cop cover-up such as this one.

It was another long visit that ended after an hour and fifteen minutes of talking and another ten minutes of awkwardly lip-reading through the glass.

14 MARCH 2011: PHONE CALL FROM FRANKLIN

By Monday evening, Franklin was on the phone again with me:

'*Hey, it's Lonnie! Where you at?*'

'I'm in Las Vegas, Lonnie, on a spokesmodelling job,' I responded quickly as it was hard for me to talk with a load of my fellow spokesmodels around, listening in.

'*But there ain't no serial killers up in Vegas!*' was his quick-witted comeback.

'No, no, no! I know that, but I'm working my "other" career. You know, emceeing, spokesmodelling, you remember?'

'*Oh, yeah, yeah…*'

And the conversation went from there. I had told him that I wouldn't be visiting him that week as I was booked on a convention in Las Vegas. However, he either forgot or pretended he forgot. I think he was just missing my visits and our conversations, which were often one-sided due to his constant chatter about other inmates.

19 MAY 2011: INTERVIEW WITH FRANKLIN

I arrived at the Men's Central Jail at the normal time, 8.45 a.m., and stood in the High Power line until 10 a.m. when we all went through security like cattle. After many other names were called in batches, it was five minutes later that Franklin's name was called by itself with no other inmates' names, at 11 a.m., and so I took my slip of paper and went to booth number A16. Just when I came around the corner he was combing his hair, probably not expecting me to be called upon quite so soon. It was very funny as his hair is so very short, yet he was combing what little he had.

We talked mainly about black history and I learned a lot. As I have already said, Franklin majored in Black History and received a C grade. He absolutely loves talking about it and it is a subject I am also very interested in. He was telling me all about how the white women, who were the owners of the plantations, would have sex with the black male servants just as their white husbands would have sex with the female black servants. When the wife of a plantation owner became pregnant by a black servant, the husband would go out of town for about six or seven months and the baby would be delivered in a black neighbourhood. Another thing they would do was swap the slaves with a different plantation owner.

Franklin told me that the high yellows are very light-skinned black people, meaning they have been mixed with a white person in either their distant or recent background. Sometimes their hair is not Afro at all and it can even be pretty straight, yet still thick and coarse.

When I asked him during the course of our conversation if he'd ever hit a woman, he made a joke and said: '*My policy is you should hit a woman at least once a week, whether they deserve it or not!*'

I hoped he was joking so I pressed the issue further: 'Come on, Lonnie! I don't think you mean that, do you? Tell me the truth, that's a bit harsh, don't you think?' He said that he has never hit his wife, the reason being because '*she throws knives*'. According to him, when Sylvia gets angry she will take a sharp knife from the kitchen drawer and hurtle it through the air, so he would find himself ducking a lot of the time.

Then he told me a story about a woman that he went out with after he came out of the Army, in the 1970s, by the name of Velvet. He was only with her for a few months as she was extremely violent although '*a pretty good piece of ass*'. The reason for this was because, he said, '*It's like this, back in those days, black women didn't give blow jobs and if they did, they would expect something in return. This woman would give them all the time and never expected it to be reciprocated – that's the only reason I was with her.*' In fact, it was never Franklin's thing to go down on a woman unless he'd been in a relationship with her for a long period of time first. Anyway, he told me that after one of her violent attacks on him, although this was very out of character for him, he ended up giving her a black eye. He insisted he was rarely ever violent to women he knew. In my view, although these women may have been considered 'loose', they weren't prostitutes and so didn't end up dead.

Velvet was a very explosive woman and after one of their numerous arguments, Franklin decided to get her out of his home and drive her back to where she lived, which wasn't too far away at the time. However, when he came back to his home after dropping her off, within minutes there was a bang at the door and Velvet was back again. This time she decided to bite down on his thumb really hard and wouldn't let go. He was forced to pin her up against the wall to try and release his thumb from her vice-like grip. She still wouldn't let go, which made him punch her in the face to encourage her to release him. It worked, however she ended up with a black eye, a busted nose and a split lip. After this incident Franklin had to keep her in the house for the next few days until the swelling had gone down and she started to look semi-normal again. Right after that, he dumped her as he saw no more use for her, and her unbalanced tendencies to get into rages outweighed her being a 'great piece of ass'. I was shocked and appalled on so many occasions talking to Franklin, and this was certainly one of those, but I never let him see that. I've learned that you gain so much more information when you pretend to be genuinely interested and understanding of the horrors your interviewee has committed, rather than show the disgust you naturally feel.

I came out at 12.35 p.m. after just over an hour and a half. I was exhausted, as I often was after my interviews with Franklin. However, I knew that I had a lot of information. Again, whichever nice deputy allowed these extended visits probably did so because they now knew I was hard at work writing a book.

2 JUNE 2011: INTERVIEW WITH FRANKLIN

On this particular day I arrived at the jail at 9 a.m. I came later than usual as I always waited so long in the line, and I was one of the first people but always the last to be called upon to go in. This time I was in the visiting room by 10 a.m. and Franklin's name was called in the usual way at 11 a.m.

He was excited to see me and clearly wanted to start blabbering right off the bat. He said that I wouldn't believe who he was '*on the bus*' with the previous day: Michael Gargiulo. Now Gargiulo is a really sick and, in my mind, mentally ill serial killer. I had interviewed him once months before and he is so crazy that I couldn't get any sense out of him. (Later, I found out that I was the only person that Gargiulo ever spoke to, and my interview with him was used on a well-known television series called *48 Hours* which aired on CBS.)

It sounds so strange hearing Franklin so casually say that he was '*on the bus*' because one gets a vision of him sitting at a bus stop and then piling into a cramped space with a dozen other people and sitting beside other bus patrons as if he were a normal person. But he obviously meant the jail bus. I happen to know these buses only too well: he would have been locked in a cage positioned either directly behind the driver or the other deputy sheriff sitting across from him. Handcuffed and waist chained, he would have been sitting away from all the other inmates with Plexiglas between them. The other inmates sit in the main section of the sheriff bus and are all chained together in one long line. Goodness knows what would happen if one of them were to trip over... It would be like a domino effect, I suppose.

Directly opposite Franklin would be the other phone booth-like cage, where Gargiulo would have been sitting with the same restraints. He then described his opinion on his fellow passenger as follows: '*That guy's a scary lookin' dude. He looks like the devil and he kept on sayin', "They ain't got nothin' on me. No DNA, no nothin'." I was scared just by bein' on the bus with him and couldn't wait to get back to my cell. That guy is a freak... You really spoke to that dude?*'

I had told Franklin that long before I met him I had done an interview with one other alleged serial killer at the Men's Central Jail and it was Michael Gargiulo. I even said that I felt the exact same way about him as he did – he looked like the devil and his eyes were as cold as ice.

I left Franklin on a good note, as I always liked to do, giving him good reason to be eager for my next visit, at about 12.35 p.m.

Numerous interviews then followed, in person and on the phone, before the trial began. This is merely the shortened version of the life story of Lonnie David Franklin Jr from his own words.

THE TRIAL

16 FEBRUARY 2016 – DAY ONE OF THE TRIAL OF LONNIE DAVID FRANKLIN JR.

After almost six years – five years and seven months to be exact – and numerous delays, the trial of Lonnie David Franklin Jr finally began. The corridor along the ninth floor of the Criminal Courts Building was packed full of sheriffs, homicide detectives in suits, news reporters, cameramen and the family members of the innocent victims; there were also members of the general public who had all heard about the prolific case starting that day.

Once inside the courtroom of Dept 109, I made my way to sit at the very back. The seat where I had sat for years was taken and so too were the rest of the benches. Most seats were filled with the family members of the victims and the rest were taken up with news reporters who had a media pass.

I had been very worried that I might not get into the courtroom, especially on the first day, as I didn't even think of getting myself a media pass, especially back when I started this book over five years ago. I had never needed one before as being an author doesn't usually require a media pass, but a case of this magnitude might have proved me wrong. I'm not currently working exclusively with any network so getting media clearance was never on my agenda. However, I made it into the room even though it was a bit of a squeeze – I think I sat in the last seat in the place.

To my right sat a very nice producer for ABC News called Sherene Tagharobi, who was typing away at the speed of light. I gave her as much information as I could on Franklin and also the media circus that had been going on in the courtroom over the past almost six years.

Just after 9.15 a.m. Lonnie David Franklin Jr was brought in. Thin and withdrawn, he was almost like a shivering rabbit as he could see the magnitude of people who filled the room to watch his life unravel over the next few months. He was wearing a baby blue dress shirt and dark glasses. I've certainly never seen him looking like that before as I've only ever seen him shackled and handcuffed in a stylish oversized orange prison jumpsuit. However, this attire was clearly for the sake of the jurors so that they could remain unbiased.

The bailiff – an unhappy-looking man with a protruding jaw – called the court to order and Judge Kathleen Kennedy came to the bench. Judge Kennedy is a woman in her early sixties with a very pleasant face and a fabulous sense of humour. However, she has never yet managed to control Franklin's lead defence, Mr Seymour Amster. We will get to him further on.

Judge Kennedy asked counsel to state their appearances.

THE TRIAL

Kristen Gozawa, Seymour Amster and Dale Alterton were representing the defence and for The People (the prosecution) were District Attorneys Marguerite Rizzo and Beth Silverman and Darren Dupree with the Los Angeles Police Department (LAPD).

Right out of the gate Seymour Amster had apparently filed a motion, one of the many he has filed over these past five plus years. What was it this time, we all wondered. This time he had an issue with handcuffs and ID badges and he wanted to make sure that the case was going to be tried only on merit alone. It was a muffled conversation as they all gathered around the Judge's bench to talk, so I hardly heard a peep. When they broke away, Judge Kennedy came back requesting that The People did not mention anything about the pictures of any of the other potential victims, to which Beth Silverman retorted in her usual way that they had 'no intention of mentioning the other victims'. Within a few moments, seventeen jurors filed in: nine women and eight men.

At 9.26 a.m. Judge Kathleen Kennedy began speaking. First, she welcomed all of the jurors into her courtroom. She stated that there were 'eleven jurors and six alternates present'. One juror had to drop out so she selected the alternate juror to stand in by selecting a random number out of six. She chose number sixty-eight, an Asian man, and asked him to move to his newly assigned seat for the trial, telling him with a laugh, 'You've just won the lottery!'

Judge Kennedy then stated she wanted to give the jurors some instructions and also the procedures for the upcoming trial. After about sixteeen minutes she finished talking to them and addressed the court, saying how hot it was in the courtroom. It's true we were all sweating and a lot of the women were fanning themselves with books. One woman, a victim's family member, asked me to tear a page out of my notebook so that she could fan herself, so I duly obliged.

District Attorney Beth Silverman, the lead prosecutor on the case, is a very hard-looking attractive woman in her late forties. She is reputedly not well liked in her field but maybe that's because she is ruthless and does her job brilliantly. For some unknown reason I have felt that she has had a problem with me from the first day. She has made it clear that if I so much as breathe incorrectly, she will have me thrown out of the courtroom. Well, I happen to know that the Judge is the one making the decision on that and she seems like a lovely woman without any preconceived notions about not wanting me in her courtroom. Putting all this aside, D.A. Beth Silverman stood at the lectern and gave a very good and powerful opening statement:

> The evidence in this case will tell a story, a story of a serial killer who stalked the streets of South Los Angeles. A serial killer who is responsible for the murders of ten women and the willful, deliberate, pre-meditated attempted murder on an eleventh. All of these crimes occurring between 1985 up until 2007.
>
> In South Central in the eighties there was an epidemic of crack cocaine. It is a highly addictive and very destructive drug. It was cheap and extremely potent and, when it first came out, had a higher purity than powder cocaine. Its distribution and its use exploded in the 1980s in South Central Los Angeles.

It left a path of destruction in this area. People lost their jobs, homes, their families and their lives by overdosing. Some women would risk everything to acquire more of this drug. Some women were willing to sell their bodies and their souls to get their next high. This drug made people extremely vulnerable and those that wanted to take advantage would do so. It was perfect for someone who lived there, knew these kinds of women, knew the area and where prostitutes would congregate. It was perfect for someone who knew the alleyways and could prey on these types of women. Someone like the defendant. It was a perfect place and time for a serial killer to roam the streets without detection.

Ms Silverman explained in great detail how these women were dumped like trash in filthy alleyways, some with dirty mattresses and trash on top of them. Some were left to rot. Most were shot at close range; one was strangled and also shot. One of the youngest victims, Princess Berthomieux, was only fifteen when she was brutally murdered. All the victims were in a state of undress and some were completely naked when found. None had IDs on them and most had cocaine and alcohol in their systems. Because of this wicked and addictive drug most victims had a history of prostitution.

All of these lost souls who fell prey to The Grim Sleeper were African-American and seemed to all be shot with the same .25 calibre automatic firearm. It was apparent that they were shot at one location then dumped at a different one – this is known as a 'body dump'. Every single one of these victims was connected to the same serial killer either by DNA evidence, firearm evidence or both.

In the lunch break I spoke to Kenneitha Lowe, the younger sister of 26-year-old victim Mary Lowe. Referring to the crime scene pictures of her older sister, she responded to myself and other local news reporters: 'I didn't want that, I didn't want to see my sister like that.' She carried on, fighting back the tears, saying, 'I feel like she's here with me now, so I'm doing this for her.'

17 FEBRUARY 2016

At 7.45 a.m. I arrived for the second day of the trial. I had arranged to meet with Lonnie Franklin's neighbours who were there in court on the previous day. We all met even before the sheriffs had arrived on the ninth floor.

Richard 'Ricky' Harris and Paul Williams have known Franklin for three decades. Paul has lived directly next door to him for most of this time. Ricky is a tall black guy with a very jovial, happy-go-lucky personality – a very gentle soul, who I was sure was religious, but I hadn't asked him that yet. He certainly liked to talk, not just talk but make sure he meets everyone within a vicinity of two feet of him. I thought I was bad, but Ricky beats me to the punch! He clearly loves people and will leave no one out of any conversation he might be having. I had met him for the first time the previous morning on the ninth floor and we got along like a house on fire. We had chatted a lot the first day of the trial, mostly off the record. He even told me in no uncertain terms, 'Man, I don' care if a whole load of those juror people come back with him bein' guilty. I know for a fact 'e ain't done none of those crimes. He wern' like that. Lonnie he'ped all the elderly in the neighbourhood, he was a good family man. I know coz I lived down the block from him for years.'

Ricky goes back over twenty-six years with Franklin and knew him well. I was surprised as to the reason he was there but he said he just wanted to see filmmaker Nick Broomfield and punch him in the face for lying to him and making him look so bad in his documentary, *Tales of the Grim Sleeper* (2014). Either way, I know Nick, and this was the last place on earth he would be – at Lonnie Franklin's trial. Despite being one of the best documentary filmmakers in the world, he tends to piss off a few people, myself included. However, I hold no grudges and he and I have remained friends to this day.

Years before, I agreed to be filmed on camera for a number of days for Nick Broomfield's documentary. However, I started to feel uncomfortable with the strange and unrelated questions that he was asking me. I even stated this to him and asked him to give me some kind of creative control as to how I would be portrayed in the finished documentary. He refused to give me any kind of creative control so I resorted to having my lawyer make sure my on-camera part, which was a lot, was removed from the documentary in its entirety. After a huge back-and-forth struggle with Broomfield and my lawyer, he reluctantly agreed to edit my part out. He did thank me in the credits, which was nice but I can safely say I dodged a bullet by making sure I was not part of his film.

As soon as I arrived at the courthouse on 17 February, I called Ricky from outside of the building. He laughed loudly and said that he was already there on the ninth floor, waiting for me!

I waited the usual long wait for the elevator (not all go to the ninth floor, mind you), and finally met up with Ricky, who was stuffing his face with some ramen noodles – at 7.40 a.m. no less!

So, after saying my hellos I wanted to sit down with Ricky and record him before we had to enter the courtroom. But before I had a chance to ask my first question, speaking through the noodles, he said to me, 'I've changed my mind!' On what had he changed his mind, I was wondering.

'Whoa, that evidence they presented in court yesterday, ooh, the picture of that lady who was shot and got away, he can't get out o' that. That's… noooooo… that's… that jus' ain' right.'

And the conversation continued between Ricky and myself:

Me: 'But yesterday you led me to believe that you felt he was 100 per cent innocent and now you've changed your mind?'

Ricky: 'No, I never said he was 100 per cent innocent, I jus' said it was hard for me to believe… somebody you bin knowing for damn near thirty years and this happened? It's hard for me to believe. Like I said in the past, Lonnie was buying cars and stealin' other cars just like it and he'd put the stolen parts on it. That was his life, and you see the po-lice [pronounced *poe-leece*] used to always raid his house but they never foun' nuttin'.'

Me: 'Why did they never find anything?'

Ricky: 'Coz, coz… to our opinion he wasn' stoopid! He didn' leave no stuff layin' aroun' to incriminate hisself. He don'ever leave nothin' behind. But they went in his house and got all that shit out that what we saw yesterday. He was very stoopid!'

Me: 'So if you've known him over twenty-six years and you're his neighbour, then how do you think he went about getting these women? When were the times you weren't with him?'

Ricky: 'He was a roamer at night. He roamed the streets at night.'

Me: 'Oh, you knew that?'

Ricky: 'Everybody knew that. Everybody knew.'

Me: 'Walking or driving?'

Ricky: 'He was driving.'

Me: 'Did he ever have an orange Pinto?'

Ricky: 'Yup…he had one of them years ago!'

I just struck gold when he confirmed this. In my interviews with Franklin, I had asked countless times if he ever owned an orange Pinto and he said he hadn't. He told me he owned a Pinto at one time, a few of them in fact, but not an orange one.

Me: 'Wow, really? He really did have an orange Pinto? Well, I didn't know that. That means he lied to me then. So what was his wife doing all this time while he was roaming the streets? And his son, what was Christopher doing?'

Ricky: 'Christopher, like you said yesterday, Christopher in't even in this state no more.'

Me: 'No, I'm talking about back then, decades ago when Lonnie was out at nights?'

Ricky: 'Christopher was always going to school. He wasn't… he din't hang with Lonnie…. nooooo.'

Me: 'What about his daughter Crystal?'

Ricky: 'Crystal was barely seen coz she was a young girl. An' young girls do what young girls do, chase young boys.' He then cracked up with laughter – Ricky is such a character. 'I'm tellin' the truth! You see, Crystal and my nephew were a couple for a while and…'

The elevator doors opened and at this I always panic in case a juror is in the vicinity – Ricky is so loud, way louder than me, and that's really saying something!

Me: 'Excuse me, you're not a juror, are you?' I turned and asked an inconspicuous-looking man standing to my right.

Unknown person: 'No, I'm not.' He responded with a shake of his head.

I still didn't feel safe as more people were coming up in the elevators. We decided to stop talking until the deputies were set up to let us through the metal detectors. They had only just arrived and were still half-asleep themselves.

As we walked down the hallway, I sat with Ricky right at the very first place on the bench next to the door just outside our courtroom, Dept 109. Same place as we sat yesterday. Again, no one was around us; the people huddling around the elevator all went to the left down the hall and some sat in the middle area meaning they weren't there for the Grim Sleeper trial. Ricky and I went to the right and sat at the very end. I even said to him that we (I meant only him) should 'lower our voices as we must be so careful that no jurors can hear us'. He duly obliged.

THE TRIAL

We then started talking again so I turned my recording device back on.

Me: 'So how did you meet Lonnie?'

Ricky: 'When he moved into our neighbourhood, almost thirty years ago.'

Me: 'What house did he move into?'

Ricky: 'Well, let me see... Paul is 1722, I stay at 1739 – I think it was 1728.'

Me: 'So if he moved into your area about twenty-six years ago, how old were you at the time?'

Ricky: 'Hey now, you wanna find out how old I am? Man!'

Me: 'OK, how old was Lonnie then?'

Ricky: 'He must've been about thirty.'

Me: 'He probably had young kids at the time then?'

Ricky: 'Yeah, he had real young kids at the time. Crystal's older than Chris.'

Me: 'What did you do with Lonnie when you hung out with him?'

Ricky: 'I din' really "hang out" with Lonnie, nobody "hung out" with Lonnie. Lonnie was a loner. We did do what neighbours do tho'. You know, we'd sit out in the front and talk a lot. He came to our barbecues and our parties.'

Me: 'Remind me of the names of the other neighbours, will you? One was Yvonne Bell, right?'

Ricky: 'Noooooo, I ne'er heard o' no Yvonne Bell.'

Me: 'Well, she was the aunt of one of the victims.'

Ricky: 'Well, she din' live in our neighbourhood.'

Me: 'OK, well, she probably lived a block or so away... Well, that's what she told me anyway.'

Ricky: 'There was Gary MacDonald, Steve Robinson, Paul Williams, Fernando.'

Although I do not know who MacDonald is, he went on to say, 'As a matter of fact, Gary is spos'd to be here, he called me last night.'

Me: 'Who was his best friend out of that group?'

Ricky: 'Nobody.'

Me: 'I thought of the guy's name yesterday when I left here who's Lonnie's best friend and that was Jerry.'

Ricky: 'Jerry, that's it! I forgot to tell you and I remembr'd when I left here yesterday.'

Me: 'Yeah, I interviewed him years ago and he didn't want to go on camera. He kind of looks like Lonnie, right?'

Ricky: 'Noooooo! Jerry looks more like this guy right here, but a little darker.'

He pointed to a quiet-looking black man, sat reading a book on our left. The man introduced himself to us and his name was Paul Sloane. He had a much smaller frame and a lighter skin than Ricky. Ricky and I had already made sure that he wasn't part of the jury so that opened up the conversation for us to talk with him.

Me: 'OK, but Jerry was good friends with Lonnie, right? Because Jerry told me that he and Lonnie were best friends and he was even there with Lonnie on the day he was arrested.'

Ricky: 'Nahhhh, he was just Lonnie's mechanic and business partner.'

Me: 'So, really? You never hung out with Lonnie?'

Ricky: 'Nooooooooo, I'll tell you what I used to do with Lonnie, I used to make money with Lonnie. Like I told you, Lonnie would, like, go to insurance sites and tow yards and get cars. He'd get his crew to go and steal a car jus' like that and then he'd take the parts off the stolen car and put [them] on the bought car. Then he would pay me one hundred bucks to drive the stripped car away for him.'

Me: 'OK, I got it. So you were receiving stolen property?'

Ricky: 'Nooooooo, I was getting rid of "stolen property". But I think I'm OK as there's a statute of limitation on that coz it's bin about fi'teen years!'

Me: 'So did you ever go to jail?'

Ricky: 'No, I never got caught!'

Me: 'Well, you know Lonnie often went to jail. You know that, right?'

Ricky: 'Yeah, well, you see, like I to'd you, the po-lice used to raid his house like it was the thin' to do.'

Me: 'How often?'

Ricky: 'Oh, it was often, sometimes like once or twice a month.'

Me: 'And what were they looking for? Stolen cars?'

Ricky: 'Car parts and stolen cars.'

Me: 'And they never found anything, why?'

Ricky: 'They never found nothin', nooooo.'

Me: 'Why?'

Ricky: 'Coz when Lonnie gets the stolen car, he'd park it on the street, ya know, down the street, but somewhere where he could see it from his window but wayyyyyyy down the block. And when he'd get ready to do it, he'd pull it in there real late at night and bing bam boom, he'd get me to drive it off the street. He'd leave nothin' behind. Nothin'!'

Me: 'OK, so he was clever. OK, so when he was using

those women, "strawberries" as you call them, did you ever see any of them?'

Ricky: 'Nooooo, that's what I keep tellin' people, Lonnie din' bring those people to his house, which is why I can' figure out why he brought this girl that close to the house. What possessed him to bring her there? But I figured out, the way they talked about it yesterday, he must din' have no gun and he din' anticipate that when he picked this girl up that he wouldn't have to go back and get his pistol. That's probably what he did. Hearin' all that stuff from yesterday, I figured… I said… that must've bin jus' what he did. That's why he brought that girl even to the neighbourhood, he realised that he din' have his gun and he wan'ed to kill her!'

Me: 'OK, I see, so he wanted to kill her but he had forgotten his gun?'

Ricky: 'He had to've done. To come that close to his house, coz why would he come that close to his house, go to his house and then come back and then shoot the girl? Coz he din' have no gun. He din' have his gun.'

Me: 'So what about the motels? Did he take them to motels? Where did he have sex with them?'

Ricky: 'I doubt it, I doubt it. Prob'ly in the car.'

Me: 'You mean that he would have sex with them in the car?'

Ricky: 'Yeah. Well, a strawberry would.'

Then Ricky turned to speak to Paul Sloane on his left:

Ricky: 'Man she don' know what a strawberry is. I was tellin' her there's a difference between a strawberry and a prostitute. There's a big difference.'

Me: 'But isn't it the same thing? If you're having sex with someone for something?'

THE TRIAL

Ricky: 'A strawberry is cheaper coz if you give them five dollars' or ten dollars' worth of dope, it's cheaper that way.'

Me: 'So did you ever use a "strawberry" with him?'

Ricky: 'Who me? Noooooooo, I'm a Christian.'

Me: 'But so what? Lonnie claims to be one too.'

Ricky: 'His wife and kids went to church every single Sunday on the corner of 81st and Western. Lonnie was not with them!'

Me: 'But Lonnie told me that he went to another church, a different one from his wife. Wasn't that true?'

Ricky: 'Yeah, he did, he did occasionally... only very occasionally.'

Me: 'Did you know the nanny that was there? I think she was white? Someone who he had sex with that also looked after the kids?'

Ricky: 'Nanny? That might be what you call it in your country but not here. Yeah, there was someone that said she used to take care of his kids but that's bull... that jus' ain' true.'

Me: 'Now, remind me of Nikkia, whose boyfriend was Gerald, Lonnie's other neighbour. She was a prostitute and a crack addict, right? Gerald was a crack dealer, right?'

Ricky: 'Noooooooo, Gerald weren' no crack dealer! Gerald's still there, he was jus' a crack user. Nikkia was on drugs when he met her. Where'd you get that from, Nick [Broomfield]?'

Me: 'No! I got everything, all my information, from Lonnie. I've spent hours with Lonnie over the years, interviewing him exclusively.'

Ricky: 'Well, what was he tellin' you about Nikkia and Gerald?'

Me: 'Oh, he would just go over the whole neighbourhood with me, telling me about everyone who lived there, including you and Paul.'

Ricky: 'What d'he tell you 'bout me?'

Me: 'He told me that you were a good friend, but it's all in my book which I've forgotten for now as it's been on hold these past few years. I haven't read it for ages.'

Ricky: 'Wait a minute… How'd'you write a book and di'nt read none of it?'

Me: 'Well, I wrote it over the years that I was visiting Lonnie after he was arrested. Then, once I had completed documenting his life story, I didn't go back and re-read it. Besides, I'm not concerned because I have his exclusive life story from his own words. He promised me he'd never speak to anyone else besides me outside of his own family members.

'Every time I interview a serial killer, I make quite sure that they are talking only "exclusively" with me. I don't waste my time going to a jail every week, and taking phone calls a few more times a week, for years, if I don't have a level of "exclusivity". Besides, Lonnie was only ever allowed two visits a week: every Thursday I would go and see him and every Saturday, his wife would go.

'You see, most of the higher-ups in the Sheriff's Department have known me since I came to America at nineteen, so I would subtly be given extra time with Lonnie. Usually, three times the amount of time than what is permitted for an Ad Seg, High Power "K-10" inmate.

'Anyway, back to what I was just saying. Lonnie used to tell me about a lady who had two sons. I really want to know who they are as I cannot remember their names.'

Ricky: 'Ahhhhhh, you might be talkin' 'bout Joe and Chuck. Miss Cole stay'd in the front, but he stayed in the back in a room.'

Me: 'Right, thank you, finally! And what's Miss Cole's first name?'

Ricky: 'I dunno... Gerther, Gerter, Gerta... somethin' like that.'

Me: 'Have you got a computer, Ricky, because I'd like you to see my blog?'

Ricky: 'No, I don' have no computer an' I don' want no computer... Nothin' like that. I don' even have an email.'

Me: 'So, tell me more about the neighbourhood, like did you ever argue with Lonnie?'

Ricky: 'Oh yeah, hell yeah, even he an' my father was feudin'.'

Me: 'What do you mean? Tell me, what did you argue about?'

Ricky: 'Lonnie was a weirdo, he was just a weirdo. He was just plain weird.'

Me: 'In what way?'

Ricky: 'In all ways. He was jus' weird. See, you don' know him the way we do... He was strange because he would do things to irritate people in the neighbourhood... like Paul. Well, Paul wanted to fight with... Nooo, I better not say nothin' coz I don't wanna say somethin' that Paul might read or hear about, and then he'd know that I said it coz I know that he and Lonnie really got into it, you know, like fightin' and stuff. My father and him got into it too. I have to axe [ask] my sista' 'bout that. I believe it was somethin' Lonnie did or said that really made my father mad. It was somethin' he did in the neighbourhood. I don' remember.'

Me: 'Was he being rude about or to a woman?'

Ricky: 'No, in his eyes all women were "strawberries" [women who sell their bodies for dope]. All women were no good in his eyes.'

Me: 'Even his wife?'

Ricky: 'She was barely there.'

Me: 'So, did they live in the same house, or…'

Ricky: 'Yeah, she lived there but she was barely there. She was like working at an "in-home care" and she would be there three or four times a week.'

Me: 'Did he tell you what kind of work his wife does?'

Ricky: 'She's a principal, a school principal.'

Me: 'Yeah, I knew that.'

Ricky: 'I din' find that out 'til he got arrested.'

Me: 'Sylvia, right?'

Ricky: 'Yeah, tha's right. She was doin' work that keeps her away from home for two or three days out of a week. But she was barely there. Then after he got arrested, she was always there. She was always there 'til they started shooting up their homes.'

Me: 'Did you ever see them hold hands in the twenty-six years you've known them from the neighbourhood?'

Ricky: 'Oh yeah, yeah, they were a family when she was there… Yeah, they had barbecues and all that.'

Me: 'Do you think in later years they shared the same bed?'

Ricky: 'Don' know.'

Me: 'Did you ever see what the inside of the house looked like?'

Ricky: 'Don' know. Didn' nobody go inside Lonnie's home. Lonnie's front yard stayed well-manicured always.'

Me: 'Did you ever see any of the women he had affairs with? Or the ones that he had children with besides his wife?'

Ricky: 'I know one girl, her name is Donna. I don' know her last name, she stayed on 80th. Evvvvvvveryone knew of Donna!'

Me: 'Yeah, I remember him speaking of Donna, but I don't remember in what context. How many kids did he have with her?'

Ricky: 'None, none.'

Me: 'And how many years were they having an affair?'

Ricky: 'Oh man, they were together for a loooooong time, like ten years or somethin'. Hey and who's that big fat man with that woman in a wheelchair?' He pointed very obviously over to the defence investigators on the case, who were close to us in the hallway. He went on to say about the man pushing the wheelchair, 'He's got a bad attitude!'

Me: 'Oh, she's part of the defence team and that's her son. She's a mitigating investigator.'

Ricky: 'What does mitigating mean?'

Me: 'They try to find reasons to defend Lonnie, anything that will take away from the prosecution, basically to weaken their testimony.'

Ricky: 'Well, he's a big ol' whale-looking guy... I'll beat him like a whale! He's nasty and he works for the defence? He got a bad attitude and I don' like him at all!'

Me: 'Hey, we have to be quiet now as the jurors are all walking down the hallway, look!'

Ricky: 'Yeah, yeah, we should be quiet – those people there are all jurors.'

★ ★ ★

Flash forward to when we all entered the courtroom:

8.52 A.M:

Lonnie was already sitting in his seat at the defence table, staring straight ahead, in the same shirt but no glasses this time. He was rarely blinking.

Another motion was made, by the defence again, so they all huddled around the Judge before the jury came in. From the little that I could hear, Marguerite Rizzo, the other District Attorney besides Beth Silverman, confirmed that she was 'not intending to introduce DNA reports or coroners' reports when a witness testifies'.

Judge: 'The witness who testifies in court is testifying to their opinion and their opinion alone. They may testify on objective facts that were recorded at the time. They will be given the facts, photos, raw documentation and will be forming their own independent opinion.'

Judge Kennedy explained: 'The Coroner's Office would perform an examination not just because they thought it was a homicide, they would do so for any unusual or unexplained death. The tragic fact that someone's body is found in an alley or in a dumpster or under a mattress or other various descriptions in this case doesn't mean that there wasn't perhaps a drug overdose or a suicide. It doesn't necessarily mean that it's going to be a homicide. But does the coroner not look at it? Or only prepare a report if it turns out to be a homicide? That's not the situation here. The Coroner's Office has certain duties to perform and to come up with their opinions, which apparently in this case, the ones they are seeking to introduce, the cause of death are homicides. I don't believe that under the case law that that transforms their report preparation into something that is testimonial under Crawford. Additionally, because it is going to be the testifying witness who is expressing an opinion, I think that the defendant's 6th Amendment rights are protected because you can cross-examine the witness that testifies, be it Dr Fajardo or whoever else from the Coroner's Office, because they are going to have an opinion and you can challenge that opinion. The defence has never been precluded if they feel that these other coroners, or DNA analysts or anybody else who performed examinations, are somehow relevant to the defence, you have the same subpoena power and you have your own investigators to find them if they are out of state, or in state or whatever it happens to be to challenge the opinions. If you feel that is something helpful to the defence and you know you've had this discovery for years of all of the opinions and reports from the Coroner's Office and the various DNA analysts that put all the hard work in this case. We've had an extensive pre-trial hearing on DNA in this case, where many witnesses testified for over eight days. So all of that is available to you to refute any opinion the prosecution is offering.

'Once again, the reports of the DNA analysts, which they are not going to introduce, were prepared for litigation. The data has all been turned over to the defence and it was utilised during that hearing over those eight days. The DNA analyst that the defence had previously did not have the qualifications to render an opinion, and I don't know if you have obtained some other expert but certainly you have the ability to challenge any opinion. I know that the defence had all the evidence analysed independently so you have the ability to present counter opinions to those that testify but I don't think that under Crawford that the prosecution is prevented from presenting the evidence in the manner that they intend to... So the motion is denied.'

As always, Mr Amster didn't take no for an answer and continued to press the Judge with another way around his plea. Unlike Judge Kennedy, this time she immediately became stronger with him and told him, in no uncertain terms, that her 'ruling stands' and that she wouldn't be changing her mind on this matter.

At 9.12 a.m. the jurors walked in.

Dr Raffi Djabourian, a doctor at the Coroner's Office, took the stand again as he had the previous afternoon.

DA Silverman: 'Yesterday I finished questioning you except for what area the injuries on Princess Berthomieux? We talked about haemorrhaging in the eye and the neck, the right side of the neck. This is all consistent with cause of death is asphyxiation in this case. You also mentioned blunt force trauma to the scalp. What is blunt force trauma?'

Dr Djabourian went on to explain that blunt force trauma is not done with a sharp object but usually a heavier object like wood, metal or stone.

DA: 'Were all injuries caused prior to death?'

Dr Djabourian: 'Yes, before death.'

THE TRIAL

DA: 'How can you be sure?'

Dr Djabourian: 'Based on physiology of the body, we know there was blood pressure so the victim was alive at the time.'

Continuing on to the next day...

Judge Kennedy [speaking directly to Dr Raffi Djabourian]: 'Sir, you have been sworn in and remain under oath.'

It was time for the cross-examination. Defence Attorney Seymour Amster went to the lectern (also known as the podium). Mr Amster is a very awkward-looking man with wild white hair. His lips are very large and, to make matters worse, he sticks them out even further when he is mad about something. As he is permanently angry, his lips always protrude, which looks just like a duck's beak, with the bottom lip even larger than the top. This makes him look like a very bad-tempered, white-haired duckling.

Amster: 'Doctor, at the time you performed autopsy, you had found no ID on the body or knew her age at the time?'

Dr Djabourian: 'Yes, that's correct, we did not have an accurate age.'

Amster: 'When you first examined her, you estimated between fourteen to twenty-one years of age?'

Dr Djabourian: 'Yes.'

Amster: 'You had this potential age by observing her physical characteristics, right?'

Dr Djabourian: 'Yes.'

Amster: 'You mentioned blunt force trauma to her scalp, in rear portion?'

Dr Djabourian: 'No, it was on the right side of the head.'

Amster: 'Could you point?'

The doctor then pointed to his own right temple, where there is a muscle.

Amster: 'So, an inch and a half above your ear?'

Dr Djabourian: 'I'd say in the middle of the head, at the side of the head.'

Amster: 'Would this be consistent that it was from a hardened object or piece of wood or metal? When this trauma was suffered, did she lose consciousness?'

Dr Djabourian: 'That would be hard to say based on one bruise. There's nothing anatomically in the brain that can tell me… that could cause the loss of consciousness. I can't exclude the possibility that there could have been a concussion from a single blow to the head.'

Amster: 'Could the assailant have hit her from the back?'

Dr Djabourian: 'Yes, that is a possibility and the hit could also have come from the front or the back – he could have hit her from anywhere.'

Amster: 'Did you observe anything you could define as defensive wounds?'

Dr Djabourian: 'No, I didn't see anything that could be described as a defensive type wound.'

Amster: 'Through your examination did you find anything consistent with forced sexual interaction?'

Dr Djabourian: 'No, there was no severe or any blunt force to the external genitalia. There was what we call "micro trauma", that is evidence of sexual activity possibly right before death. Nothing like any significant tears or contusions or lacerations of the external organs or genitalia.'

Amster: 'Was sexual activity prior to death looking like it could've been consensual?'

Dr Djabourian: 'So, yes, it would be consistent with consensual sexual activity.'

Amster: 'Thank you, no further questions.'

District Attorney Beth Silverman then cross-examined the witness.

DA: 'Dr Djabourian, the "micro trauma" you mentioned to the vaginal area, you said it could be consistent with consensual sex, but could it also be sexual assault?'

Dr Djabourian: 'Yes, but also knowing that she was probably underage so it couldn't have been, but I don't want to get into the laws or anything.'

DA: 'So it could be consistent with forceable?'

Dr Djabourian: 'Yes, it could be.'

DA: 'For example, she could have had a gun held to her head?'

Dr Djabourian: 'Yes, that could be one of the many possible scenarios.'

DA: 'Do you have expertise in the area of sexual assault injuries?'

Dr Djabourian: 'Yes, I've had a few cases where there have been significant sexual assault injuries.'

DA: 'Have you had sexual assault cases with no clinical or medical findings?'

Dr Djabourian: 'Yes.'

DA: 'How many sexual assault cases have you dealt with over the years?'

Dr Djabourian: 'I would say about ten to fifteen.'

DA: 'Your cause of death in this case was not caused by the blunt force trauma, correct?'

Dr Djabourian: 'That is correct. She did not die from blunt force trauma.'

DA: 'She died from strangulation?'

Dr Djabourian: 'Yes, she died from asphyxia. Yes, strangulation.'

DA: 'Thank you. I have nothing further, Your Honour.'

★ ★ ★

'The People will call Mr Mark Fajardo to the stand.'

The Los Angeles County chief medical examiner – Mark Fajardo – took the stand. He was a highly strung (in a good way) flamboyant character, who seemed eager to make a great deal of eye contact with the jury. Knowing his job uses complicated wording, he made sure to speak in layman's terms as best he could for the jury and the rest of the court to understand. Dr Fajardo held his right hand up and swore to tell the truth, the whole truth and nothing but the truth. He also stated his full name.

DA: 'Good morning, Dr Fajardo, is this the first time you've testified in Los Angeles?'

Dr Fajardo: 'Yes, it will be my first time.'

DA: 'Tell us about your occupation.'

Dr Fajardo: 'I'm the chief medical examiner coroner of Los Angeles County. I'm in charge of the Coroner's Office here in LA.'

DA: 'When were you appointed to that position?'

Dr Fajardo: 'Since August 2013. The CEO of LA County appointed me. I'm currently responding directly to the LA County board of supervisors.'

DA: 'Tell us about your responsibilities as the chief of the LA County Coroner's Office.'

Dr Fajardo: 'I oversee the entire department, which consists of over 216 employees, a budget of thirty-two million. I have twenty-eight doctors on staff, a team of investigators and toxicologists. Basically, our job is to investigate sudden, unexpected and violent deaths and determine the cause and manner of death of those individuals.'

DA: 'What was your prior position before coming to LA County?'

Dr Fajardo: 'I was a chief forensic pathologist at Riverside County and I'd worked with them for over thirteen years.'

DA: 'And you've conducted a number of autopsies?'

Dr Fajardo: 'I've conducted over 5,000 autopsies.'

DA: 'Out of those 5,000-plus autopsies, how many of those were homicide cases?'

Dr Fajardo: 'Over 300.'

DA: 'Tell us about the different bureaus in the Coroner's Office.'

Dr Fajardo: 'We have four bureaus: We have Operations, they are the investigators who actually go to a scene. They are my eyes and ears and they write a report surrounding somebody's death.

'Then I have my toxicology lab, they do toolmark analysis, collecting of evidence and running the toxicology. Then I have my three doctors, my medical unit who do the actual autopsies. Finally, I have my administration, which is the infrastructure of the department. For example, any time you need a report or you need to collect the property of loved ones, you go to my brick building and that's where public services is.'

DA: 'So they are the ones who would give out a death certificate, autopsy report, things of that nature?'

Dr Fajardo: 'Correct.'

Dr Mark Fajardo went on to explain in great detail what his team does at the scene and once the body has been picked up and examined. The toxicologist (or criminalist, as they are also called) can determine what is in the blood of an individual. They examine the 'toolmark' residue and scan for a gun's 'hot residue'. Sometimes they are called out to a scene, particularly if there's a homicide. They would analyse and document the clothing for law enforcement and/or obtain a sexual assault kit.

The investigators will go to the scene and find out the facts, look at the body, interact with law enforcement, then write the reports surrounding the facts of the death. They collect all the information available on the outset of the crime.

DA: 'What's your prior background in training and education?'

Dr Fajardo: 'In 1988 I received my Bachelor of Science degree in biochemistry from Cal Poly. In 1993, my medical degree from UC Davis. From 1993–1998 I trained in anatomic and clinical pathology and forensics. Forensics is my field. It's a field of specialised medicine that marries law with medicine to determine cause and manner of death. After that, I did a year of forensic pathology, also at UC Davis.'

DA: 'So you are a licenced medical doctor?'

Dr Fajardo: 'I am.'

DA: 'So are you certified? Are you board certified?'

Dr Fajardo: 'Yes, I am board certified by the American Board of Pathology and Anatomic, Clinical and Forensic Pathology.'

Dr Fajardo explained that the The Los Angeles Coroner's

Office is the largest in America. In a year, 60,000 people die in Los Angeles County, but not all of these are coroner cases. Of those, only about twenty or thirty thousand are actually reported. Of those, the Coroner's Office only do autopsies and examinations on about 9,000 of them – that's more than any other jurisdiction in the US. There are over sixty law enforcement agencies throughout LA County. He seemed like a very knowledgeable man and knew many interesting statistics.

Dr Fajardo went on to explain about the procedures that happen from the time his office receives a call. If somebody dies of natural causes in a hospital, for example, that's never reported to his office. However, if they die of a 'sudden unexpected death', as in a motor vehicle accident, then the Coroner's Office will be notified: 911 will be called, Fire will roll out, law enforcement will roll and get to the scene and then they'll call the coroners. This call is received at 'first call desk' and from this point the investigator who has been assigned will then go out to the scene and talk to law enforcement and the fire department and gather up all the facts. For example, 'What kind of car was it?', 'How fast was it going?'

Dr Fajardo: 'We get all that information back to the office and write a report. Sometimes we send out a van to transport the deceased person and bring them back to the office. Then we determine whether it would need full autopsy or not.

'If a law enforcement officer thinks that a sexual assault might have occurred, then they call our office and we dispatch a criminalist to the scene to collect a sexual assault kit, then they will preserve all the evidence collected.'

DA: 'So if you receive a call that there is a dead naked

female body in an alley then that would be a situation where you would dispatch someone to perform a sexual assault kit?'

Dr Fajardo: 'Absolutely!'

DA: 'If you have a dead naked female in an alleyway then would you definitely perform a sexual assault kit?'

Dr Fajardo: 'Definitely! Regardless of whether an autopsy is performed or not, blood will always be collected so we can ensure who that person is, for their DNA and also to find out if there were any substances that contributed to their death.'

DA: 'What is in the packaging, for example, of the sexual assault kit?'

Dr Fajardo: 'The sexual assault kit is a kind of a box that consists of all kinds of slides, swabs and combings and what have you. Other instances of examinations are if a knife is impaled in sometimes a head, or a ligature around the neck or bindings around wrists or ankles, a deputy medical examiner will be the one to examine that and evaluate whether it shouldn't be removed.'

DA: 'Are they photographed after they are processed for autopsy so any injuries or marks can be readily available to be observed and examined for the medical doctors?'

Dr Fajardo: 'Yes, absolutely!'

To most of DA Silverman's questions Fajardo would answer 'Yes, absolutely,' unless he was explaining something. I felt that although Dr Fajardo was very knowledgeable in his field, this was possibly a sign of nerves.

DA: 'If someone commits suicide in their home it's usually pretty easy to identify the body, but if someone is found dead in an alley and is referred to as a "Jane Doe", for example, how then would she be identified at the Coroner's Office?'

THE TRIAL

Dr Fajardo: 'This is one of our main functions, to identify an individual usually by fingerprints. Most are done this way. Sometimes we resort to dental or finally we might have to resort to DNA. But the majority is using a California driver's licence or fingerprints.'

DA: 'What are the other major functions at the Coroner's Office?'

Dr Fajardo: 'We have to identify the individuals, we have to safeguard their property, determine cause and manner of death and then issue a report on those findings.'

The cross-examination went on to find out how they keep their records safe and Dr Fajardo explained very clearly how they keep over twenty years' worth of reports on site. Some are even archived and are stored in a very secure manner at the Coroner's Office.

Dr Fajardo: 'We keep them all indefinitely, forever.'

He continued to explain the difference in examining suicides versus homicides and what the minimum requirement is to be a coroner. The qualifications are simple: they have to have a California driver's licence and must be a licensed medical physician. There is a manual and every two years they have to revise that manual. This particular Coroner's Office examined all of the eight homicide cases that we were discussing that day.

Dr Fajardo explained in detail about decomposition of the body in layman's terms by saying, 'When we die our body's natural destruction is at war with all the bacteria within our body. Our pancreas starts to fall apart because of the acid in a bag in our stomachs, just basically opens up. There's bacteria in our intestines and they have free range once we die, basically the destruction of the human body. Skin slipping is when we are alive our body has a sort of glue that holds our skin on our body – that's when even hours after death the skin can slip off the body.'

After we took a short break, Dr Fajardo was asked to open a small envelope, with a pair of scissors, which contained another envelope containing a projectile, minimally deformed, meaning it hit hard tissue in the body, such as a bone or the spinal column. If the projectile was not deformed then it would probably have been shot into the soft tissue of the victim, like skin or an organ. This projectile was one of the three bullets used to kill Henrietta Wright.

★ ★ ★

22 FEBRUARY 2016

That morning I took the train as I knew I'd be in court all day. I arrived at 7.35 a.m., which was way too early, but that's usually when I get to talk to Franklin's friends and neighbours. I'd spoken to Paul and Ricky over the weekend so we were starting to become well acquainted.

We all walked in at 8.35 a.m. I held the door for Diana Ware, who walked with her cane so very slowly as she has done for the past five and a half years. God bless this dear lady who has come to court so diligently over these years to get justice for her stepdaughter, Barbara Ware, one of The Grim Sleeper's victims who was so brutally murdered. Like most days, Ms Ware had been sitting outside the courtroom on the bench right next to the door, just waiting to go in and see who might well be her daughter's killer: Mr Lonnie David Franklin Jr.

THE TRIAL

At 8.55 a.m. the prosecution walked in and DA Beth Silverman went up to the family members, mainly the Alexander family, and asked, 'How was your weekend?' To which they responded with their pleasantries.

At 8.58 a.m. Seymour Amster waddled in at the very fast pace he always does.

At 9.15 a.m. Franklin was walked in by the usual bailiff, wearing a grey dress shirt and slacks. This time he looked straight at me and nodded a 'hello'. I would not have mentioned it here except for a reporter from the *Daily Beast*, who was sitting next to me and asked me, 'Was he saying hello to you?' I had to let him know that he was correct and that Franklin was – I certainly wasn't going to respond back to him though for fear of being thrown out of court.

I told him that Franklin has given me his exclusive life story and that might have been the reason he acknowledged me that morning in court, the way that he did. I really don't know why he would do that on that particular day after so many years of just looking straight ahead when he sat in the courtroom for all his pre-trial hearings and arraignments.

At 9.17 a.m. Judge Kennedy took her seat at the bench.

There was some talking going on (that I could barely hear) between the bailiff, the Judge and both counsels, as there was confusion about a person in the room by the name of Sonya Mongol. An attractive black woman who sat two seats away from me, she had a very sour look on her face. She made sure not to make any eye contact with anyone. I believe she was going to be called upon as a witness, but that idea was immediately quashed. Judge Kennedy addressed Ms Mongol and told her in no uncertain terms that she could 'leave the courtroom now'.

Mr Seymour Amster then suddenly jumped in by saying that he wanted Margaret Prescod, the founder of the advocacy group Black Coalition Fighting Back Serial Murders, as a witness for their side. The prosecution retorted that wasn't going to happen and she must be 'excluded'. Amster kept on explaining why he would need her and that she wasn't going to be a 'guilt phase' witness and would only be a 'penalty phase' witness, 'But I can make it without her if I have to,' he insisted.

At 9.21 a.m. the jurors came in.

It was rather strange as they all came in the regular door of the courtroom, the one we all use, not the typical jurors' door. The Judge apologised for keeping everyone waiting and mentioned how cold it was in the courtroom that day.

Dr Denise Herold took the stand. She was an elderly woman with what I would consider to be a Chicago accent (although I wasn't certain on this), with long brown hair.

Ms Silverman opened with her first line of questioning:

DA: 'Good morning, Dr Herold. We were discussing the sexual assault kits for Bernita Sparks. What evidence did you collect?'

Dr Herold: 'Anal swabs, oral swabs, vaginal swabs, nipple swabs and contact swabs [this I will explain later], loose fibres and pubic hair combs – a fine-toothed comb is used to collect that. The sexual assault kit consists of one envelope, one box, many swabs and slides.

'They also have to collect "trace evidence" in a possible homicide case, especially when the body may have been "dumped".'

THE TRIAL

DA: 'What do you test for with that?'

Dr Herold: 'Well, for fibre evidence, for example, it could be acrylic fibres, which could be from things like sweaters or car seats. With hair you would analyse it the same way you would the fibre evidence, but you also look at it for "hair growth form" to see if it can be evaluated for DNA typing.'

Cross-examination from the defence:

Amster: 'Can you find blood type in hair fibres?'

Dr Herold: 'Not to my knowledge.'

The Judge then interjected with a very important question. She asked: 'Is that the correct phrase, Mr Amster, "hair fibres"?'

The Doctor stated that the word 'hair' is the correct word to use and not 'hair fibres' as Amster had said. Therefore, Amster continued on by saying that he apologised and would start using the word 'hair' only from then on.

Dr Herold: 'Hair collected from the 1980s that was collected can be tested for DNA.'

(DNA consists of two kinds of DNA: one is half from the mother and half from the father; the other is mitochondrial DNA, which is only passed from the mother to the offspring.)

Dr Herold continued to explain that she had taken fibres from the body that are always longer than they are wide. 'Soot and stippling' always have a roundish, disc-like shape.

Amster asked if she'd taken a swab from any other part of the body to which she responded that she had. She'd taken a swab from the left ankle because it was uncontaminated from any other blood or cosmetics. DNA could not be taken from the clothing as the body fluids had leaked into the clothing due to the decomposition of the body. The DNA would have been so degraded if it had been tested.

At 11.28 a.m. Amster continued with the testimony of Dr Herold. This time they started to discuss Alicia 'Monique' Alexander. I felt so sad that this was going to be discussed, as about six members of the Alexander family were sitting in front of me. These were the two brothers, her sister, uncle and both of her parents. The parents and brothers were usually always there without fail every day but now nearly all the family was here together. I prayed there would be no crime scene pictures of their daughter, yet this was a trial of a serial killer, so I knew it would be unlikely. However, there weren't any photos from the crime scene shown on this day, thank God. However, we were told that her body was so decomposed that it had to be put in a 'decomp' freezer to prevent it decomposing any further and to ensure that any tissue or material needed for evidence could be extracted as they needed to from the body. Tests were taken on the body and given to the LASO – the Los Angeles Sheriff's Office.

★ ★ ★

11.32 a.m. Heidi Robbins was sworn in. She was a very attractive woman with blonde hair, in her mid to late fifties. Ms Robbins had been working as the director of administration at the Sheriff's Crime Lab for eleven years. She ran the latent prints and the CSI Unit for the county. Latent prints are prints that cannot be seen and therefore have to be lifted by dusting and analysed back at the lab. She had five teams and had worked with the LASD for thirty-one years. A criminalist with the Coroner's Office in 1985, she then transferred laterally to the LASD thirty-one years ago and currently worked in the Firearms and Narcotics Unit.

In 1980 she was a senior criminalist at the Coroner's Office.

She explained what 'body dumping' means.

Robbins: 'When you have a body that has been transported after death, it is important to gather the trace evidence from, for example, the material the body might be wrapped in, like a blanket or sheet.'

Robbins herself has personally collected evidence from between 100 to 200 crime scenes, prior to their autopsy.

DA: 'On Saturday, January 30th 1988, were you called to report evidence of a case who was later identified as Lachrica Jefferson?'

Robbins: 'Yes, I was.'

DA: 'However, on that form there was handwriting which came from the criminalist stating: "Criminalist: possible AIDS," on the actual form. For what reason?'

Ms Robbins explained that in the 1980s, there was little knowledge about the transmission of HIV/AIDS, although it was known to be a disease spread by sexual activity and needles used to inject drugs. Therefore, for the protection of the staff who were dealing with the body, they used extra precautions not to touch it because a napkin with the word 'AIDS' had been placed over the face of the victim.

At approximately twelve noon we broke for lunch and my friend Burt had invited me to his new office across the street from the Criminal Courts Building (CCB) in the Hall of Justice. Burt had transferred from Crescenta Valley Station to SIB – Sheriff's Information Bureau – and had invited me to come over and see his new office in my lunch break. CCB, which is where I am every day, is located at 210 West Temple Street, and the Hall of Justice, where SIB is located, is right across the street at 211 West Temple.

It was great to just walk across the street and see Burt, plus numerous other people I know, who I hadn't seen for a while and were also there today. As I was waiting in the lobby, Chief Beck came down in the elevator, with his entourage, to the lobby area where I was standing. He said hello to me with a smile. However, I'm sure he says that to everyone in his path. I've only met him a few times and that was at big events over the years so I doubt he would remember me.

After I spent most of my lunch break visiting Burt and going around SIB and seeing the fabulous office, I walked back across the street to the CCB and we all went back into the courtroom at 1.31 p.m., followed by the jury members, who were coming through the main doors that we all walk through (they came in about 1.34 p.m.).

Cross-examination by Seymour Amster:

Amster: 'So you obtained a sexual assault kit from the victim?'

Robbins: '"Obtained"? I think you mean that I "collected" it?'

Amster: 'Yes, that's right.'

Robbins: 'Yes, I took nipple swabs, oral, anal and also inside the vaginal cavity area swabs.'

Amster went round and round in circles trying to make it look like the victim could have been just randomly raped by some unknown person, but Ms Robbins was able to hold her own and explain how this was not the case.

Ms Robbins was excused at 1.50 p.m.

★ ★ ★

Ms Supria Rosner was then called to the stand and sworn in. A younger-looking woman with long brown hair, she was about thirty-eight years of age. She was a criminalist with the LAPD, assigned to testing DNA evidence in the Forensic Science Unit. A technical leader, she oversaw all the training and had thirty DNA analysts and sixty DNA technicians working with her.

A person's DNA (deoxyribonucleic acid) consists of half of the mother's DNA and half of the father's. DNA is in almost every cell in our bodies, especially in muscles and other soft tissue. Everybody is made up of their own unique DNA except for identical twins, who have almost identical DNA and genetic profiles as they are born from the same fertilised egg.

She was to testify about the testing of Barbara Ware, as Ware was tested for DNA in 2004. Having more than two DNA numbers on any area tested is indicative of there being more than one person's DNA, one 'contributor' as it is professionally referred to.

Barbara Ware's DNA and Lonnie Franklin's DNA were combined in eleven out of the thirteen areas tested on Barbara Ware's body. So this was confirmation that Franklin's DNA was included with Ware's DNA.

We left at 4.04 p.m.

★ ★ ★

THE GRIM SLEEPER

Early the following morning, at 6.40 a.m. I received a frantic call from Ricky Harris, saying he'd been 'thrown out of the courtroom and isn't allowed back'. And could I get there sooner than the time that I had planned on being there.

I couldn't believe it, that he of all people would have been thrown out. He did explain that he was sitting there, minding his own business as he usually does, and the defence just laid into him, telling him that he could no longer be there as he was going to be called upon as a witness for the defence.

Well, apparently this was the very first time Ricky had heard of that. In fact, he felt so strongly that if his friend of almost three decades, Lonnie Franklin, really committed these atrocities, he wants them (the state) to 'fry his ass'! His words entirely.

Sad, but true. Ricky cared about Franklin for many years and he trusted him as a friend and a neighbour. However, if Franklin had committed the crimes of which he stood accused, then he, Ricky, would be the first one to make sure he received the death penalty. This is a far cry from Franklin's other neighbour and friend from the other side of the road. However, this other friend and neighbour was willing to stand by Franklin all the way to the end.

I knew what I had to do before I went into the courtroom after the lunch break at 1.30 p.m. and that was to talk to whoever could get Ricky Harris back into the courtroom. As I rode the elevator to the ninth floor I knew that I wanted to talk to Detective Dupree first and foremost. I could see that he was on the phone, once I had made it through the metal detectors, so I walked down the corridor and sat with some of the victim's family members and shared my usual pleasantries with them. They are such a loving and decent family, it breaks my heart every day to know the horror and sadness they have gone through.

As soon as I saw Detective Dupree off the phone I went up to him and explained the situation about Ricky Harris. He told me that he had been trying to get hold of Ricky for years and hadn't heard back. I told him that Ricky had been living in Atlanta, Georgia, for the past year as his aunt was dying, but he was here now and wanted to be 'no part of the defence'. I added that he really wanted to get back in the courtroom, and Detective Dupree told me that it was the defence who threw him out, not him. I knew that it wouldn't have been Dupree but I certainly didn't want to talk to the defence.

I saw Dale Atherton (the second part of the defence team) coming towards me as I waited by the door to go in. When he gave me his usual warm smile, I felt that was the opening for me to speak to him. Besides it was for Ricky anyway and not myself.

Me: 'Dale, could you please let Ricky Harris back into the courtroom as I can assure you he won't be a good witness for you by any means. He came here from Atlanta and needs to be here and sit in on the case. Even though before he might've thought Lonnie was innocent, now it's a very different story.'

Dale responded that Seymour Amster was the main guy to speak with and I really should take it up with him. I immediately told him my concerns in talking to him and could he please do it for me.

So, Dale went off back down the hallway to speak to Seymour Amster on behalf of myself and Ricky to get him back in the courtroom. He then came back to me and said, 'I'm sorry, but Mr Amster is in a conversation with someone and I cannot butt in.'

A few minutes later Mr Amster came storming down the hallway so I had to seize my opportunity right then.

Me: 'Mr Amster, could I just ask you to please reconsider your decision in asking Mr Richard Harris to leave the courtroom today. I can assure you that he would not be a good witness for you at all. He came all the way here from Atlanta to sit in on this case as he's known Lonnie for almost thirty years and for no other reason.'

In his usual abrupt and out of control manner, Amster responded with, 'Well, I'll just have to see about that by the end of the day.' At least that gave me some hope that he'd be let back in soon.

At 1.30 p.m. we went back into the courtroom after the lunch break.

Franklin was walked in and was wearing a dark blue shirt, beige slacks and a tie (that had already been folded); he awkwardly placed the circular part over his head before the jury walked in.

At 1.36 p.m. the jurors walked in, still coming through the main door that we all walk in.

Ms Supria Rosner was the witness testifying and confirming that the DNA found on the bodies of both Bernita Sparks and Barbara Ware was indeed that of the defendant, Lonnie David

THE TRIAL

Franklin Jr. Meanwhile the defence, Seymour Amster, was doing his best to mitigate this claim:

Amster: 'You seem to have no idea how many cousins or relatives Mr Franklin might have that might not be in the database, do you?'

Even the Judge chuckled to herself at another one of his outrageous questions. Amster went on to try and convince the jury that the policies and equipment for testing the DNA might not be quite up to par.

Judge Kennedy: 'Again I don't understand your question, Mr Amster.' And then turning to the witness, 'Do you?'

Ms Supria Rosner explained that after thorough testing the chance that the DNA might be someone other than Mr Franklin would be 1 in 81 quadrillion or seven times the population of the earth.

A number of times, Mr Amster seemed to be frantically searching for something, walking back and forth from the podium to his chair and back again, looking under his papers, knocking the DA's chair as he went. He was clearly out of sorts.

The next witness to be called to the stand was Cristina Gonzalez. A senior criminalist for Los Angeles County, she had been there for twenty-six years. She explained how she came to the conclusion, with her decades of experience working in DNA analysis, that the DNA found on the body of Princess Berthomieux did in fact belong to the defendant Lonnie David Franklin Jr.

We adjourned for the day at 4.08 p.m. and when the jury was released, we then were free to go.

24 FEBRUARY 2016

Franklin was wearing the same blue shirt and beige slacks as the previous day. His trousers seemed far too big for him due to the amount of weight he must have lost by being in jail.

Cristina Gonzalez was still on the stand from the previous afternoon, testifying under cross-examination about her collection and research of the DNA taken from the victims. To me it seemed that she was basically having to defend her professionalism and the correct procedures and protocol used in collecting and analysing the DNA, just as she did the previous day.

In the lunch break, my goal was to get Ricky Harris back into the courtroom as I had promised him. So, at about 1.10 p.m., long before we were due back, I very graciously went up to Seymour Amster, who was doing his usual pacing of the corridor. I asked him if Richard Harris could please be allowed back into the courtroom. There was a very large number of people gathered in the corridor, especially near Dept 109, so perhaps because he had an audience in the corridor, Amster reddened and immediately raised his voice, flapped his hands and shouted, 'Would you stop interfering with my procedure!' I responded that I was sorry, however I was speaking on Ricky's behalf as, 'You have clearly told him that he is not allowed in the courtroom, which is why I am asking on his behalf.

'After all,' I continued, 'he has flown here from Atlanta for the trial and he blatantly refuses to be a witness for you, the defence.' But Amster simply shouted back at me, 'Mr Harris has been excused and that's all there is to it. Now, stop interfering with my process.' He then stormed off back into the courtroom. After that exchange, I certainly didn't want to land myself in trouble for 'interfering' so I sat back on the bench waiting to go back into the courtroom.

I found it strange that every time we waited in the corridor, on each recess and on lunch, we were sitting next to all of the jury members, homicide detectives, victims' family members, Franklin's friends and news reporters wrapped up in the case. To me this seemed dangerous as jurors aren't deaf and everyone was talking to each other.

We all walked back in through the main door at about 1.38 p.m., followed by Lonnie Franklin who was walked in by the bailiff through the side door as usual. Franklin was again putting his tie on in his seat. He was still wearing the same blue shirt and beige slacks as the previous day.

The bailiff was in a very heated discussion with a black woman seated in front of me (she was sitting where the victims' family members usually sat). The bailiff was asking her nicely who she was and what her association was with the trial. Was she a family member of a victim or the defendant?

Bailiff: 'Would you please identify who you are? I am coming at you nicely and professionally and asking you who you are here for. If you don't tell me who you are, I will have to remove you from the courtroom.'

Woman: 'I don't have to tell you nothin'. I'm a family member of someone. I was a kid when she died. I ain' telling you who she was.'

Bailiff: 'You are being uncooperative and I'm going to have to remove you from my courtroom. This is my courtroom and I need to know who is sitting in here.'

The woman sat with her arms defiantly folded across her

chest as the bailiff leant in to her very closely and said, 'OK, step out of the courtroom right now.' She resisted, and I could see all the other sheriffs closing in on her, including the defence and Detective Dupree. It looked like a takedown was about to happen but then she got up and stormed out, escorted with no fewer than four sheriffs, one of them being the bailiff.

At 1.43 p.m. the jurors walked in the main door.

Seymour Amster rose for the continuation of the cross-examination of Ms Gonzalez, who was still on the stand.

Amster: 'So, are you saying that it's not at all possible in the entire world's population for there to be the same...'

Judge Kennedy cut him right off, sternly, and said, 'Mr Amster, we've been through all this the last time you cross-examined this witness. Move on!'

With that, Amster didn't say another word, he just gathered his papers and stormed back to his chair, sliding his feet as he does, with his neck protruding at least a foot ahead of the rest of his body.

Finally, the witness was released.

★ ★ ★

At 1.52 p.m. LAPD Sergeant Allan Seeget came to the stand.

Sergeant Seeget currently worked out of Rampart Division and oversaw the Training Unit. He had been with the LAPD for thirty-two years. He used to work at Newton station in South Central Los Angeles, where he was a patrol officer. This crime scene is where Barbara Ware was found: at 1356 East 56th Street.

DA Silverman: 'Sergeant Seeget, on Saturday, January 10th

1987 at 12.30 a.m., just after midnight, were you called to an alley located in the 1300 block of East 5th Street?'

(Later, I spoke with retired homicide detective Cliff Shepard, who said there is no such address: it was in the 1300 block of 56th Street, not 5th Street – 'That's fifty-one blocks' discrepancy,' he said.)

Sergeant Seeget: 'Yes, I was.'

DA: 'Was it a call for a dead body?'

Sergeant Seeget: 'Yes, it was a call for a "possible" dead body.'

DA: 'What were the weather conditions? Was it dark out? What did you see?'

Sergeant Seeget: 'It was very cold that night and it was still dark. In fact, me and my partner had to use our flashlights and walk up the alley (Robert Diaz was my partner at that time). We saw lots of trash and debris all over the alley.'

Judge: 'Sergeant Seeget, you can say what "you" saw but you cannot say what "we" saw.'

The Sergeant turned to look over at the Judge, who was sitting directly to his right.

Sergeant Seeget: 'Yes, Your Honour, I understand.'

Turning back to Beth Silverman, DA, again, he said: 'I then saw a dead body.'

DA: 'Could you show us?' (motioning for Seeget to use his laser pointer on the monitor).

With his pointer Seeget showed us the position in which the body was found, which was to the right of the picture on the side of the alley. He pointed to a jean-clad leg and explained that the debris was stacked up on top of the victim. He had called for additional units to come to the crime scene and put up the yellow tape so that no one else could enter that area without signing in and signing out of a log. At least one coroner, one criminalist and at least one investigator always show up at a crime scene which appears to be that of a homicide.

Throughout this Lonnie Franklin looked straight ahead as he does every day. He never looked left or right when seated in his chair. Also, he never looked at the ELMO (the projector screen).

DA: 'Did a serial killer task force arrive at the scene?'

Sergeant Seeget: 'Yes, at least eight officers arrived at the scene.'

Hang on, I thought, the serial killer task force wasn't even formed until 2007, so how could it have been possible for a serial killer task force to be on hand two decades before? Something didn't make sense here and I planned to ask Detective Dupree about it in the afternoon recess.

More horrifically graphic crime scene pictures were shown of Barbara Ware and her lifeless body. We saw close-ups of her face with blood all over it even though she was shot in the chest. My guess is that the blood on her face came from when she fell to the ground somehow after being shot. The victim's mother, Ms Diana Ware, was noticeably absent from her seat and I was so glad that she wasn't in the courtroom that day. I'm sure she was advised not to attend as it would have been too difficult for her to see. God bless that woman! I'm sure her daughter is looking down on her from heaven, knowing how much her mother loved her and had dedicated the past three decades to putting her daughter's killer away.

Above: Police removing items from Franklin's home in South Central Los Angeles after his arrest in July 2010.

Below: LAPD chief Charlie Beck addressing reporters after Franklin's arrest.

Images © Gary Friedman/Los Angeles Times via Getty Images

Above: Enietra Washington (centre), the only known survivor of Franklin's attacks, stands with relatives prior to the press conference announcing his arrest.

© Mike Nelson / EPA/REX/Shutterstock

Below: The Grim Sleeper's victims displayed on screen as Deputy District Attorney Beth Silverman delivered her opening statement at the start of Franklin's trial on 16 February 2016.

© Al Seib/Los Angeles Times via Getty Images

Deputy District Attorney Beth Silverman and Seymour Amster, representing Franklin, often clashed during the trial proceedings.

Above: Franklin during the trial – he would be found guilty of the murders of nine women and one teenage girl and sentenced to death.

Below: Kenneitha Lowe (right), the sister of victim Mary Lowe, and Tracy Williams (left), a cousin of the victim, after the conclusion of Franklin's trial.

THE TRIAL

Ms Silverman asked Sergeant Seeget how many homicide crime scenes he'd been called out to over the years, to which he responded, 'Well over a hundred, but that's a tough one to be exact on, that.'

Silverman then asked the question which she asked most first responders, 'What exactly is a body dump?' She clearly wanted to drive this answer home for the jury and everyone else in the courtroom so that we could be perfectly clear on what it means. It would prove, without a shadow of a doubt, that each of the bodies was killed somewhere else then transported to the various crime scene locations.

Sergeant Seeget answered the same way as everyone else: 'She was killed elsewhere then brought to the dumping location. Our investigators did numerous tests that would confirm this.'

Seymour Amster was then due to take the lectern. We waited and waited while he was banging around on his desk, large, overly full manila envelopes piled in disarray on top of each other. Amster was making a heck of a lot of noise yet saying nothing and certainly didn't apologise for the wait. He then started looking under the desk for something. He was slapping documents down on the desk, clearly making a spectacle of himself, though none of us knew why. No one said anything, but we all looked at each other. The Judge rolled her eyes subtly.

Then Amster decided to stay in his seat area and started speaking in a high-pitched, shrill voice. He didn't even go to the podium, he just rose from his seat and shouted to the witness on the stand:

Amster: 'Did you receive a call to go to that location?'

Sergeant Seeget: 'Yes, I received a radio call, which was a possible 187 [the penal code for murder]. The PR [person reporting] stated that it was the dumping of a body.'

Amster wanted to focus on the graffiti on the wall near the body and asked if it appeared to be fresh graffiti. We all know what he was implying: he wanted the jury to think that the murder was the work of the person who put the graffiti on the wall, i.e. a gang member. (Graffiti was everywhere on almost every wall in South Central Los Angeles, especially in the eighties.) Sergeant Seeget seemed to know full well what he was implying and therefore responded with a definitive 'No!'

DA Silverman then cross-examined the witness with only a few 'to-the-point questions'.

DA: 'Did the graffiti appear fresh to you?'

Sergeant Seeget: 'No.'

DA: 'Did the graffiti appear to be typical of all the other graffiti in South LA?'

Sergeant Seeget: 'Yes.'

DA: 'Thank you, no further questions.'

* * *

Donald Hrycyk, a detective who'd been with LAPD for forty-two years, was then called to the stand. Detective Hrycyk was stationed at 77th Division for three and a half years. Over his extensive career, he has covered well over sixty homicides. He responded to a homicide call at about 1.15 p.m. on 12 August 1986 (his partner was Jay Johnson). The victim turned out to be Henrietta Wright.

Detective Hrycyk described the scene as 'filled with trash,

trash bags, mattresses, looked like a transient could have been sleeping there'. It was clearly a 'body dump'.

Just before we took the afternoon break and after the jury were let out, the Judge raised a point. In fact, she became a little irate with DA Beth Silverman, saying she didn't want her to use the names of the victims.

DA: 'But every time a slide is shown, the victim's name is always at the top so the jury see it anyway.'

Judge: 'I'm not going to argue with you, Ms Silverman. When I make a ruling, it stands. That's it.'

DA: 'Fine!'

And with that heated exchange we were released on a break.

I spotted Detective Dupree in the hallway and went up to him – he is so easy to talk to and always has time for people. I told him that I was confused that a 'serial killer task force would show up to a crime scene in 1987, yet as far as I knew the serial killer task force wasn't formed until 2007'. He knew why I was confused and stated, 'That's what Margaret Prescod, would like you to think, but we had various serial killer task forces formed earlier on.'

Margaret Prescod is the founder of the Black Coalition Fighting Back Serial Murders. Prescod believes that the cops weren't doing their jobs over the years, and knew there was a serial murderer killing young black women in the South LA area yet they didn't even try to close the cases. In her opinion it's because these females were black that the killer wasn't caught for almost thirty years. Prescod is an advocate for women's rights, civil rights and is also a black rights activist.

Anyway, I didn't know that a task force was formed before

2007 and I needed to get to the bottom of this. As I knew Detective Dupree's time was limited during the trial, I knew I had to get someone else to expand on what Dupree was trying to tell me, so I planned on calling Detective Cliff Shepard that night. This call will be documented later.

Meanwhile the mystery woman who was thrown out of the courtroom was sitting right outside the whole time we were on break, making no eye contact with anyone. I was intrigued to know who she really was and I'm sure so too was the bailiff.

We came back after the break and Detective Hrycyk explained that he responded to a crime scene at 9.15 a.m. on 12 August 1986 at 9414 South Western Avenue, South LA, a parking lot adjacent to an alleyway, with his partner, Jerry Collins. When he showed up to the scene there were already a number of uniformed officers in the area of the body. There was a dumpster on the south-east corner adjacent to the alley, with two lids: one lid was open and the other was closed. It was an overly full dumpster. Detective Hrycyk then spotted a foot with a grey sock on the open side of the dumpster.

The detectives made sure to always wear gloves to preserve the integrity of the crime scene. There were ligature marks on the right side of the victim's neck.

DA: 'Were there similarities between this crime scene of Bernita Sparks and the homicide we spoke about before, Henrietta Wright?'

Detective Hrycyk: 'Yes, both were shot in the chest. Both were African-American women. Both were dumped in the South Central area location. Both were dumped in trash or covered in trash. Neither had any identification. Both were either in or adjacent to an alleyway. Both were covered to disguise the body and there were no .25 calibre casings at either crime scene.'

Amster: 'Good afternoon, Detective. On January 10th 1987 you were responding to the crime scene of... oh... no wait... Ha, ha, ha....' Seymour exploded in hysterical laughter, leaving the other people in the courtroom trying to piece together where the potential joke was. 'Ha, ha... I must've gone back too far, sorry about that. Ha, ha, ha... I meant on August 12th 1986, you went to a crime scene with your partner, Detective Collins, correct?'

Detective Hrycyk: 'Yes.'

Amster: 'Part of your duty is to request a latent fingerprint analyst to come to the scene. Correct?'

Detective Hrycyk: 'I don't recall.'

Amster: 'Well, do you recall seeing an examiner there?'

Detective Hrycyk: 'No, I don't recall.'

More laughter came from Amster as he rummaged through his paperwork, frantically searching for something. What could possibly be so funny? Nothing about this case was a joke.

Amster: 'So you mentioned that when you arrived on the scene that a transient might have been sleeping there?'

Detective Hrycyk: 'Yes, it's possible that that area might be an area where a transient might sleep there.'

Amster: 'Are you familiar with the type of people that frequent that area?'

After much going round in circles so that Amster could make his question clearer, Detective Hrycyk finally responded.

Detective Hrycyk: 'Well, yes, it's an area where there are

people on drugs. It's an African-American area, there are transients there and a lot of graffiti.'

Amster: 'Thank you. Nothing further.'

This was where we adjourned for the day. As we left, the mystery woman was still sitting on the bench, earphones in her ears, right outside the courtroom. It was very strange indeed.

★ ★ ★

Once I arrived home to write up the events of the day, I decided to call my friend, Detective Cliff Shepard, to clarify my confusion regarding this Serial Killer Task Force and when it all began. Maybe there was more than one task force? I was looking forward to finding out.

Cliff: 'In 2007, I was working for a homicide supervisor by the name of Rob Bub. He was in the Cold Case Unit at that time and was aware of cases that occurred in the eighties. When Janecia Peters' murder came in, in 2007, I was on a day off and Captain Jackson was told that the same DNA matched six or seven other victims. Detective Kilcoyne overheard this conversation and they all decided to form a task force from that very day forward, which began at approximately the end of April in 2007.'

Where my confusion arose from was how a serial killer task force was also around in the eighties? Cliff let me know that it was the Southside Slayer task force. The Southside Slayer is another serial killer I have interviewed extensively by the name of Chester Turner, currently on Death Row. Yet the twist here is that in some of the Franklin murders, Turner's DNA was also found on or inside the bodies of various victims.

THE TRIAL

This was touched on during the trial but it didn't amount to anything as there was numerous other men whose DNA was also found on the bodies. Yet Franklin also always seemed to be linked. Turner had already been convicted for the murders he committed and is currently serving his sentence out on Death Row.

Turner was also killing women who were selling themselves in the sex trade, in the South Los Angeles area, at the same exact time as The Grim Sleeper. Hence this would make sense. So yes, there was a serial killer task force that came to the scene of the murder of Barbara Ware. However, it wasn't the same as the one assigned to the Grim Sleeper case. This was very interesting for I had no idea that there were a few serial killer task forces set up, which went back over a few decades. We will see what transpired next...

★ ★ ★

25 FEBRUARY 2016

I arrived at court a little later that day, at about 10.45 a.m. It was the morning recess so everyone was in the corridor. Detective Dupree always says hello to me and I sat with the same girl I always sit with – M.W. She's a writer for television and I always give her as many tips as I can because she wasn't covering this case from the beginning. I told her that Enietra Washington, the star witness, was sitting two people away from us on the bench as we were talking. She subtly looked over and I explained that this meant she would be the next witness to testify on the stand.

Enietra Washington was sworn in at 11.08 a.m.

Enietra had a strong stature and carried herself with a huge air of confidence. She breezed in, wearing a short dress, her hair was up and she was sporting long blue fingernails with blue dangly earrings and a blue bag to match. She was wearing glasses and I could immediately tell that she was someone you wouldn't want to mess with. Franklin kept his gaze fixed to the back wall of the room and didn't look over at her, not even once.

DA Beth Silverman opened the questioning:

DA: 'Ms Washington, can you please tell us how old you are?'

Enietra Washington: 'I am fifty-seven years old.'

DA: 'Could you tell us what you do for work?'

Enietra Washington: 'I work for LA Unified as a CAN – a nurses' assistant.'

DA: 'I want to draw your attention back to the evening of November 19th, early hours of the morning of November 20th 1988. How old were you at that time?'

Enietra Washington: 'I was twenty-eight or twenty-nine. Well, my birthdate is 10.17.1958.' She was only a year off.

DA: 'On that evening were you walking near or on Normandie and 91st Street?'

Enietra Washington: 'Yes, I was.'

DA: 'Where were you coming from?'

Enietra Washington: 'A friend's house.'

DA: 'Where were you going?'

Enietra Washington: 'To my friend Linda Lewis's house to change clothes to go to a party at 84th and Denker in the South LA area.'

DA: 'Were you going somewhere together?'

Enietra Washington: 'We were going to a party.'

DA: 'As you were walking to your friend's house to change your clothes, did you notice anything that caught your eye?'

Enietra Washington: 'Yes, as I was walking in front of a store, I noticed an orange Pinto that was parked in front of the store as I was walking by. It was on the corner of Normandie and 90th or 91st Street. It reminded me of Hot Wheels, you know those l'il miniature cars that my kids used to have. I was shocked that it was a Pinto as you jus' din' see them anymore. It was orange and it was all fixed up, it had rims and a racing stripe and the flares.'

DA: 'You said it had racing stripes? What does that mean?'

Enietra Washington: 'A car design.'

DA: 'Where were they?'

Enietra Washington: 'Down the side of the car and up the middle of the hood. They were white stripes.' She went on to describe the Cragar rims and the tyres, which looked like the ones usually found on Porsches.

DA: 'How do you know all this?'

Enietra Washington: 'Coz I like cars and my "play brothers" liked cars and would teach me about cars.'

DA: 'What are "play brothers"?'

Enietra Washington: 'Someone I grew up with in the neighbourhood that didn't have no brothers or sisters. Someone you can learn about girls and guys.'

DA: 'Did you have a "play sister"?'

Enietra Washington: 'I had a couple. Linda was a "play sister" and a friend.'

The testimony went on and Enietra explained that the

Pinto was not on the main street, it was parked in front of the store on a side street. It was on 91st Street, not the main street. Enietra said that she saw a short man leave the store and go to this vehicle – she wasn't sure how short he was, she didn't pay much attention to that. He walked around the side of the car and caught her looking at it so then he said something, but Enietra didn't pay him any attention, she just kept on walking.

The next thing that happened as Enietra was walking by was that the man yelled at her, so she turned around to see who he was yelling at. She kept walking towards where she was staying on 90th or 91st (with Linda) and realised he might be yelling at her, so she ignored him.

The man then drove up to her within about a minute of yelling at her. She was still on the pavement so he drove alongside her. He was on her left-hand side as she was walking, therefore the passenger side of his car was closest to her. He spoke to her through the rolled-down passenger window.

Enietra Washington: 'He was hollering at me through the car window and I said, "Excuse me, you cannot holla at me through a car window, you have to get out and talk to me."'

She hadn't heard what he had said. So he stopped the car and got out. He approached Enietra and the main thing she noticed was that he was so short.

Enietra Washington: 'And I don' like short men.' (She giggled with her response.)

She noticed the individual was neatly dressed – 'He wasn't scruffy-looking. He wasn't raggity-looking [ragged-looking], he looked like someone that looked like he'd just come from work. He looked approachable.'

THE TRIAL

The man had khakis on and a short-sleeved button-down uniform shirt, which made her think he'd just got off work. He asked Enietra what she was doing and where was she going. He even had the nerve to ask her if he could take her to her friend's house before her party. She told him with an attitude, 'No, I'm good! I'm good!' But he kept on pressing her and asked exactly where she was going, and expressed strongly that he wanted to take her there. She kept emphasising that she was 'all good' and didn't need a ride. In fact, she could have even walked, it was so close.

It was perhaps strange that although they had never met before, neither asked for the other's name. The man pushed her even further and asked if he could go to the party with her. Although taken aback, Enietra said it would be fine for him to go to the party too because at that time parties were open for anyone to go to.

The man then pushed for the fourth time, asking to take her to her friend's house, and again she responded, almost laughing at his insistence, that she was fine, that she was all good and really didn't need a ride. At this he seemed to suddenly change his demeanour and said, 'See, that's what's wrong with you black women, people can't be nice to you.'

DA Silverman repeated these words back and then asked: 'Then what did you do next?'

Enietra thought about it and said that she felt that she might have come off wrong for him to say something like that, so she decided to change her mind and told him that he could take her over to her friend's house. DA Silverman remained curious as to why she would change her mind, and Enietra said that it was because of his remark, and how she felt that she might have come off as standoffish to him. She then felt sorry for him because she knew he was a short man, so her attitude changed.

Enietra Washington: 'See, I have a theory about short men, they all have a Napoleon complex!'

DA Silverman pressed this issue about her 'theory' on short men and she was quick to respond.

Enietra Washington: 'Look, I'm a big woman and most short men have this attitude about themselves like, "I'm gonna take you down and I have this Napoleon complex," or somethin' like that, and I'm like, "Ugh! No thank you." I just don't even get myself involved.'

Even though Enietra is only 5ft 7in, she still speaks of herself as a 'big woman'. She has a very large presence and a lot of self-confidence along with great posture so she appears even bigger and taller than she actually is.

Right before getting in the car with this man, he kept asking Enietra where the party was going to be as he seemed to really want to go. She said it was open and he was welcome. The man wasn't overweight, he seemed fit to her. However, as she was wearing tennis shoes, she knew he was short because she was towering over him. She remembered that he was African-American and only a little older than her.

Enietra was carrying her handbag at the time and inside was her ID, a few dollars and some make-up. She let herself in the passenger side door of the man's car and he removed some children's school books from the passenger seat so she could sit down. She noticed a toolbox on the floor, a mechanic's or plumbing toolbox.

When she got into the car, she noticed that the interior had white diamond tuxedo leather seats. That's material which is laid into a diamond shape with leather tucked into the pattern. They seemed to be personalised seats, not the typical standard ones. It was certainly a customised car according to Ms Washington. There was even a pearl ball handle on the gear shift.

Enietra Washington: 'There was fur across the dashboard too. He had it all "pimped out" too, coz I was looking.["Pimped out" in layman's terms simply means "customised".] It was also a low rider but without the dice on the rear-view mirror.'

Enietra then asked who made the car all 'pimped out', and 'He said he did it hisself.'

The man never asked Enietra about herself, they just talked about the car, and still he never asked her name. She gave him directions for her friend's house and he appeared to be driving in that direction at first. Enietra was wearing a beige mini-skirt and jacket set with a shirt underneath. She was also wearing white tennis shoes along with her underwear and also biker shorts over her underwear.

Enietra Washington: 'After he started going in the right direction, when we got to Western and Denker, he made a left turn instead of keeping straight. He then turned left on Manchester. I told him he was going the wrong way and he told me he had to go to his uncle's house to pick up some money.

'When he got onto Western he made a right, from Manchester. He drove down to 79th or, I don't remember, but he made a right turn on, maybe on 80th Street? I could describe it to you but I cannot remember the numbers.'

The man drove a few houses down and then parked by a tree. He parked directly in front of the house, not in the driveway of the house. He got out and talked to someone (it was a man's voice, Enietra thought), then he went into the house. Although Enietra heard a man's voice, unfortunately, she didn't see him. He turned on the corner of the street. She remembered an apartment building on the side and a mechanic's shop on the corner. The house had a diamond shaped window on the front of it. The man was gone about ten or fifteen minutes so she waited in the car and smoked a cigarette.

DA Silverman put a photograph of the map of the houses in the area on the ELMO (monitor). Enietra was given the laser pointer to point out the location of the house and the place where she stopped. Using a marker to mark an 'X', she marked the area outside of a house which was green in colour right next to an orange house.

When he got back in the car, the first thing the man said was for Enietra to stub out her cigarette – 'There's no smoking in my car.' She complied by tossing the cigarette out of the car window.

The man had music blasting in the car but she paid very little attention to him even when he started driving again. He proceeded straight ahead then made a right turn on the first street. The next thing that happened was he called her someone else's name, like Brenda, not her real name. Enietra responded quickly with, 'That's not my name.'

Enietra Washington: 'He then said something and I turned to him again and everything just went really, really eerily quiet. Like one minute the music was blasting then all of a sudden it wasn't blasting no more.'

DA Silverman wanted her to try and remember what exactly happened next, when the man called her Brenda and right before things went really quiet. What did he do at that time?

Enietra Washington: 'I thought I saw him reach across hisself, but I didn't really pay no attention, I didn't really see nothing.'

The man reached across himself towards the driver's door with his right hand but she didn't see if he retrieved anything or not. Enietra felt like it was a strange situation and instinctively decided she needed to get out of the car, so she started to reach for the passenger door handle to open it, whereupon the man became very sinister and told her firmly, 'Don't you touch that door, bitch, or I'll shoot you again!'

Enietra was shocked as she'd felt nothing if he had shot her once already. She then said, 'Oh? You shot me?'

Enietra Washington: 'Oh, OK, so he shot me. You know when you hear when you get shot, you feel burning, but I din' feel nothin'! I din' see him shoot me! I din' feel the gunshot! I din' hear no gunshot! His voice sounded angry but wasn't yelling, he was just… He was just… menacing.'

DA: 'Did he seem out of control or calm?'

Enietra said that he was calm and didn't even raise his voice. She then asked him why he had shot her and he said, 'You bin doggin' me out!' DA Silverman asked her to clarify that statement and she explained that it meant that he said he had thought she had been 'disrespecting him'. He still kept calling her the name Brenda again. Enietra couldn't understand how she was being accused of 'doggin' him out' when she didn't even know the man. She kept laying into him with, 'I don't even know you so why would you shoot me?' The whole time she never wanted to look down on herself as she was afraid of what she would see. At some point though she did look down and saw some blood on her chest and her jacket. Then at that point she knew that she had to get out of the car.

She kept asking why the man had shot her and he just kept rambling. But he had confused her with someone else and so, after telling him that he was wrong, Enietra kept begging him to take her to the hospital, but he said that he couldn't do that. She begged once more and said he could even drop her off a block away and she would walk herself to the hospital. She kept mentioning her kids to him and warned, 'If I die then I'll come back and haunt you.' Referring to her children, she then went on to say, 'They better not want for nothin' coz I'm going to come back and haunt you.' She didn't mention who or how old they were, she just mentioned them because she figured that would get him to take her to the hospital. She tried to appeal to his human side especially because of the school books she had seen in the car and that he had put on the back seat.

DA Silverman wanted to know if Enietra was trying to appeal to his conscience, to which she responded, 'Well, I was just tryin' to appeal to something, I don' know.'

But he didn't take her to the hospital, he just drove around for a while as she was fading in and out of consciousness. She even woke one time and she said that he was on top of her. In a semi-conscious state, all she could mumble was for him to get off. She remembered trying to push him off but then she faded out of consciousness again. Another time, she remembered a flash went off as he was flashing a camera in her face and seemed to be taking pictures of her. She remembered with certainty that it was a Polaroid Instamatic.

Although Enietra had no idea where the vehicle was at this time, she knew that the car was stopped and that this man was still on top of her as she lay dying in the front passenger seat. She felt a lot of pressure on her chest, like an elephant was sitting on top of her, but she wasn't sure if that was from the gunshot or from the man being on top of her. Conjuring up as much strength as she could, she tried to push him off and then told him how much he was hurting her.

Enietra Washington: 'I then woke up again with his face down between my legs. He was trying to kiss me down there.'

She continued to fight him off by pushing him away but then he pushed her and grabbed at her to stop her pushing him. Her skirt was pulled up above her thighs but her shirt was still half-on. His clothes seemed to stay on throughout this horrific ordeal. When she tried to get out of the car, he pushed her out and then kept driving.

DA: 'Were you raped?'

Enietra Washington (quietly): 'Yes, I was.'

DA: 'Then how do you know you were raped?'

Enietra explained that the reason she felt she was raped was because 'the man's face was down there and he was on top of me'. This convinced her she was raped. The DA then asked if she felt for certain that she'd been penetrated, but Enietra couldn't recall as she was going in and out of consciousness at the time. She believed he must have done so when she was passed out. The atmosphere in the courtroom was completely silent throughout Enietra's testimony. She spoke so convincingly and brought everyone in the courtroom right there with her in that car, slowly dying yet doing all she could to live.

We then broke for lunch at about twelve noon and reconvened at 1.30 p.m.

★ ★ ★

Enietra was sitting on the stand for the longest time, sometimes staring directly at Franklin, yet he kept his gaze straight ahead, at the wall in front of him, not blinking and seeming to not even move a muscle.

In her dying state, Enietra reached as best she could for the passenger door handle to get her out of the car once and for all. Once she got it slightly open, the man then pushed her completely out of the moving vehicle. She then landed on the cold hard street and just lay there for an indefinite amount of time. Meanwhile she talked to herself in her head, telling herself that she had to 'get my ass outa' the street!' She gradually rolled onto the kerb, by now almost dead and losing blood fast. By then it was dark, so it would have been hard for anyone to see her lying there. She didn't know where she was, she just wanted to get to the main street. After 'feeling on cars' to make her way down the street and into the light, she was holding on to the parked cars to guide the direction in which she was dragging herself, and finally pulled herself along the road near to a street called Denker. She was still fading in and out of consciousness as she made her way to the main street and then finally to Linda's house.

Enietra Washington: 'I started beatin' on her door, but she weren' there. I jus' kept beatin' on her door, coz I wanted her to call the police. But she was at the party. So I figured I'd wait on her porch. I just laid down on one of the steps on her porch... I was still fading in and out.'

Linda and her husband finally pulled up in the car, in their driveway. Linda got out and started 'fussing' over her friend, saying they'd waited all that time for her and she just didn't show up. Enietra kept trying to interject with, 'Call 911! Call 911!' Confused, Linda asked why on earth she would have to call the police.

Enietra Washington: "'I've been shot. I've been shot. Call 911!" She didn't see at first and then she came up to me closer and saw that I'd been shot and then she started screamin' and hollerin' and everyone came out of their doors. They were all hysterical and then she raced for the phone to call 911.'

The next thing was the paramedics' arrival while she was still lying on the porch of Linda's house. They placed a mask over her face and told her not to fade out, to stay awake. She told them she was shot. They cut her clothing away from her chest and then the next thing she remembers, she was rushed to the emergency room at the Harbor-UCLA Medical Center, in an ambulance. One of the doctors at the hospital said, as they were cutting her clothes off, that they couldn't give her anything as she had been shot in the chest – they had to cut her open while she was awake as the bullet was still travelling. She remembered the doctor slicing down the side of her ribs and she remembered screaming but nothing else after that until she woke up under a white sheet in the hospital.

Enietra stayed in hospital for around three weeks, recovering from major surgery. The surgery was done on the right side of her body and immediately above the centre of her chest as well. She still bears the scars today.

There were three main doctors, including the surgeon Dr John Robertson, looking after her in the hospital. One of them she called 'Superman' because he looked just like Clark Kent. Enietra remembers being interviewed at least twice by law enforcement while still in the hospital.

The DA put two photographs of Enietra on the ELMO (monitor). One was a picture of her as she was in her hospital bed. The other was of the bullet hole lodged in her chest. Her property was never returned to her by the hospital (I would guess it was being taken care of by her friend Linda), so she didn't have any of her possessions nor her ID. This was odd because she remembered that when she rolled out of the car, she did have her belongings and her bag with her at that time.

Once released from the hospital she accompanied police to the exact location where the Pinto stopped (when the man said that he was supposedly getting money from his uncle). This was in December of the same year, 1988.

The DA then asked Enietra if she was prescribed medication at the hospital and/or medication to go home with. She answered yes to both questions and said that it took her about a year to recover fully from the shooting. She did not work during the time of her recovery.

DA: 'On that date of November 19th 1988, prior to the time you got into this Pinto, had you pursued any type of drugs that day?'

Enietra Washington: 'Yes.'

DA: 'What did you consume?'

Enietra Washington: 'Cocaine and marijuana. Marijuana laced with cocaine. I took it about three or four in the afternoon.'

THE TRIAL

DA: 'Did you have any alcohol?'

Enietra Washington: 'No.'

DA: 'How many hours had passed between you taking the marijuana laced with cocaine that you got into the Pinto?'

Enietra Washington: 'About four or five hours later.'

DA: 'Did you feel when you were walking and before you got into the Pinto that you were under the influence of anything or unaware of your surroundings?'

Enietra Washington: 'No.'

DA: 'When was the last time you consumed any illegal drugs since that date?'

Amster: 'Objection!'

Judge: 'Overruled... OK, sustained on irrelevance grounds.'

DA: 'Have you consumed any illegal drugs last night or today?'

Enietra Washington: 'No!'

On the ELMO, DA Silverman placed a photograph taken by the assailant on the day she was in the Pinto. Enietra was asked if she pulled up her blouse or her skirt while in the Pinto, to which she responded with a firm 'No!' both times.

DA Silverman asked Enietra if she ever saw the individual who shot her ever again on her release from hospital.

Enietra Washington: 'I believe I did. By my house in Inglewood [the address that was on her driver's licence], nowhere near where I was staying before.'

DA: 'Where did you see this individual?'

Enietra Washington: 'He was walkin' down my street. I happen' to be standing outside.'

DA: 'Did he look familiar to you?'

Enietra Washington: 'Kind of.'

DA: 'What was said?'

Enietra Washington: 'He said to me, "Do I know you?" And I said, "Am I s'posed to?" Then he turned and walked away. I didn't think it was the man at first and then I thought, oh my God, it was him. I just shook it off. This was about a year after I left the hospital.'

Then DA Silverman put picture on the ELMO, and asked Enietra if she recognised who the person was. She said she did; DA Silverman asked who he was and Enietra immediately said, 'The person who shot me.' There were gasps in the courtroom for she made no qualms about what she said and continued to say anything that came into her head. Good for her! I thought. She seems to be a person with absolutely no fear.

Enietra remembered testifying in 2011 for a grand jury at this same courthouse; she was shown this same photograph and back then also identified the same man as the person who shot her. DA Silverman asked if this was how the person looked in 1988 to which Enietra replied that he did.

DA: 'Looking at this photograph, do you see this person in the court today?'

Enietra: 'Yes, I do!'

DA: 'Can you please point him out?'

With great confidence and strength, Enietra threw her right arm out in front of her and pointed to the defendant, Lonnie David Franklin Jr, who was still staring straight ahead at the wall behind the Judge. She described his clothing and that he was sitting at the end of the table.

DA Silverman then asked very slowly but surely, 'How certain are you that this was the person who shot you?' To which Enietra firmly replied before the District Attorney could finish off her question: 'One hundred per cent!' DA Silverman then asked, 'Does he look the same to you as he did in 1988?'

'Minus the hair,' Enietra chuckled. 'But he still looks exactly the same,' she added.

The Judge then called for Seymour Amster for the cross-examination.

Amster: 'I believe you testified today that sometime you saw the individual outside of your house. Now, I don't want to know the address of your home and I'm not even going to ask you for your add…'

Enietra Washington: 'Well, you ain' gonna get it anyway even if you did ask!'

She cut him off and the court laughed as one. Good for her, we all thought. It was very evident, the disgust she had for Mr Amster, even before he stood at the podium to question her.

In an effort to discredit her testimony as much as he could, Amster asked Enietra all kinds of questions to which her response for each was a firm 'No, I didn'!' or 'No!' or even 'I doubt it!' Amster then went over to show her the document he had from the police report, intending to see if it would refresh her memory.

Unfortunately, when he got to where Enietra was sitting, he then tripped and said he was sorry. She immediately responded with 'No, you're not!' Again, the courtroom chuckled.

Amster: 'Did you see the individual sitting on the bus with you one day?'

Enietra Washington: 'Yes, he did a couple of times but that was before he came to stand outside my house.'

Mr Amster kept fumbling around after he asked each redundant question. Pacing between his chair and the podium and then back again, he slid across the floor as he went, his neck jutting straight out in front of him.

Amster: 'At any time did you say to Linda, "They shot me"?'

Enietra Washington: 'No, I did not!'

Amster: 'At any time did you say to Linda, "They raped me"?'

Enietra Washington: 'No, I did not!'

Amster: 'At any time when you were telling Linda about what happened to you did you use the word "they"?'

Enietra Washington: 'No!'

This continued with Amster asking similar rhetorical questions. But then he asked an important question.

Amster: 'At any time after the incident did you tell law enforcement that this individual had acne scars on his face?'

Enietra Washington: 'I may have as I thought I'd scratched him.'

An interesting answer as I know from Franklin himself and all of his friends that he never had acne at any time in his life. I have been very close to him when I interviewed him and there isn't a single scar on his face. This was a very damning question and a damning response.

On a side note, I sometimes read the newspapers and articles on the internet to see what was being written about this case. Sadly, many newspapers weren't just copying what another reporter had written, but they were copying their mistakes too. Today, I decided to read what had been written in the Grim Sleeper case and to see what the papers were saying about the trial.

Mentioning no names, I was shocked to see the blatant mistakes in some well-respected newspaper publications. To make matters worse, the same six or seven mistakes were the exact same mistakes that were in the other newspapers and online magazines. To name just a few mistakes of that day, I will list them below. Various newspapers stated that:

1. Enietra Washington said that during the attack she lost her bag containing her driver's licence.

   This is very wrong! When Enietra rolled out of the Pinto after being shot almost to death, she did have her bag with her. She very clearly stated on the stand two days earlier that she had it when she was taken to the hospital. However, it was not returned to her by the hospital when she was released from there to return back home.

2. 'That's what's wrong with you black women. Men can't be men to you.'

   According to the newspapers this was the 'exact' quote of Franklin's words to Enietra Washington when she kept trying to reject his suggestion of driving her to her friend's house. This is also wrong! The correct quote was in fact: 'That's what's wrong with you black women, people can't be nice to you.' Several of the top newspapers stated this because they copied each other and once the first one made that mistake, the others all followed.

3. Enietra said the man went inside and when he came back out he told her to toss her cigarette out the window before heading off in the wrong direction.

Also wrong! In actual fact, after 'the man' got back in the car, he headed in the right direction for a few blocks and then after a while he turned in the wrong direction.

OK, maybe you don't think these mistakes are really that bad, even though there were quite a few other errors made like this that I read that morning on a number of other online publications, including getting the ages wrong for some of the victims. I won't mention them here for I don't want to appear petty. However, the most outrageous mistake of all is this next one:

4. After Franklin was arrested, police searched his property and say images of Washington were found inside.

This might be true but this hadn't even been mentioned in the trial as yet. This is very damaging indeed for the prosecution. Yes, District Attorney Beth Silverman put a picture of Enietra on the ELMO (projector) showing when she lay dying in the assailant's car. However, she made no mention of the fact that this picture was taken from Franklin's home during the search. This was written in one newspaper and then blatantly copied to a whole lot of other publications.

THE TRIAL

Continuing with Enietra Washington on the stand... Seymour Amster continued to grill Enietra about the information she gave to law enforcement regarding the interior and exterior of the orange Ford Pinto. He also asked if she had told law enforcement whether or not he had inserted his finger into her vagina. She said that she might have said that, but when asked if she'd told law enforcement if he'd kissed her, she said she did tell them that.

Amster continued to question Enietra in greater detail as to whether she could remember if Franklin had ejaculated inside her 'with an erect penis'. Naturally, she was very uncomfortable. When asked if she had 'felt moistness in her vaginal area', she answered in a much quieter tone of voice: 'I felt nasty down there. Something was nasty down there on me, which was something other than saliva but I didn't want to look there and find out. All I knew was I didn't like the way it felt and I needed help.'

He continued to press her for information of what she may have told the nurse in the hospital and even asked if a condom was used. Obviously offended, Enietra said, 'Are you suggesting it was consensual?' To which Amster seemed to have no response and he blatantly ignored her question.

Moving on, he continued to ask her a lot more questions that didn't seem relevant at all. Basically, after he kept the courtroom waiting for extended periods of time, fussing with his paperwork, he would come back with questions that included, 'Do you remember telling law enforcement that he had big hands?' Each question started with 'Do you remember telling law enforcement...' followed by something like, 'he wore a gold chain?' or 'he wore a white shirt under his work clothes?' or 'they raped me?' or 'they were in the car with me?' And so on, and so forth.

Once Amster had finished, DA Silverman got up to ask one final question on re-direct:

DA: 'You mentioned that you said you were going dancing... Where were you going dancing?'

Enietra Washington: 'At the party.'

DA: 'No further questions, Your Honour.'

After Enietra left the stand, she confidently walked off the podium with her head held high and her dress flowing as gracefully as she had when she walked in. All eyes were on her except of course for those of the defendant, Franklin.

★ ★ ★

The next witness to be called by the prosecution was Miros Surrena. She is retired from the Los Angeles Police Department, where she worked for almost twenty-six years. In 1988 she was assigned to 77th Division where she worked patrol and was on loan to the detectives for the rape section. Ms Surrena went to Harbor-UCLA Medical Center to retrieve evidence of a bullet from an alleged rape victim by the name of Enietra Washington. She flew in from Idaho to testify in this case.

★ ★ ★

2 MARCH 2016

After being forced to miss four days of the trial the previous week due to my work as a spokesmodel for the annual technology convention in Orange County, I arrived at the courtroom that morning and caught up as much as I could on all I missed. From one of my sources, I won't say who, I was told that on the days I missed the previous week the following happened:

Dr John Robertson, the surgeon who removed the bullet from Enietra Washington and who saved her life in November 1988, was one of the witnesses who testified for the prosecution.

Another witness who testified was Hawthorne Police Sergeant Chris Cognac. He knew one of Franklin's alleged victims before she was killed. Princess Berthomieux was a young female of fifteen who was well known to police as someone who 'was no stranger to the streets' despite being so young. In 2002 Berthomieux had been attacked by a man, not Franklin, and Sergeant Cognac had charged her assailant, but during the subsequent trial, Berthomieux could not be found: she had been murdered by the man considered to be The Grim Sleeper serial killer. Authorities believe she was one of the youngest victims.

Inglewood Police Detective Daniel Milchovich was the next to be sworn in and take the stand. He was the patrol officer who responded to the crime scene where Berthomieux was found naked in an alleyway on 9 March 2002. Like most of the others, there wasn't much to go on from this crime scene since there was little evidence collected other than the body. It was clear, yet again, that this was a 'body dump', meaning Berthomieux had been killed somewhere else and then dumped at the location.

Another witness, who was also an LAPD detective, Roger Allen, testified that he had investigated the murder of Valerie McCorvey back in July 2003. She too had been dumped at the location where she was found, due to the lack of physical evidence at the scene.

Seymour Amster did his best to make it look as though the LAPD hadn't investigated the scene to the best of their ability, using an incredibly far-fetched example relating to orange peel. The peel from an an orange found near the body was not examined, and Amster seemed to make these peelings such a focal point that he was almost laughed right out of the courtroom.

One of the star witnesses was an undercover LAPD detective who had posed as a busboy at a pizzeria, where Franklin had been attending a children's party. In the early afternoon of 5 July 2010, John's Incredible Pizza in Buena Park was in full swing with a possible serial killer partying among them. This undercover detective carried a plastic tub collecting plates and carefully placed Franklin's discarded plates, with food still on them, in a separate metal pan with a tray placed on top to conceal it.

7 MARCH 2016

I arrived after the first witness had been sworn in. It was about 10.15 a.m. and Theresa Curtis was already on the stand. Ms Curtis was an attractive, petite Hispanic woman with long brown hair. She was on the stand on the Friday morning explaining how she strategically collected the items from Lonnie Franklin's garage.

Franklin was sitting in his chair facing straight ahead wearing a yellow shirt, black trousers and a dark black tie.

Detective Curtis is a detective with the LAPD and had

been with the Robbery Homicide Division for just under five years when she was called out to Lonnie Franklin's address on 9 July 2010. She no longer worked in the RHD unit but was still with the LAPD.

District Attorney Marguerite Rizzo was asking the questions that day. Ms Rizzo is an attractive blonde woman with a softly spoken voice. Although I have never spoken to Ms Rizzo, I assume her to be a very nice person.

Ms Rizzo placed on the ELMO various photographs of the overly packed 'central' garage belonging to Lonnie Franklin. This garage was called the 'central' garage because on either side were two other garages. One was called the east garage and the other was called the west garage. That day we were discussing the central garage.

The central garage was so filled with stuff that you would think a homeless pack rat might have happily lived in it. There were two televisions, a white microwave, plastic bags, boxes of oil, cleaning bottles, electrical cords, light bulbs, tapes, VHS holders, paperwork, books, home improvement items, car parts and car radios to name but a few things.

DA Rizzo put up more photographs on the ELMO, showing all areas of the garage along with a Polaroid of Enietra Washington. OK, so now it had been mentioned, for the first time, that day, that the Polaroid of Enietra was found among the mess in Franklin's middle garage. DA Rizzo wanted to know whether Detective Curtis recognised the picture from seeing it that day, back in 2010. She confirmed it was indeed one of the Polaroids they had seized from the central garage that day.

There was a VHS box and tape holder filled with money which was also recovered, and that was all counted by Curtis's supervisor. She didn't recall how much money was taken into evidence as she wasn't the person doing the counting.

DA Rizzo walked over to Detective Curtis, gave her an envelope and asked her to open it and then explain carefully what she was doing and what was inside.

Detective Curtis spoke slowly.

Detective Curtis: 'I'm breaking the red seal and opening the envelope. Inside there are three pieces of paper.' She opened the first piece of paper, saying that it was a 'Notice to Appear', a citation of sorts: 'The name on the citation is Lonnie David Franklin Jr.' She went on to open the next piece of paper and Ms Rizzo put this document on the ELMO. It was clearly a military document, perhaps from Franklin's time in the Army. The third piece of paper was a vehicle registration with Franklin's full name on it as well.

This concluded the prosecution's questions.

It was now Seymour Amster's turn for the cross-examination.

Amster shot up from his seat and raced to the podium like a duckling chasing his mother across a busy street. He wanted to confirm that she, Detective Curtis, was the 'collector' of the evidence collected at the garage on 9 July 2010. Curtis confirmed that her team had handled the entire search of the garage and didn't search any of the other areas. When Amster was placing the pictures on the ELMO, Franklin tilted his head slightly to the left, and for one of the first times, was looking directly at what was being shown on the ELMO (he had recently started to look up at the screen more often).

THE TRIAL

Amster: 'Could someone else have access to the Polaroid photograph that was found at the scene?'

DA: 'Objection! Speculation.'

Judge: 'Sustained.'

Amster: 'What did law enforcement have to do to get the photograph?'

He then called for everyone to 'go to the sidebar' as he often does. The sidebar is where both sides, including the Judge, huddle to the left of the courtroom to secretly talk without the jury hearing. All we could see was Amster flapping his arms about, with his elbows firmly tucked into his waist, making a spectacle of himself. DA Beth Silverman just kept shaking her head in disgust and not making eye contact with him at all. Within about eight minutes they all dispersed back to their seats and Silverman was still shaking her head all the way.

Amster: 'Do you put everything into the property report?'

Detective Curtis: 'In this case I did not. The property report was written by another detective showing all items that are received and booked in to evidence.'

Amster: 'Can you refresh the recollection... let me rephrase the question... Can you recall the items you collected? Could any of them be sold in a retail store?'

The Judge looked confused and so did the witness. It was objected to by the prosecution on the basis of 'relevance'. Amster then continued to ask if she had had to move the items in the garage to get to where that Polaroid was. He asked her what items she removed to get to the photograph? How many items had she moved?

Detective Curtis did not recall anything other than she had

removed a box of motor oil that was moved out of the way to see the Polaroid.

Amster: 'Did you look in the box of oil?' Amster continued his questioning as the Judge rolled her eyes. Amster then put up more pictures on the ELMO all relating to the Polaroid of Enietra Washington, showing where it was found in the central garage. He wanted to see if someone else could have had access to that Polaroid besides the witness herself. How many television sets had she seen in the garage, he wanted to know. Could she have moved a partition to get to this Polaroid? He went on with the same line of questioning as before.

Amster (referring to the Polaroid): 'What did you move to get to it?'

He then seemed to run out of the same generic questions and asked to speak to everyone, yet again, at the sidebar. They all huddled around again, each clearly looking begrudgingly at the other, realising that this was yet another stalling tactic from the defence. Dale Atherton, the second defence lawyer, to me seems a very decent man but as yet he hadn't said much as he was so very new to the case. After they all dispersed back to their seats, Amster continued.

Amster: 'Did you take a record of everything you seized in that garage?'

Detective Curtis: 'I don't recall.'

Amster: 'Could you describe the contents you saw when you were there?'

Curtis: 'There were so many items – there were boxes, oil cans, cleaning bottles, plastic bags, hanging electrical cords, home improvement items, paperwork, books on shelves... There were items everywhere.'

After Amster tried to make the question sound different each time to no avail, he then asked another question. Again it was so similar to the last one that he said for the fifth time that day, 'I will withdraw the question.' It's amazing how many times he said that he must 'withdraw the question' which was always a question that he was already halfway through asking. He had done this every day since we began the trial. So far, the prosecution had never had to withdraw anything they'd said.

After Mr Amster had been apparently faffing around for numerous minutes, he then asked the same question yet again. This continued throughout the day with him withdrawing his original question then asking the exact same thing as he'd asked before but in a different way each time.

★ ★ ★

After we came back from lunch it was 1.39 p.m. when the jury walked in through the main door. Franklin was already sitting there, with his glasses on this time and staring straight ahead.

Amster approached the witness with a large envelope stating Lonnie David Franklin Jr's name on it and he asked her to open it. Suddenly all the power went out, the ELMO switched off, the microphones went down and some of the lights went off too. Amster roared with hysterical laughter. We all looked at each other to see if we'd missed the joke but it really was just a power outage. Amster just kept laughing and laughing. After a few minutes, a deputy went back behind the Judge's wall, tripped the electrical breakers and then all the power went back on again.

The picture we were looking at now came right back to full view on the ELMO. It was of the inside of the central garage at Franklin's home located at 1728 West 81st Street. I found it so strange to see a white microwave, two televisions and a cabinet filled with car radios in the garage along with all the other junk. What a pack rat he was!

After Amster was done with his somewhat monotonous and long-winded questioning, on the exact same point, he had no further questions and shuffled and slid his way across the carpet back to his seat.

The DA wanted to know about the procedure the police go through when money is found and how it is collected and booked in to evidence. Detective Curtis explained that she had to advise her supervisor of this and he documented the money from that point forward.

Nothing further.

★ ★ ★

At 2.30 p.m. the next witness was sworn in and took the stand. He was a rather rotund Hispanic man by the name of Detective Luis Rivera.

DA Silverman asked Detective Rivera what his profession was and he answered that he had been with the LAPD for twenty-seven years, a detective for fifteen years and a detective with RHD – Robbery Homicide Division – for a total of nine years.

DA: 'Did you participate in a search warrant at the location of 1728 West 81st Street on July 7th 2010?'

THE TRIAL

Rivera: 'Yes, ma'am, I did. I was assigned to search the south-west bedroom.'

DA: 'How many people were there with you, in your team?'

Rivera: 'Approximately five of us.'

DA: 'What did you find in the south-west bedroom?'

Rivera: 'In a filing cabinet drawer I found a receipt for a .25 automatic handgun purchased at Western Surplus.'

DA: 'What did you do with it when you found it?'

Rivera: 'I took it outside and I pulled it out and it was then photographed and it was taken in to evidence by Detective Rick Jackson.'

Detective Rivera was assigned to another search, this time of Franklin's vehicle. He then went to Al's Towing, which is located on 6100 St Andrews, where Lonnie Franklin's 2001 Honda Accord had been towed.

Rivera: 'In the pocket of the back passenger seat I found an ID card issued by the City of Los Angeles Sanitation Department in the name of Lonnie David Franklin. I posted this in to evidence.'

The DA walked over to where the detective was sitting and showed him the picture of that photo ID with Franklin's picture on it. The detective confirmed that this was indeed the picture he had found back in July of 2010.

Nothing further and no cross-examination at that time.

★ ★ ★

The next witness called to the stand was Denaro Arredondo, a tall Hispanic man with jet-black hair and a full black moustache. He stated his full name for the jury and explained his occupation and what duties he performed with the LAPD.

Detective Arredondo: 'I am a firearms examiner with the LAPD. I've been with the LAPD for twenty-one years and have been a firearms examiner for the past sixteen years. I respond to crime scenes, analyse evidence, collect the evidence out in the field and then book it in and then provide testimony.'

DA: 'Were you assigned to go to a large-scale search warrant on the dates of July 7th through July 9th 2010?'

Detective Arredondo: 'Yes, ma'am.'

Detective Arredondo was assigned to a team of two to three members and they named themselves Team F. He was assigned to search, along with the others, the central garage on 9 July 2010 in the early hours of that day. DA Rizzo put a photograph on the ELMO of the cluttered central garage from various angles, and the detective explained, 'The garage was filled with clutter, debris, motor components, cardboard, lubricants, electrical components, vehicle repair components, car parts, motor oil… It was very convoluted and difficult to navigate due to all the clutter.'

DA Rizzo's main reason for her specific line of questioning was to find out what exactly was in the garage, where it was located, what the detective had removed from the garage and how he removed it. This was to see how he was able to find the Polaroid of Enietra Washington.

Detective Arredondo: 'Once I was able to clear out some of those items, the picture was clearly visible. When I pulled back some of the dry wall, I pulled it down a little bit, I could see the Polaroid just lying there. I was standing right over it and I could see it very clearly. The photographer, who was one of the detectives, took the picture of the Polaroid before it was handled by anyone from my division. The photograph of the Polaroid was taken before anyone even collected it, so it wasn't even touched by anyone.'

The DA approached the witness with an envelope with a red (LAPD) seal on it labelled 'Detective Dupree'. The witness opened the envelope with the Polaroid of Enietra Washington collected from the west wall behind the dry wall of the central garage.

There followed cross-examination by Seymour Amster:

Amster: 'Were you the first officer to see this Polaroid photo in your opinion?'

Detective Arredondo: 'Yes.'

Amster (pointing to the dirt on top of the Polaroid): 'Was that the correct amount of debris that was on the Polaroid when you saw it or was there more or less?'

Detective Arredondo: 'Yes, to my knowledge it is the same amount of debris on the picture of the Polaroid today as it was when I found it in 2010.'

Yet again, Amster kept pressing the issue and repeated the same question but in a different way: 'So you had to remove items before the Polaroid was accessible to you, right?'

The Judge interjected rather sternly with, 'Mr Amster, you've asked that question five, six, seven, eight, nine times already! You cannot keep asking the same question over and over and over again. Now move on!'

After quite a few minutes of rustling, clearly looking for something that he seemed not to find, Amster put a document up on the ELMO. Then suddenly he laughed and spluttered an apology. Through his laughter he let us know that it was the wrong photo, still laughing hysterically as he frantically tried to remove the document.

After so much wasted time, Judge Kennedy ended the day a few minutes before 4 p.m.

Once the jury had left the courtroom, we were all left there as the defence, prosecution and Judge wanted to discuss which witnesses would be coming up next on the side of the prosecution and how much longer it would be to present their case. This discussion almost immediately turned into a conflict with everyone bickering, especially the DA and the lead defence, Seymour Amster.

DA Beth Silverman said that she planned to finish presenting the prosecution's case by the end of that coming week. She named the next witnesses she planned to call for the following day: Rafael Garcia, Lisa Mallory, Charlene Johnson, Jeff Lowe, Sharlene Cruz, Ray Davis and three others. I couldn't believe that she would be calling so many in one day when we had so far been going through a maximum of three witnesses per day.

Seymour Amster said he had an objection to the prosecution calling Ray Davis as a witness, because he'd reviewed Davis's file and found out that he had some kind of a gun charge and was charged with attempted murder in 1990. After a few minutes the Judge then asked DA Beth Silverman a question.

Judge: 'You have stated the amount of witnesses that you will be calling in tomorrow and I was just wondering, on what planet that might happen on?'

Ms Silverman responded that they would call them over the next two days and already there were five witnesses who had stayed outside all day that day.

THE TRIAL

Then the dispute began between DA Silverman and Amster regarding the defence not being prepared in a 'timely manner', and Amster was highly evasive as to whether or not he was going to put certain witnesses on the stand when it came to his time to present his case.

DA Silverman: 'Yet again the defence's discovery is going to be in the eleventh hour, delaying the trial yet again.'

8 MARCH 2016

Ricky Harris had called me early the previous morning saying that the defence had subpoenaed both him and Paul Williams to be in court that day and for me to 'hurry up and get there'. I arrived by 9.45 a.m. as I knew that we weren't going to be in session until 9.30 a.m. due to the Judge having other cases to deal with.

As soon as I got there I saw Ricky and Paul talking to the defence investigators. I'm not going to say any more here as I've been asked by certain people not to mention their names, but what I can say is what happened next with Ricky. He came bouncing down the corridor to greet me in his usual way and then we sat down to talk quietly, when he told me that he was not going to accept the subpoena due to the fact that he didn't want to be a witness for someone who he felt had most certainly committed the crimes of which he stood accused. He was very serious about this and wanted to go into the courtroom he had been banned from by the defence due to him being a 'potential witness for the defence'. He explained how he most definitely didn't want to be a witness of any kind for the defence. Prosecution maybe, but not the defence!

I told Ricky that we could go in and sit together and see if he could stay without being thrown out. As we walked down the hall, he pointed to a man and started laughing.

Ricky: 'Hey, hey, Vic! I want you to meet someone. This guy here, this guy, this guy is me, he's me!'

I didn't know what he was getting at. There was an elderly light-skinned black man sat hunched up next to a pillar, seemingly also not knowing what was going on either. I held out my hand to the man and introduced myself. He said his name was 'Richard... Richard Harris.' Ah, now I got it.

Ricky laughed and said, 'See, I tol' you this man here, he's me! I'm Richard Harris and this man here's Richard Harris an' he don' know nothin' about this case or why he's even here. He got subpoenaed coz of his name and he din't even live near none of us in South LA, he's from the west side!' Laughing in his flamboyant way, he then said, 'The defence subpoenaed the wrong guy!'

And so the day began.

I went into the courtroom and Lonnie David Franklin Jr was sitting there in a lime green shirt and beige trousers, looking straight ahead. The witness on the stand was Rafael Garcia, one of the criminalists searching Franklin's house over the period of time from 7 July through to 9 July 2010. He was testifying about the ballistics and the .22 calibre gun used in the killings. On the ELMO were three different photographs of the gun, the magazine and the bullets, along with a ruler to measure the length and width of the gun. Five inches long and five inches in height, it can easily be concealed in a pocket, so it's often called a 'pocket pistol'. DA Marguerite Rizzo was asking the questions.

There were four live rounds of ammunition found.

The DA (Ms Rizzo) approached the witness (Garcia) with a large white envelope with red tape around it. She asked him to carefully open the envelope and explain what he was doing. Garcia pulled back the red seal, which is known as the 'LAPD evidence seal', he then reached inside and pulled out the Titan .22 calibre gun, tied with a zip tie to prevent it from being discharged, along with another small envelope which was also inside.

The Judge explained to the jury and the rest of the court that the reason for the zip tie tying the gun was to prevent it from discharging for the safety of the courtroom. Any time a weapon is brought into a courtroom it must be tied with a zip tie so there is no way of it being accidentally discharged.

Garcia had also found an Army jacket in the hallway of Franklin's home and inside, among other items, was a driver's licence, business cards and a Vons club card. The driver's licence was placed on the ELMO and it said: 'A0612197. Lonnie David Franklin Jr, DOB 08.30.1952. 1728 W. 81st, Los Angeles 90047. 5ft 7in. 170lbs.'

After a short recess, we all came back into court. Paul Williams was sitting next to the defence investigators and Ricky and I were only a few seats away. Seymour Amster looked over at Ricky and kept shaking his head and was whispering to his co-defence lawyer, Dale Atherton. Amster was becoming increasingly redder in the face as he spoke. Something was about to happen and it did.

Amster: 'One second, Your Honour... I have a Mr Paul Williams in the courtroom today who has been subpoenaed by the defence and I've placed him on call.'

Judge Kennedy then looked at Paul and said, 'Sir, Mr Williams, do you understand what it means to be placed "on call"?'

To which Paul responded that he did. She said that if he changed his phone number he must let the defence know and that he was on call for the duration of the trial.

'OK, thank you,' she said and he was then free to go.

Amster: 'Your Honour, we also have here in the courtroom Mr Ricky Harris. We were unable to serve him with a subpoena and I don't want to get into it, but he is a potential witness in this case. He's in the courtroom right now and I...'

Judge (looking very confused): 'OK, who's Mr Harris?' (Ricky raised his hand.) 'Mr Harris? Mr Ricky Harris?'

'Richard Harris,' Ricky then said, to which the Judge apologised and called him 'Richard Harris' instead of 'Ricky'. This entire time, Franklin had turned around fully in his chair, nodded to me very subtly and then looked over to Ricky and then back to me again. He gave a semi-smile basically acknowledging that he knew I was there every day and he knew why. I didn't respond in any way.

Amster: 'I don't feel I have control over him to make sure he stays out of the courtroom, we will do our best to serve him a subpoena.'

Judge Kennedy: 'Mr Harris, the way it works is like this. When someone is a witness and not one of the detectives testifying in the case, they are not permitted to be in the courtroom when other witnesses are testifying. Mr Amster has identified you as a potential witness for the defence. I see you are shaking your head but it's up to him and not you to decide whether or not you will be called upon to testify. So you are not going to be allowed to remain in the courtroom. You can remain in the hallway if you like but you cannot be in the courtroom.'

'OK, I'll go, bye bye,' Ricky told the Judge flippantly. I could see that he was annoyed but I did see the Judge's point and explained this to him later on. He then turned to me and said, 'Call me later.' I of course acknowledged him and confirmed that I would.

★ ★ ★

After Ricky Harris left the courtroom and at 11.12 a.m. the jurors were then allowed back in. Mr Garcia was on the stand and continued talking about the driver's licence and the gun, which was taken in to evidence. Previously Mr Garcia had carefully opened the envelope with the red LAPD evidence seal and had shown the contents, which was the gun with the zip tie firmly securing the handle.

No further questions from the DA.

The Judge then asked if the defence he wanted to cross-examine the witness. Amster immediately jumped up from his seat and wanted to know what kind of analysis Garcia had done on the gun and also the magazine. The Judge suggested that he could take the envelope over to him to be reminded of what he had analysed.

Amster was permitted to 'approach the witness' to give him back the envelope again. He uncoordinatedly rushed over at a great rate of speed, holding the large envelope out in front of him, and landed awkwardly at the witness stand. I blinked and the next thing I knew was the gun seemed to have bounced out of the envelope and fallen to the floor! Yes, Amster had dropped the gun on the floor right by the witness.

Mr Garcia shot back in his seat immediately and Amster roared with laughter. Even the Judge raised her eyes and said with a smirk, 'This is exactly why we have the zip tie on, for everyone's safety.' Everyone in the courtroom erupted at that point.

Amster wanted to know who the initials were that were on the smaller envelope. They were of the toolmarks examiner with the initials D.S.R., that is Daniel Seth Rueben, who was Garcia's co-worker.

Amster then cross-examined Mr Garcia about his search of the north-west bedroom on 8 July 2010.

Amster: 'What were your duties when searching the north-west bedroom? What were you searching for?'

Garcia: 'To look for firearm evidence and photographic evidence, any type of photographs.'

Amster: 'Is it fair to say that, ha, ha, ha, ha... you searched that entire room and you found some clothing?'

Garcia: 'Yes.'

Amster: 'Are you familiar with clothing that's... well... clothing that has been worn by men?'

At this the courtroom erupted in fits of laughter.

Judge: 'I suppose, Mr Amster, you could explain that.'

To which Amster then repeated his question again in a much higher octave this time and speaking through his laughter, 'Well, I don't know, are you familiar with clothes normally worn by women?'

Garcia: 'Yes.'

Judge: 'It's just a loaded question, I don't know.'

Amster (loudly and condescendingly, still laughing): 'OK. IN... THAT... ROOM... DID... YOU... OBSERVE.... CLOOOTTTHINGG?'

Garcia: 'Yes.'

Amster: 'OK, and was the clothing that you observed, would it be normally worn by a man or normally worn by a woman? Or both?'

Garcia: 'Erm, what I recall is clothing which would be worn by a man.'

With much confusion and more questions of this nature, Garcia perhaps understandably responded a number of times with, 'I don't recall.' Then Amster put a photograph on the ELMO of clothing hanging from the door of the bedroom being searched. He was pointing to an item of clothing that was a little larger than the others and wanted to know if it looked to the witness like it was a dress or a shirt or what? Naturally, the witness didn't recall as it wasn't an item that had been taken into evidence.

Amster: 'Did you... I will withdraw the question. Also in this closet I am pointing to this item, I'm pointing to the shirt. Did you see what size the shirt was?'

The Judge rolled her eyes as Mr Garcia responded with, 'No, I don't recall the size.'

Amster: 'I'm now pointing to a closet, do you remember if there were clothes in there?'

Garcia: 'Yes.'

Amster: 'Did you write down an inventory of the clothes in that closet?'

Garcia: 'No.'

Amster: 'Was anyone else besides you in that room?'

Here, the Judge was forced to clarify: 'He means were there other officials, law enforcement, in that room while you were collecting the evidence?'

Amster: 'Who were they?'

Garcia: 'There was a photographer and two other members of the laboratory.'

This went on for about another ten minutes while Amster was asking if the documents Garcia had found had any other name on them besides Lonnie Franklin. To which Garcia responded with a firm 'No,' each time. Amster was implying that some of the clothing might have belonged to a woman yet none of us knew where he was going with this. He pointed with the laser pointer at a drawer and asked how many drawers were in the chest of drawers. Again no one could understand where he was going with this line of questioning.

There were numerous remote controls in the drawer not seized by law enforcement.

The questioning went on and then back to whether the shirts were either male or female. Amster then had to withdraw the question a number of times. About five to eight minutes went by of silence when the defence should have been saying something. Instead there was silence and the whole courtroom was left waiting.

A few times Judge Kennedy had to rephrase the defence's questions to make the process go a little more quickly and smoothly. Amster was just not making sense to anyone, especially the witness. He wanted to know if any latent fingerprints were taken or any swabs of the items were taken at the scene. Many objections were called out and the Judge sustained them. Amster then asked for the sidebar, yet again, to which the Judge responded with a firm 'No.' It was apparent that she too had had quite enough.

No further questions and Rafael Garcia was free to go.

★ ★ ★

The next witness called to the stand was a tall attractive black woman with very short hair, Tracey Benjamin. She was sworn in and explained her job as a chief detective with the LAPD. Amster interjected with something I couldn't quite hear, but he was asking if he could have a few more minutes to review something. Judge Kennedy allowed this, but of course, Amster took the usual over-extended amount of time compared to a normal attorney.

DA Beth Silverman was asking the questions and asked how long Benjamin had been with the LAPD, which was twenty-six and a half years thus far: she had been with RHD for about ten years.

DA: 'Were you one of the detectives who assisted in a multi-day search warrant from July 7th 2010 to July 9th 2010 at the location of 1728 West 81st Street in Los Angeles?'

Detective Benjamin: 'Yes.'

DA: 'What area were you responsible for searching?'

Detective Benjamin: 'The dining room.'

Detective Benjamin found her items on the china cabinet in the dining room. The picture shown on the ELMO was of a person from her investigating team wearing a mask and pointing to something at the top of the china cabinet, with two notebooks of two of the field officers placed in the air next to the item. One of the items she collected was a box of photographs.

Amster then cross-examined the witness about the official police notebooks in the picture, which was a shot taken as part of the evidence collected. He wanted to know if Detective Benjamin had looked inside the notebook. Whose handwriting was in it? Who provides these notebooks? How were the notebooks purchased by the LAPD? Who else could manufacture them and how they were manufactured? He wanted to know if anyone had tried to swab or take latent fingerprints of those notebooks. Amster asked this question to a lot of witnesses regarding evidence collected. After he had to withdraw this question at least four times in this one short cross-examination, he went on to ask if there were any other documents that Detective Benjamin might have seen on the credenza that she had been searching in the dining room. She replied that she had not seen anything else.

No further questions.

★ ★ ★

The next witness was called to the stand. Lisa Mowery was sworn in.

DA Silverman: 'Could you tell us how you are employed, please?'

Lisa Mowery: 'I work for the City of Los Angeles Bureau of Sanitation. I've been employed by the City for twenty-four years and with the Bureau of Sanitation for seventeen years.'

DA: 'What is your position with the Bureau of Sanitation?'

Lisa Mowery: 'I am the chief financial officer with oversight of our financial, administrative and personnel programmes. This includes all personnel records, everything from employment applications to reviews to emergency appointments, as well as assignments for personnel.'

The DA then asked if she reviewed the personnel records of an individual by the name of Lonnie David Franklin Jr. She replied that she did. When the DA read out the information belonging to Franklin, she confirmed that it was correct, but the Judge would not allow her to read out the social security number belonging to Franklin.

According to the DA, there were three addresses in Franklin's personnel file, including his main residence of 1728 W. 81st in Los Angeles. There was also an address of 1707 W. 85th Street in Los Angeles and 443 W. 111th Place in Los Angeles. The witness confirmed that these three addresses were in Franklin's file. She also confirmed that the first date of Franklin's employment with the City was in April of 1981 until 30 June 1982 and his job title was garage attendant. He was assigned to the LAPD Central facility, downtown LA, in the Central garage. Franklin's duties included vehicle maintenance and towing disabled vehicles. On 1 July 1982 he was given a new job title of maintenance labourer, which is unskilled labour – picking up bulky items, riding with a truck operator on any of their refuse trucks. From June 1985 until February 1989 he was a trash truck driver in the City of LA. He would have worked at the South Central Collection Yard, with his duties including picking up trash, debris and large objects from alleyways and all other areas in non-commercial areas of Los Angeles.

In the 1980s the City went from two-person teams to one-person. The name for these one-person vehicles is

Truck Operation 1 Man. The location for the landfills open for operation at that time was in the San Fernando Valley by the name of Lopez Canyon Landfill, and the trash truck operators would make their dumps at this location.

The DA showed a photograph on the ELMO of a few truck operators standing among refuse at the Lopez Canyon landfill.

Nothing further.

Cross-examination from Mr Amster.

Amster: 'Good afternoon, ma'am. Do you have the personnel records of Mr Franklin from June 1985 until February 1989?'

Lisa Mowery: 'No.'

Amster: 'Do you have any record of where he was travelling at that time?'

Lisa Mowery: 'No.'

Amster: 'Do you have any record of who he was travelling with at that time?'

Lisa Mowery: 'No.'

Amster: 'Do you have any… I'll withdraw the question. Do you have any record of what hours he worked on any given shift?'

Lisa Mowery: 'No.'

Amster: 'Would the driver have a designated route if he worked for the sanitation department between the time of June 1985 until February 1989?'

Lisa Mowery: 'Yes.'

Amster: 'Ma'am, you stated that some of the… some of the refuse dump areas in the City of Los Angeles during this time period was the Lopez Canyon Dump, correct?'

Lisa Mowery: 'Yes.'

THE TRIAL

Amster: 'So how many people worked at Lopez Canyon Dump on any given shift?'

Lisa Mowery: 'I don't know.'

Amster: 'What is the procedure when someone drives a truck to the Lopez Canyon Dump and how do they unload it?'

Lisa Mowery: 'At that time there would be someone directed to a portion of the landfill that was active on that particular day so that they would know where to empty the load.'

Amster: 'At that time was the City of Los Angeles concerned about potential health problems on a load that a sanitation truck driver unloaded?'

DA: 'Objection! That's irrelevant!'

Judge: 'Overruled.'

Lisa Mowery: 'No.'

Amster: 'So the City of Los Angeles would not be concerned about if an individual truck driver would bring a dead body and have it contained in his truck?'

DA: 'Objection!'

Judge: 'Sustained.'

Amster: 'Are there standard operating procedures for the City of Los Angeles to have an inspection concerning the items dumped at a particular location?' I am assuming Amster wanted to prove that even with inspections, no body was ever found.

Lisa Mowery: 'I don't know.'

Amster: 'Are there any procedures done to ensure that a dead body had not been dumped at the Lopez Canyon Dump during the period of June 1985 until February 1989?'

Lisa Mowery: 'I don't know.'

Amster: 'During the period of June 1985 until February

1989, did the City of Los Angeles maintain a log of what driver would check out a truck that they were utilising and and then check back in when they were done using it?'

Lisa Mowery: 'I don't know. I know we have similar procedures today but I cannot speculate what exactly they were doing back then.'

Amster: 'Were you employed by the City of Los Angeles during the period of June 1985 to February 1989?'

Lisa Mowery: 'No.'

Amster: 'Are you familiar with how personnel records were maintained by the City of Los Angeles for the period of time between June 1985 until February 1989?'

Lisa Mowery: 'No.'

Amster: 'Are you familiar with how personnel records were maintained by the City of Los Angeles for the period of time between April 1981 to June 30th 1982?'

Lisa Mowery: 'No.'

Then Amster suddenly grew very red in the face, waved his hands around more frantically this time and shouted: 'So all the information you've given us today has been based upon information and procedures that you do today but not that even existed back in the 1980s?'

Lisa Mowery: 'The information was based on the information contained in the documents that I reviewed.'

Amster: 'But you are not familiar with the record-keeping procedures back in the 1980s, were you?' I felt he was trying to discredit her.

Lisa Mowery: 'No.'

Amster: 'So all your information is not based on personal knowledge, it's just what you reviewed in that file?'

Lisa Mowery: 'Yes, my personal knowledge of what is in that file.'

Amster: 'So you are just speculating that the procedures used today are the same way they were used in the 1980s, correct?'

Lisa Mowery: 'No, I never stated that.'

Now, Amster was getting to a fever pitch and raising his voice as loud as he could while saliva was flying out of his mouth from all angles. His head was protruding out from his neck and his hands were now placed firmly on his hips as he continued to basically scream at the witness.

Amster: 'Are you familiar that from time to time your department is required to maintain records in a different way depending upon what the Controller's Office wants by the City of Los Angeles?'

DA: 'Objection! Irrelevant.'

Judge: 'Sustained.'

Amster: 'So you have absolutely no idea what the requirements were, or how records should have been maintained, or how they were even preserved back in the 1980s, do you?

'No further questions!'

DA Beth Silverman posed her final questions to the witness about the records in a much clearer and more concise manner. The witness was able to explain clearly how similar all the procedures and documentations were from the current day to back in the eighties – it was just that a different person was conducting the checks back then. She had been reviewing all of those documents in the courtroom because the person who had documented everything back in the eighties had since passed away.

Amster went up one final time and asked a number of redundant questions to which her answer was a firm 'No,' on every one of them.

Nothing further and the witness was excused.

★ ★ ★

At 2.19 p.m. the next witness was called to the stand. Detective John Luke had been employed by the LAPD for twenty-eight years and had been with the RHD for seven years.

DA Silverman: 'Did you assist in a search warrant at 1728 W. 81st Street in Los Angeles on the dates of July 7th, 8th and 9th of 2010?'

Detective Luke: 'Yes.'

At this the Judge looked at Seymour Amster and said, 'Well, if you're going to make a face like that, I don't know what it means.' Judge Kennedy was referring to the kind of a face that Amster pulled when motioning that, yet again, the defence wanted to go to the sidebar. She then turned and faced the jury and said with a smile, 'This is how I keep my girlish figure, folks,' referring to the amount of times she had been called to the sidebar every day, which was keeping her extremely fit. They all laughed.

This testimony was similar to that of the other detectives from the Robbery Homicide Division of the LAPD. Detective Luke explained his findings and what he booked in to evidence.

★ ★ ★

The next witness, Sharlene Johnson, was called at 3.03 p.m. She had been with the LAPD for almost twenty-one years and with RHD since 2006. Johnson was also part of the team of about twenty who searched the home of Lonnie Franklin over the three days starting on 7 July through 9 July of 2010.

Detective Johnson searched the western garage at the residence on 8 July 2010. In this garage she found a Toyota Corolla. There was a photograph of the western garage placed on the ELMO. The witness explained to DA Rizzo that the moment she entered the garage all she could see was 'total chaos' – 'The hood of the car was partially open, there was stuff under the hood, there were things all over the car, under the car, on the trunk, on the walls, things hanging from the ceiling, bicycles, bicycle tyres, a refrigerator, cabinets stacked on top of things. There was stuff everywhere.'

She had found a Polaroid camera and a box of bullets on an open cabinet. A photograph of the Polaroid camera was placed on the ELMO.

DA Rizzo walked up to the witness and handed her an envelope for her to describe what was inside as she opened it. Detective Johnson explained that it had her name, her serial number and the red LAPD evidence seal. Inside was the Polaroid camera that she had seized at the location on 81st Street on 8 July 2010. She confirmed all of this.

On cross-examination, Seymour Amster asked if she was a detective with the LAPD. Despite her previously explaining all of this in great detail in her testimony with the DA, he still asked this seemingly redundant question.

After withdrawing his questions a number of times, he then asked, 'Did you direct the criminalists to collect the biological evidence when you were in the garage?' Detective Johnson responded that she did. Amster then asked if she had directed anyone on the team to collect any latent fingerprints but she had not. He asked if she had moved anything from the roof of the car to see the camera more visibly. She said that she didn't remove anything but it was possible that someone else in the team might have removed items to make the camera more visible.

Amster then asked if there were items on top of the Polaroid camera or if there was any stuff on the camera. Detective Johnson placed the camera back in the envelope and was subsequently released.

★ ★ ★

At 3.37 p.m. the next witness was called to the stand. Lieutenant Michael Oppelt was sworn in. Oppelt had been a lieutenant with the LAPD for six years and would have been with the LAPD for a total of thirty-five years the following month. He was the acting commanding officer for the Criminal Gang Homicide Division in South LA. Lieutenant Oppelt has worked in the same position in other divisions over the years and he had been in charge of the homicide division for the past eight years.

DA Silverman: 'On July 7th through July 9th of 2010, did you have a role to play in a search warrant that was performed at 1728 W. 81st Street in Los Angeles?'

Lieutenant Oppelt: 'Yes.'

DA: 'And what was your role?'

Lieutenant Oppelt: 'My role was to be the officer in charge of the event directed by the two main detectives that were on the case, Detective Kilcoyne and Detective Coulter.'

THE TRIAL

The centre of the photograph showed the aerial shot of the location of Franklin's residence on 1728 W. 81st Street. It showed the LAPD 'easy up' and the command centre, which was an RV, a recreational vehicle. Lieutenant Oppelt explained the reason for having a command centre along with the RV: it was so that there was a main point of contact to take and examine property taken from the residence, from vehicles and from the garages.

A woman by the name of Doreen Hudson was the commander and the person in charge, with Lieutenant Oppelt, at the time. She was in charge of assigning the tactical team to carry out the search warrant of various areas of the residence on that Monday morning. They decided to have a team of three search outside of the residence and a team of three search inside. (Of course there were many others, this is just the two teams of investigators that Hudson and Oppelt assigned to the scene.) On top of this there was someone from the firearms unit and component unit, photographers, a SID support person and an RHD detective all assigned as well.

There were eight vehicles on Franklin's property in his garages at the back of the house, outside of the garages and also on the street. These were all impounded and subsequently searched in order to accommodate the actual searches of the various garages. This occurred more so on 7 and 8 July so that investigators could navigate more easily when searching inside the garages.

DA Silverman went on questioning the witness for a while longer until we adjourned for the day just after 4 p.m.

★ ★ ★

THE GRIM SLEEPER

Well, the last few days had been interesting, even more so with the growing contentiousness between DA Beth Silverman and the defence, Seymour Amster. On the Wednesday the underlying disdain the two of them seemed to have for each other came to the forefront and nothing was going to stop them attacking each other publicly, even in front of the jury this time.

Quoting below from *LA Times* reporter, Stephen Cesar, who put it so eloquently:

> The defence and the prosecution clashed Wednesday over whether prosecutors should have previously disclosed that an earlier witness had a conviction for attempted murder. The witness, Ray Davis, a former friend of Franklin's, testified that he once saw Franklin with one of the victims in the case.
>
> Defence attorney Seymour Amster complained that he had never seen such an oversight by a prosecutor and called the late notification 'egregious.' Davis' testimony, he argued, should be stricken from the record.
>
> Superior Court Judge Kathleen Kennedy rejected his request, saying Davis could return to testify about his conviction.
>
> 'She doesn't matter enough,' the defence attorney responded. 'I feel pity for her, but that's as far as it goes.' 'I know you and Ms. Silverman don't much care for each other,' Kennedy said, referring to Deputy Dist. Atty. Beth Silverman.
>
> Some in the audience gasped and others laughed.

Silverman shot back, asking the judge to silence Amster for his comments and allow her a chance to respond. Nothing improper had occurred, and Amster was engaging in pointless, personal attacks, she said.

'I don't care what he thinks,' Silverman said.

Amster complained that the judge was characterizing his personal feelings toward the prosecutor, but Kennedy interjected.

'I haven't been living under a paper bag for the last five years,' Kennedy said. 'I have observed hours and hours and hours of your conduct, her conduct, everyone's conduct — personal attacks, raising your voice.'

It is quite shocking as to how this had been going on between the two of them in the courtroom for more than five and a half years. Sometimes the Judge has even thrown them both out until they can come back in, and I quote: 'leave your egos at the door'. She has even warned them both, in no uncertain terms, to grow up, basically. However, this was the very first time that the jury had to become part of their ongoing dislike for each other. Although this didn't help the case at all, I suppose it did add some humour to a very dark subject that they would be forced to endure for at least a few months more. Throughout all of this, and throughout the entire trial, Franklin would blankly stare at the wall in front of him. He showed no emotion and barely made a sound, not even a cough or a sneeze.

District Attorney Beth Silverman is an attractive, tough yet brilliant woman, and to see her in action, you can't help but respect her. Sadly, there was nothing professional or 'attorney-like' about Seymour Amster. This unprofessionalism was compounded by all of his games, stalling tactics and complete lack of effort in carrying out his duties, which is why this case was delayed for so long. At this time and since we were now in the full swing of the trial, he seemed to want to delay it even further by asking the same redundant question over and over again.

Every single day, the Alexander family was in the courtroom patiently waiting for justice to be served for the murder of their daughter and sister. They were such a close-knit, loving family, who sadly lost their precious loved one, Alicia 'Monique' Alexander, back in 1988 at the tender age of just eighteen years old. So far they had not missed a single day of court since the pre-arraignments all began over five and a half years ago. God bless them all and might justice be served!

Over the past few days we had seen numerous criminalists testify: Henry Tuazon, Jeffrey Lowe and Daniel Rubin. Tuazon and Lowe found all sorts of women's underwear strewn across the garages at the back of Franklin's residence. The previous day a good friend of Franklin's testified, Ray Davis – however, it upset the defence a lot due to his criminal background. But he was not on the stand for long and might return if called upon again.

That day, witness Daniel Rubin took the stand again and for the entire day this poor man was subject to scrutiny and abuse generated by Seymour Amster, once he was allowed his cross-examination.

Mr Rubin is a toolmark expert and criminalist. He sounded as though he was either from back East somewhere or Chicago. My guess would be that he hailed from Brooklyn, New York

THE TRIAL

City, due to his strong accent and very apparent disdain for Mr Amster's antics. After being questioned by Amster for hours and hours with a redundant, degrading, offensive and an argumentative line of questioning, his demeanour was such that often times I felt as though he would like to reach over the witness stand and strangle the defence.

After withdrawing the question over a dozen times and being told by the Judge repeatedly that his line of questioning made no sense, Amster continued breaking down Mr Rubin's very professional examination of the bullet.

Amster: 'Did you identify one of the bullets from the test fire with some type of number or something you could refer back to for comparison purposes?'

Rubin: 'Yes.'

Amster: 'And what did you call them?'

Rubin: 'I called them test fire 721A.'

Amster: 'How many reproducible marks did you find on 721A?'

DA: 'Objection!'

Judge: 'Sustained. Mr Amster, he's told you several times already that he doesn't count marks.'

Amster went on to ask the same question again eight more times in different ways and it was clearly making Mr Rubin more and more frustrated. Finally, he just turned to the jury and shook his head and wiped his brow all in one motion. What made it more outrageous was when Mr Rubin had to answer the same question and he did so with the same answer each time. It got to the point where he would then put a full stop in between each word of his answer when he spoke. For example:

Rubin: 'I have answered this question numerous times before. I. DID. NOT. NEED. TO. COUNT. THE. MARKS. ON. THE. BULLET!'

Again, Amster, who refuses to ever give up, kept pressing.

Amster: 'OK, so the bullet you… I withdraw the question. I want to confirm that the bullet that you were examining was from a .25 calibre handgun, right?'

Rubin (with a huge sigh): 'Yes!'

Amster: 'So how many .25 calibre firearms are in the County of Los Angeles that this bullet could have been placed in to discharge that particular bullet?'

Rubin: 'I. DO. NOT. KNOW!'

Amster: 'Is the .25 calibre automatic firearm a readily accessible firearm for purchase?'

DA: 'Objection! Irrelevant.'

Judge: 'Overruled.'

Rubin: 'Well, that would depend on the circles that you travel with.'

At this the courtroom erupted in fits of laughter. Amster clearly relished the attention and laughed for the longest time.

Rubin: 'Well, if I was to patronise a gun store who was a distributor of those firearms then I would find them to be more available, but if I went to a gun store in another part of town who was not a distributor then it would be less available.'

This went on and on, and then Amster pressed further with trying to discredit the witness by making him try to remember whether the exact toolmarks were present on the murders of Barbara Ware and Henrietta Wright. He just wanted to make sure that they were from the same gun.

Amster: 'Were all of these toolmarks present on the Ware bullet present on the Wright bullet?'

Rubin: 'That I don't recall.'

Amster: 'Do you remember if there were some toolmarks that looked different on the Ware bullet to the toolmarks on the Wright bullet?'

Rubin (rolling his eyes again): 'As I've said before, I don't have a recollection one way or another on that.'

Amster: 'When you compared the bullets, do you look for marks that are present on one and not present on the other?'

Rubin (sarcastically and in a very high-pitched tone): 'Yes.'

Amster: 'Was there a single striated toolmark?'

Rubin: 'When you say "single striated toolmark", do you mean just one line?'

Amster: 'Yes.'

Rubin: 'No, it wasn't! As I've said before, it was an entire pattern. As I've said before, I. DO. NOT. COUNT. THE. LINES!'

Amster: 'Can you describe in your notes what this striated toolmark looked like?'

Rubin (with a look of complete shock at being asked the same question): 'No.'

Amster: 'And you cannot say that the pattern you saw on the Jackson bullet number 4 that you felt existed on the Wright bullet number 111 was the same pattern you saw on the Washington bullet number 10?'

Rubin: 'Correct!'

Amster: 'Nor on the Alexander bullet number 14?'

Rubin: 'Correct.'

Amster: 'Nor on the Sparks bullet number 57?'

Rubin: 'Correct.'

Amster: 'Nor on the Lowe bullet number 3?'

Rubin: 'Correct.'

Amster: 'Nor on the Ware bullet?'

Mr Rubin rolled his eyes again for the umpteenth time to the jury, this time wrinkling his brow.

After more lengthy and seemingly pointless questioning by the defence, which went round in circles all day after withdrawing the question numerous times, breaking down and roaring into uncontrollable laughter at nothing, waving his arms so much, elbows firmly at his side (as if trying to take off), referring to items by the wrong name and being corrected by the Judge on a number of occasions, and after putting the wrong photographs on the ELMO, Mr Amster finally gave up and said that he had 'Nothing further.' Phew!

The Judge turned to DA Beth Silverman for her to then ask the witness more questions, and she did.

DA: 'Mr Rubin, at some point in the defence questioning I think there was the question that asked… that long question… whether or not you know the number of firearms in Los Angeles County that could have fired this unique bullet that you matched to this gun. What was your answer?'

Rubin: 'ONE!'

DA: 'OK, as I wasn't sure what your answer to his question was. So as you understood the question regarding how many guns there were, whether we're talking about Los Angeles County or all of California, you're saying there's only one gun that could have fired that particular bullet, right?'

Rubin: 'Yes!'

DA: 'And that would be that Titan FIE that we looked at yesterday and today. The only gun we've looked at?'

Rubin: 'Yes!'

Defence: 'Objection! Vague.'

DA: 'Of all the guns that exist in the world, how many guns could have fired that particular bullet that was pulled out of the body?'

Rubin: 'One! The only gun that we have examined here in the court. YES!'

DA Silverman went on to confirm the answers to the questions that Amster had asked the witness, but in a much clearer way, to clarify the main points for the jury.

Most of the witness's responses were a firm, 'YES!'

She had nothing further.

And if you can believe it possible, Amster got up again to ask more questions even though it was the end of the day. Even though we had just four minutes to go, I left the building.

★ ★ ★

15 MARCH 2016

Criminalist and ballistics expert Alison Manfreda was on the stand again, as well as the previous Friday, giving her testimony very well indeed. This time Franklin was wearing a deep blue, almost denim-looking shirt and staring straight ahead.

Seymour Amster was using his somewhat demeaning and derogatory tone of voice when cross-examining the witness. He was challenging her in almost the same way as he had with criminalist Daniel Rubin (who was on the stand all day on the Thursday), even using the same seemingly redundant line of questioning.

Amster: 'How many toolmarks did you see on the bullet?' 'How many striations did you see on each bullet you tested?' 'Did you see how many marks there were when you tested it under the microscope?' 'Did you measure the area of the markings?'

To which her answers were continuously, 'No, I did not,' 'As I've said before, I don't count the toolmarks,' 'I'm going to try and make sense of that question.'

Here, I wanted to simply compile a few of the defence's never-ending questions along with the similar answers from the witness to follow the rhetorical questions so I don't make it too long and drawn-out. You catch the drift, I'm sure. The Judge often interjected with: 'Did you understand that question?' To which the witness would respond: 'I did not, no.' The Judge then said, 'Apparently not. We better try that one again, Mr Amster.'

Amster continued to challenge the witness by asking if she 'utilised physics' when comparing the bullets, which of course she didn't. He then asked if she 'considered the velocity' in determining if the bullets matched, which she had not either. He even asked if she had used 'kinetic energy' when comparing the bullets, which of course she hadn't.

He also persisted with the same seemingly redundant question of 'How many?' For example, 'How many striations were there on the bullet?' he asked, despite knowing full well that they don't count the striations. He also wanted to know how many patterns were on the bullet, knowing full well that nothing is counted per se.

Amster: 'Did you take a photograph of the test-fired bullets?'

Alison Manfreda: 'No, I did not.'

Amster: 'Did the microscope which you were using have the ability to take a photograph?'

Alison Manfreda: 'Yes, it did.'

Amster: 'Yet you still didn't use it to take a photograph?'

Alison Manfreda: 'I didn't need to as I could see it with my eyes.'

Amster: 'How many clusters of striations did you find on each bullet?'

Judge: 'Mr Amster, she has told us repeatedly that she DOES. NOT. COUNT. THE. STRIATIONS. NOR. THE. CLUSTERS.'

This line of questioning went on and on and Ms Manfreda really held her own on the stand, with the defence continually asking the same question after being repeatedly told not to.

After the lunch recess we came back into the courtroom and Ms Manfredo was on the stand again. The Judge walked in with her robe gaping open. Underneath she was wearing a very brightly coloured striped outfit.

Amster: 'So what do you look for when examining the bullet?'

Judge (with a long sigh): 'You have asked that I don't know how many times, Mr Amster!'

Amster: 'OK, so you believe that your eyeballs can determine the exact height, width, weight and all the characteristics of the bullet then? And you believe, withdraw the question, so you are certain that the two bullets have the exact same toolmarks as each other?'

This line of questioning went on and on all day so it really wasn't very interesting at all, which is why I won't elaborate any further here.

★ ★ ★

16 MARCH 2016

I arrived a little later than usual today, at about 10.30 a.m., and saw most of the jury sitting on the benches along the hallway. The detectives were all talking with each other at the end of the hallway, which was odd as it was a little too early for the first recess of the day.

Detective Dennis Kilcoyne was talking to Detective Darren Dupree. Kilcoyne is a very tall man with a small grey moustache. He has a very large and commanding presence and I'm sure can be very intimidating when he wants to be. The lead detective in the hunt for The Grim Sleeper for many years before Lonnie Franklin was arrested, he also played a big part in forming the Serial Killer Task Force in 2007. He has since been retired for the past three years at least. My guess was that he would be called upon to testify that day as this was the first day I had seen him since the trial began.

I was confused as to why everyone was in the hallway and just assumed that the recess had started early. Detective Dupree let me know off the record that 'We're starting late today because Mr Franklin missed the bus!' Somehow that statement sounded hysterically funny to me as I was imagining Lonnie Franklin running down the street, chasing a bus that had pulled out from the kerbside and left him standing there at the bus stop. After a short moment I realised he must have been referring to the Sheriff bus. But really, how could the Sheriff bus have left without him? I told Detective Dupree that had I known, I could easily have picked him up on the way as I drove my car in that day. He laughed.

We finally were let in, way late. Franklin was wearing the same dark blue shirt and grey tie and black trousers as he had worn the day before. His glasses were firmly on and his eyes were fixed straight ahead.

The first witness, Detective David Holmes, was called to the stand. He had been with the LAPD for eighteen years and was currently assigned to the RHD – Robbery Homicide Division.

DA Rizzo: 'On July 7th 2010 were you assigned to investigate a series of murders that took place in the late 1980s to 2007?'

Detective Holmes: 'Yes, I was.'

DA: 'And you were partnered up with Detective Dupree?'

Detective Holmes: 'Yes, I was.'

DA: 'And do you see the Detective in the court today?'

Detective Holmes: 'Yes, I do.'

Detective Holmes described Detective Dupree and pointed to him where he was sitting in front of him in the courtroom. He spoke of how he, Detective Holmes, transported Lonnie Franklin from the jail at 77th Division to RHD, which is located in downtown LA at the LAPD headquarters. The detective identified the defendant in court, describing what he was wearing – a blue shirt and grey tie. Holmes waited with Franklin in the interview room for Detective Kilcoyne and Detective Coulter to arrive. He took him to the restroom first, then, after the interview was taken, he assisted in taking swabs from the inside of Franklin's mouth before taking him down to the LAPD jail, where his blood was then taken too.

Both were placed in an evidence envelope and then brought back to RHD and given to Detective Coulter.

On the ELMO, DA Rizzo placed a photograph of an evidence envelope with three vials of blood. This photograph was described and confirmed by Detective Holmes.

There was 'nothing further'.

Judge: 'Mr Amster?' She looked to him to see if he had any cross-examination questions. Of course, he did!

Amster: 'At any time when you were with Mr Franklin, did you read him his Miranda Rights?'

This means that when a person is arrested, they must be read an official document, called Miranda Rights, to let the detainee know that anything he or she says can and will be used as evidence against him/her so they have the right to remain silent if they want to. They are as follows:

'You have the right to remain silent. Anything you say can and will be used against you in a court of law. You have the right to an attorney. If you cannot afford an attorney, one will be provided for you. Do you understand the rights I have just read to you? With these rights in mind, do you wish to speak to me?'

DA: 'Objection! Relevance.'

Judge: 'Sustained.'

Amster: 'I have nothing further.'

Detective Holmes was then released.

★ ★ ★

At 10.24 a.m. the next witness called to the stand was Lieutenant Michael Oppelt. He had previously testified so this was his second time testifying. This time he was decked out in his full LAPD uniform; last time he was in a suit.

DA Silverman questioned the witness about the search on 8 July 2010 of the eastern garage, where there was a mini refrigerator. Lieutenant Oppelt confirmed that he took part in this search. On the ELMO was a picture of the fridge with the door open, and inside was a photograph of a female and also a black bra, which I believe was also found in the fridge. There was a VHS tape cover with $10,000 in cash also found in the fridge, along with more photographs of other various females in an envelope in the door of the fridge. In a lock box (similar to a safe), an additional $7,000 was found in cash. So Franklin was not only facing the death penalty but he would now be faced with a guaranteed audit by the IRS as soon as they found out about this.

When Amster got up for his cross-examination, he asked the same question as he had asked to every other investigator, detective and criminalist so far.

Amster: 'Did you see any item of evidence being processed for latent fingerprints, or biological evidence?'

To which each person, including Lieutenant Oppelt, said that they hadn't, as this kind of testing was not done at the scene but done 'at the integrity of the lab'.

★ ★ ★

The next witness called to the stand was my favourite – Detective Darren Dupree. Detective Dupree had been with the LAPD for twenty-six years and with RHD (as a homicide specialist), where he was currently assigned as a detective, for the past ten years. Dupree is a very good-looking black man who looks about forty. However, that would mean he began work with the LAPD when he was just fourteen! Anyway, going on the amount of time he's worked with the LAPD, I can only guess that he might be fifty.

When he began at RHD, and for the first four years, he was assigned to the Redrum Unit (murder spelt backwards). Throughout his career, Dupree has worked gangs and homicide units and some units were both gang and homicide units. Most of his time with the LAPD has been as a detective with both gang and homicide divisions.

DA Silverman: 'Detective Dupree, where did you grow up?'

Amster: 'Objection! Relevance.'

Judge: 'Sustained.'

DA: 'Are you familiar with the South Central area?'

Detective Dupree: 'Yes.'

DA: 'How?'

Detective Dupree: 'Because I grew up there.'

DA: 'Were you there in the 1980s?'

Detective Dupree: 'Yes.'

DA: 'Was there a problem with crack cocaine at that time?'

Detective Dupree: 'Yes.'

DA: 'Are you familiar with prostitution in that area?'

Detective Dupree: 'Yes.'

DA: 'Are you familiar with the hotels in that area that was described by Detective Trujillo in the area of Western Avenue?'

Detective Dupree: 'Yes.'

DA: 'What are the names of those hotels that Detective Trujillo was describing that are known for high business of prostitution?'

THE TRIAL

Detective Dupree: 'The Mustang Motel [inaudible], Fox Motel.'

DA: 'Did you review all of the cases that are being prosecuted for this trial?'

Detective Dupree: 'Yes.'

DA: 'What is your relationship to this case?'

Detective Dupree: 'I am the last remaining member of the task force. One week prior to the defendant's arrest, I joined the task force.'

The witness went on to say that soon after he joined the LAPD in 1991 he was immediately assigned to the gang unit as he grew up in the area. When questioned about the crimes, Detective Dupree confirmed, 'None of them were gang-related,' much to the defence's dismay.

There were a lot of cries of 'Objection! Vague!' or 'Irrelevant!' coming from the defence's table when it came to DA Silverman referring to the crime scenes as 'crime scenes'. All of these were 'Overruled,' but for some reason, the defence seemed to have a problem with the places where all of these dead women were found being called 'crime scenes'.

DA Silverman found these objections to be as ridiculous as the Judge did, especially as every picture placed on the ELMO clearly always stated the words 'crime scene' somewhere to describe each image. Therefore they were all overruled and DA Silverman was able to use the correct wording when referencing each of the 'crime scenes'.

The DA went back to question Detective Dupree regarding the distance from the defendant's residence to each of the crime scene locations.

At 11.58 a.m. we broke for lunch.

THE GRIM SLEEPER

★ ★ ★

At 1.36 p.m., Detective Dupree was already waiting on the stand when we returned after the lunch break. DA Silverman asked him about the four VHS tapes, now converted to DVD, which were part of the evidence. He had reviewed them all. On the ELMO was a still photograph of the video we were about to see: it was a tape without audio. Then it was played.

All we saw on the video, for about seven minutes, was a man identified by Detective Dupree as the defendant Lonnie Franklin. He was fooling around sexually with a woman. It was clear that he had set up a hidden video camera to record the event that was about to take place. You see a woman undressing herself and Lonnie Franklin's mouth on her chest area. Then you see Franklin taking his clothes off only from below the waist and then she reaches her hand in to his groin area. Paper towels were used too. It seemed that he didn't penetrate this woman but a sexual act did take place in the seven minutes we watched this awful video.

The location where the video was shot was not a recognisable location to Detective Dupree. Did that mean it was not at Franklin's home, I wondered. Or did it just mean that Dupree didn't recognise it as being Franklin's home although it may well have been?

Detective Dupree was part of the tactical team that cleared the residence but wasn't part of the team that did the search. However, the location where the video was taken was not mentioned in the questioning.

After the video was played, it was time for the defence to cross-examine the witness.

THE TRIAL

Amster: 'You were part of the tactical team that was there on the day of the search?'

Dupree: 'Yes.'

Amster then asked if there was a detective also there besides Dupree, to which Dupree's response was that the other detective was not there on that day.

Detective Dupree was free to leave the stand and Mr Amster demanded of the Judge that he must still 'remain on call' for the entirety of the trial. This is always confirmed each time a witness leaves the stand. The Judge responded sarcastically with, 'Yes, I think he'll be around.'

Then at 1.54 p.m. Detective Dennis Kilcoyne came to the witness stand and was sworn in. Kilcoyne was the lead detective in the Grim Sleeper case from the very beginning. As stated earlier, he is a very tall man with a grand presence. He has a very kind face, which is nice to see with a man who has a job as hard and as cruel as his.

DA Marguerite Rizzo questioned the witness about his testimony from before, where Kilcoyne was head of the task force in 2007, which culminated in the arrest of the defendant, Lonnie Franklin. This was confirmed by Detective Kilcoyne. When asked to point out the defendant in the courtroom and state what he was wearing, he pointed to the man at the end of the counsel table and said he was wearing a blue shirt, a grey tie and black glasses. Detective Kilcoyne told the court how he interviewed Franklin on the day of his arrest, 7 July 2010, on the fifth floor of the LAPD headquarters, which is where RHD is located. The videotaped interview was with Detective Paul Coulter and Franklin and began at 12.50 p.m. It was forty minutes long, but the videotape was rolling for approximately three hours. We were about to see the forty-minute version in court that day.

During the showing of this interrogation video we saw Detective Holmes come in and take the handcuffs off Franklin, and then he asked if he needed anything, to which the defendant responded that he needed to '*urinate... go to the bathroom*'.

We could then see Detective Holmes start to get up to take Franklin to walk down the corridor, however the video was rolling only in the interrogation room. All we saw was a blank video with three empty chairs and a table for a few more minutes. DA Rizzo paused the video after we sat and watched the blank room for those minutes and then asked Detective Kilcoyne what Franklin was doing at that time.

Kilcoyne: 'I assume he was going potty!' The courtroom all laughed.

Throughout the interview Detective Coulter did most of the talking and at a quarter of the way through he started to take out a photograph of each victim, one by one, saying directly to Franklin that his DNA 'juice' was on each and every one of those women. Meanwhile Franklin kept denying ever knowing any of the women, at which Detective Coulter became really heated up and strongly stated that the defendant was 'insulting his intelligence' by denying ever knowing any of these females. Some of them Franklin even referred to as '*butt ugly*'! When Detective Kilcoyne started to talk, he came in for the kill right away.

Detective Kilcoyne: 'Mr Franklin, you have a major problem, OK? July 7th 2010 and up to twenty-five years ago. You've had this problem, at least that we are aware of, for twenty-five years. You creep out, you pick up these ladies that work Western and Figuroa in the middle of the night. You have sex with them, you kill them and you dump their bodies in alleys throughout the City of Los Angeles, mostly not too far from your house. You see the number of faces here [pointing to the photographs on the desk]? That's how many families are affected by this, families that have been suffering with this for twenty-five years... parents. You're a parent, you have young children. What do you think it would feel like to have your little girl murdered and dumped in an alley and not know how that came to be for twenty-five years, yet somebody left their DNA signature like their thumbprint on these bodies.

'These women had a life and families, they had loved ones. That's your little girl out there and some guy that's got a problem dumping them in alleys as if they are trash. It's like a dog pissing on a fire hydrant... That's you, you're leaving your mark every time you do this. Well, know the science has caught up with you. Mr Franklin, your signature is on every one of these women, there's no denying that and there's no getting out of it. You need to man up and tell us what caused this to happen, what caused Mr Lonnie Franklin, when he's not working on a car or out with his wife and children, why he's out creeping at night and cannot control himself. How did this happen?

'We know an awful lot about you, much more than you have any idea of. Especially with the comment you made a while ago, saying you "don't creep at night". We know that you cruise Western Avenue, looking for whores, every night.'

★ ★ ★

THE GRIM SLEEPER

Lonnie Franklin arrived wearing a very bright yellow shirt and black trousers. The courtroom was very empty that day presumably because most people know that the testimony of DNA and ballistics experts can be quite dull and repetitive.

Going back to the previous Monday, 21 March, after Mr Amster completely lost all control of himself, his opening statements in front of the jury were quite good. Amster listed a number of victims and the areas in which each were tested for DNA. He went on to explain that the DNA lab used confirmed that Franklin's DNA was not found on a number of areas that were tested. This of course raised doubt in the minds of the jury.

The few days that I missed of the trial the previous week were, according to my sources, very dull and repetitive. That day we continued dealing with the defence's witnesses, and most of the previous week (and also today) consisted of various analysts from the Sorenson DNA Lab, which is located in South Salt Lake, Utah.

Emily Jeskie from the Sorenson Lab was on the stand all day long, giving her testimony of how she and her colleagues collect and analyse the DNA. She talked of the analysing process her lab undertook for three of the victims: Barbara Ware, Enietra Washington and Jenecia Peters.

Amster opened with: 'Was saliva testing done by your lab?'

Emily Jeskie: 'Yes.'

Amster: 'What were the results?'

Emily Jeskie: 'Negative.'

Amster: 'Was blood testing done?'

THE TRIAL

Emily Jeskie: 'Yes.'

Amster: 'And what were the results of that testing?'

Emily Jeskie: 'It was positive but insufficient DNA so it was inconclusive.'

Even though most of Emily Jeskie's answers were 'negative', I was confused when she replied with the word 'positive' in her testimony as I thought that would mean that Franklin's DNA was found. However, afterwards she stated that it was 'inconclusive'. I will explain why this is so later on in this piece.

Mr Amster went on and asked if sperm was tested and Ms Jeskie responded with a 'yes' and that it was proved to be 'negative for Franklin's DNA'. Often she stated that there was 'insufficient DNA detected to determine a contributor and/ or a profile'. She said that there were thirty items tested from the Barbara Ware case and a few of them are listed below:

Left-hand fingernail clippings
Pubic hair
Vaginal and external anal swabs
External genital swabs
Oral swab
Right and left nipple swabs
Vaginal slide
Anal slide
Oral slide
Panties
Bra
Shoes
Victim's head hair

THE GRIM SLEEPER

Victim's facial hair
Hair removed from victim's shirt
Right-hand fingernail scraping kits
Right-hand fingernail clippings
Reference sample for Barbara Ware.

Each one was analysed and the results were mostly 'negative' or 'inconclusive' or 'insufficient DNA was found'. Ms Jeskie explained that the more 'male DNA that is present' reduces the DNA that can be analysed to determine who the contributor could be. So basically, it could not confirm that Franklin's DNA was present but it also could not exclude him.

Most items tested, especially the vaginal areas, had at least four lots of male DNA present when tested, so this weakened the confirmation of a known contributor.

Amster was still questioning the witness, *his* witness, all morning. Then we broke for lunch.

★ ★ ★

At 1.35 p.m. we were all seated back in the courtroom and the jurors entered. Ms Jeskie was patiently waiting on the stand. Mr Amster kept asking the rhetorical question, 'Were the steps [testing of the DNA] done in a competent manner?' She repeatedly responded with 'Yes, they were.' Meanwhile Amster rustled around, shuffling back and forth as he always does as if racing to catch a train, his white hair blowing all around him. After at least ten minutes of silence except for the sound of his shuffling, the Judge spoke up and said, 'Let's go, Mr Amster. Come on!' He responded that he had 'lost an exhibit' and was looking for it. So we continued to wait.

Finally, he found what he was looking for. The exhibit was placed on the ELMO and depicted a graph of the DNA showing how it peaks up and down and the parents who are the contributors of a person's DNA.

DA Marguerite Rizzo was then allowed to cross-examine the witness.

Ms Rizzo: 'How many times have you testified as an expert in court in your life?'

Emily Jeskie: 'About thirty-seven times.'

DA Rizzo: 'How many times have you testified in California?'

Emily Jeskie: 'This is the fifth time.'

DA Rizzo: 'Did you perform the analysis on three victims by the names of Barbara Ware, Enietra Washington and Janecia Peters?'

Emily Jeskie: 'Yes, I did.'

In her cross-examination DA Rizzo pointed out that if she leaned over Mr Atherton (the second defence) or Detective Dupree right then and touched their jackets, wouldn't her DNA be present on their clothing? She also used the analogy of being in a Starbucks getting coffee and if she leant on the counter, 'Wouldn't my DNA be on the counter and vice versa, wouldn't the DNA of the person who sat there, be on me?' This line of questioning was essentially to weaken the testing abilities of the Sorenson Lab.

Mr Amster so repeatedly objected to DA Rizzo's comments that she could hardly get the words out – 'Objection! Speculation,' 'Objection! No evidence,' 'Objection! Vague,' 'Objection! Relevance,' 'Objection! Compound,' and so on and so forth. Judge Kennedy overruled most of these objections with a sigh of frustration. Meanwhile DA Rizzo continued with her questioning. Then, suddenly, a very loud and tuneful mobile phone went off and carried on ringing for a number of rings. This is a well-known pet peeve of Judge Kennedy's so we all looked around at each other in fear and trepidation. Ringing phones and sheriffs' loud radios she will simply not stand for and will throw anyone out on these grounds. Eventually, the clerk raised her arm up, mobile phone in hand, apologising profusely. At this the Judge laughed and said, 'Well, I guess I can't throw her out, can I?' We all laughed along with her.

DA Rizzo wanted to know what the Sorenson DNA Lab charges for someone to be a witness. The answer is it charges $2,000 per day, and on top of that are the charges to test for DNA on the items to be tested. For example, in Barbara Ware's case there were at least twenty-four items tested and the total cost was $21,670. I couldn't believe it! Then for Enietra Washington, who had at least eighteen items tested, I believe there was a charge of $26,000 for those tests to be made. For Janecia Peters, there were only nine items tested yet the bill came to a whopping $8,665! I must be in the wrong line of work then, I thought.

Anyway, it was a long day and a long week prior, as we were still covering Sorenson Lab, the private lab that the defence hired to do the DNA testing.

30 MARCH 2016

I knew that the Grim Sleeper trial would be slow-going today for two reasons:

THE TRIAL

1. Seymour Amster, the defence, was presenting his case;
2. Seymour Amster was still comparing the Sorenson Lab's DNA results to the state's DNA lab results.

With this in mind I went down the street for the second (full) day of the Tanaka trial. It started an hour before the criminal court so I was there by 8 a.m. as I would be almost every day. I spent the entire day in that trial, which ended at 1.30 p.m. with no lunch, then came back to the CCB and went into the Grim Sleeper trial after they came back from lunch. I asked my sources (mostly sheriffs, who sit in on the trial most days, not the bailiff, I might add) what had gone on, and I was correct in that it was just DNA testing; also, Amster had called back a female witness: Detective Benjamin. She had testified before I arrived there.

When I arrived, soon after 1.30 p.m., Detective Dupree was on the stand although he had no idea why, as he'd told me the previous day. He was laughing as he said it. So I was so glad to be there for his testimony. After much shuffling and racing back and forth, Amster finally slammed his binder down on the podium and proceeded to question Detective Dupree.

Amster: 'Now, I'm not going to ask exactly where you lived when you grew up in South Central as I wouldn't do that, I want you to tell us the vicinity in which you lived in 1985.'

Detective Dupree responded with his full address. That didn't surprise me – he's honest as the day is long and not afraid of anything. He also likes to help in any way he can, so perhaps to prevent Amster from bumbling further, he responded quietly and strongly with the full address where he resided as a teenager in the eighties.

After Detective Dupree left the stand, Doreen Hudson came to the stand. An employee of the LAPD for thirty-nine and a half years, mainly she has worked for the crime lab. She was there very briefly and recapped the testimony that she gave before.

4 APRIL 2016

It has been a few days since I last wrote but the events of the Grim Sleeper trial have been very much the same, day after day after day. Not only because Seymour Amster, the lead defence, likes to play games and drag his feet, but also because comparing the defence's DNA results from the eleven victims (one was an attempted murder) from the Sorenson Lab to the DNA results from the state-approved lab is a tedious and time-consuming process. As I stated earlier, it's not just blood and sperm that is tested and at great expense, but also hair, swabs, slides, fibres, etc, all tested to the most infinitesimal detail.

It seems to me that Mr Seymour Amster has called in each and every individual from the Sorenson Lab in Utah to testify on their findings. Highly unnecessary, I believe, but perhaps in his mind, it all helps to delay the process of a slam-dunk trial. This is however incredibly costly for the taxpayers paying his salary too.

On a side note, because of the repetitive nature of the Grim Sleeper trial, I have also been able to cover another trial down the street at the Federal Building in which I have a personal involvement. To make it short, it is the trial for

THE TRIAL

a former under sheriff of the Los Angeles County Sheriff's Department by the name of Paul Tanaka. He is accused of many things, among them 'conspiracy to obstruct an FBI investigation'. The FBI brought the case to trial and I have been there every day and will continue to cover it until it ends in the next few days. As I have already mentioned, this trial finishes every day at 1.30 p.m. with no lunch break. The Grim Sleeper trial, a few buildings up the road, reconvenes after lunch at 1.30 p.m., hence I have managed to make every afternoon at the trial.

The reason for my attendance at the Tanaka trial is because this is a matter I am very close to, as I've been involved with the LASD, in various capacities, since I moved to America as a teenager. It's devastating that so many innocent sheriffs, who were in positions subordinate to Paul Tanaka, have now lost their jobs, been convicted of crimes they didn't commit, by simply 'following orders from above', and/or made a plea. Hence their lives have now all been ruined.

I have heard many retired captains testify and all were very powerful in their testimony. I've heard the sleaze-bag Gilbert Michel testify. He was the deputy who smuggled the mobile phone into the jail to inmate Anthony Brown, after making a cash deal with an undercover FBI agent in late July 2011. Not only did he commit this disgusting crime, still wearing the LASD badge, but when caught he took down other deputies with him, accusing them of 'excessive force'. This very bad apple slipped through the net of one of the best law enforcement agencies in the world, and I'm ashamed that he was ever given the title of deputy sheriff. Thank God it was only for a short time.

219

Today and Friday we heard Tanaka testify. On Friday his defence – Dean Steward and Jerome Haig – put him on the stand. He quivered, lied, had selective memory loss and basically looked like a complete phoney to all and sundry. He buried himself with his testimony on the Friday and that was with his own defence questioning him. Today, matters became much worse when he was cross-examined by AUSA Brandon Fox and Ed Hardy. AUSA Fox didn't mince his words when asking about Tanaka's association with the well-known deputy gang, The Vikings, which he presumably ran while working as a sergeant in Lynwood. This lasted a number of gruelling hours, and we heard more of Tanaka's untruths and the placing of blame on the one person above him – Lee Baca – along with his close subordinates.

I started to write my book on this subject a year earlier, but put this on hold pending a trial. It's just a bit of a coincidence that both the Grim Sleeper and the Tanaka trials began around the same time. I can only focus on one book at a time, hence I am continuing on with The Grim Sleeper. My book on the LASD and the FBI will have to wait a few more months.

After the day ended today, I walked over to CCB (the Criminal Courts Building) and rode the elevator to the ninth floor. I hadn't even walked in to sit down when Amster's scream came through the double doors, this time screaming at the Judge – yet again! I walked in right after lunch recess had ended and the jury weren't back in the room yet. Here's how it went:

Judge: 'You'd be screaming bloody murder, Mr Amster, if they'd done that to you!'

THE TRIAL

What a pun, I thought, but what on earth could they have been talking about? I realised immediately that yet again, Amster had not given the name of the witness that he wanted to call up next. He was screaming that he had just handed the prosecution the name of the witness, which he had written on a small Post-it. The court erupted as we all thought, 'He just cannot be serious!' But he was, and to his mind, he is.

As Judge Kennedy showed her disdain for Amster's complete lack of professionalism in scribbling the name of the witness (who he was calling on today) on a Post-it to show the prosecution, he piped up.

Amster: 'Well, I respectfully disagree, Your Honour, because we have had to deal with so many surprises from the prosecution's side and they...'

Judge Kennedy: 'Stop, stop! I'm not asking you what you say they did or didn't do. You're like the kid that deflects everything when they're in trouble by saying, "Well, my brother did this and that..." when questioned about something, you know what I mean. But right now we are talking about you, Mr Amster!'

She went on to say: 'You are not going to ever do this again, Mr Amster. You're not going to write a note in the middle of the day of what witness you are calling up next. You have to give thirty days' notice and that's the rules. You could have even told them on Friday, or told me as I know you two don't communicate well. Now, let's bring the jury in.'

I couldn't believe I'd just come out of a highly professional courtroom in the Federal Building and walked up the road to the Criminal Courts Building and straight back into the apparently never-ending circus of the Grim Sleeper trial. What a contrast! Believe it or not, today there was yet another witness on the stand from the Sorenson Lab, testifying about the DNA. Even Detective Dupree almost fell asleep, he told me, listening to these highly repetitive and seemingly unimportant testimonies that had gone on for well over a week.

When the witness was allowed to continue, with the jury present, the same questions were asked of him as they have been asked of all the witnesses before:

Amster: 'Was the DNA testing done in a competent manner to the best of your knowledge?' The witness on the stand, who I believe was from the Sorenson Lab, answered in the exact same way as all the other witnesses had done before: 'Yes, it was,' along with answers such as 'Yes, DNA was found, but there were too many contributors to determine whether we could determine a match.'

The previous day, after I left the Federal Building, the jury went to deliberate in the Paul Tanaka trial. I walked over to the CCB as I had done each day. Thinking that yet again the defence would still be focused on the DNA comparisons, as they had been all that morning (I was told this by my tipsters) and all the previous week, I was pleasantly surprised.

I walked into the courtroom as a criminalist and firearms expert by the name of Rafael Garcia was on the stand. On the ELMO was a picture of one of the guns found in Franklin's home. Another picture was a view of the hallway and the west closet showing an image of the jacket in which the gun had been found. The firearm was in the picture next to this one. It was of a semi-automatic pistol: a Raven .25 calibre auto.

THE TRIAL

DA Silverman asked if these types of guns are designed for 'easy storage' to which Amster objected straight away.

The objection was overruled and the answer from Mr Garcia was: 'Yes, absolutely. It is designed for easy storage and concealment, one that a person might carry in their pocket.'

Mr Garcia was handed an envelope on two separate occasions in his testimony, both of which he opened slowly and pulled out a small coin envelope with a magazine inside. Also in the large envelope was a gun with a flex tie on it so that it wouldn't go off accidentally.

The second envelope Mr Garcia opened held a .380 automatic 'Hi-Point' firearm. This was displayed for the court to view in a larger format on the ELMO. It seemed like a larger gun than the previous one, which almost certainly couldn't have been concealed too well. This gun was also tied with plastic flex ties for safety in the courtroom and had six live rounds of ammunition inside.

Before I walked into the courtroom, my sources told me that during the search of the hallway and also the closets of Franklin's home, a machete and approximately nineteen mobile phones were found there. Also found were pornographic items, including videos.

We ended the day on this witness, Rafael Garcia.

★ ★ ★

18 APRIL 2016: 8.30A.M.

We have not been in trial for the past week due to the defence – Seymour Amster – needing 'more time to prepare'. Yes, apparently five years and nine months was not enough. Therefore, two Fridays ago, the jury was sent home until 18 April, today, so that Amster could get new experts to testify.

That morning, I arrived at the court by 8.30 a.m. and had my usual chat with Detective Dupree. We sat outside the courtroom waiting for the bailiff to open up the door to Department 109. Dupree admitted that he too was confused by the continuing antics of Seymour Amster, and confirmed to me that the jury wouldn't be back until at least that coming Thursday at the earliest, or even the next Monday. That past week, Detective Dupree told me that Amster wanted to bring in as a witness David Lamagna, a firearms expert. Of course this would be the defence trying to negate and discredit all of the prosecution's firearms experts who had so brilliantly testified over the past few months.

The reason for the jury being 'out', yet the court still in session was so that he, Amster, could prove that his witness was sufficiently credible to be put on the stand in front of the jury. DA Beth Silverman had a major problem with this.

We walked into the courtroom at 9 a.m. and I sat in my usual seat. Six middle-aged-to-elderly men walked in with DA Silverman, some of whom I recognised from previous testimonies. The men were all firearms experts. Ms Silverman greeted everyone in the courtroom, and was especially loud that day for some reason. She actually made a few funny and derogatory comments concerning Mr Amster, which made perfect sense to all who were listening – that was most of the gallery.

A few minutes after 9.10 a.m. Amster arrived, shuffling in at his usual pace with his usual puckered facial expression.

THE TRIAL

By contrast, Dale Atherton, another public defender who was hired to work alongside Amster, walked in and gave me a lovely smile and a 'good morning' as he always does – such a nice man.

At 10.01 a.m. Franklin was brought in by the bailiff. This time, the defendant was in his orange prison jumpsuit and also waist-chained. As soon as he made it to his seat, the bailiff was more than happy to reach across and handcuff Franklin to his chair. Such overkill!

We started with more friction between DA Beth Silverman and Seymour Amster, and Judge Kennedy assumed her usual stance as the referee. This time, Amster became so heated that he decided to address the gallery and turn right around and wave his hand at all of us.

Judge Kennedy: 'Mr Amster, turn around and face the court!'

Amster apologised but continued to rant about how he wanted to put his witness, Mr David Lamagna, on the stand.

DA Beth Silverman was quick to come back with, 'He is just not qualified.' She said that Mr Lamagna was not part of the scientific community at all and wasn't even qualified in this type of science and expertise. Amster had brought him in as a 'firearm and toolmark expert' and he would be cross-examined by Ms Silverman to prove that he is not. On the other hand, the prosecution's six witnesses were highly qualified and the proof was in their training, experience and the law enforcement agencies in which they had spent most of their careers.

Ms Silverman accused Amster of 'insulting' her witnesses and said that alluding to Mr Lamagna as being of a 'higher level' to those witnesses was an utter disgrace and completely disrespectful.

DA Silverman (to Amster with a snarl): 'Show a little respect!'

Amster: 'There was no insult intended. We're not insulting these individuals, we're saying the prosecution hasn't done their homework!'

There were gasps around the courtroom at this comment.

Amster: 'The court asked me, "What is Mr Lamagna going to testify about?" and we specifically stated forensic topography and surface metrology! We said this multiple times, so I don't understand why they're now saying that somehow they are "ambushed". We've said it multiple times!'

In an effort to stop the bickering between defence and prosecution, Judge Kennedy simply said, 'Why don't we just put him on the stand then?'

By 10.45 a.m., Mr David Lamagna was on the stand.

Mr Amster did his usual line of asking seemingly redundant, rhetorical questions, and even his own witness looked to the Judge for help at times. In between rolling her eyes, she would look down at Amster and say, 'You've just asked that question a number of times, Mr Amster. Ask something new.'

Then, suddenly, Amster said, 'I believe the prosecution is laughing and snickering at me and also laughing during the testimony of my witness.'

Then the witness, David Lamagna, backed this up: 'Yes, I actually find it quite offensive.'

Like a kindergarten teacher who has finally reached her limit, the Judge came back at DA Beth Silverman: 'Ms Silverman, let's just stop making faces, OK?'

Ms Silverman apologised and we started up again.

Amster not only continued on with his monotonous, repetitive line of questioning, he would also give the answers and all the information in his rhetorical questions. After more rolling of her eyes, the Judge had had quite enough.

Judge: 'I don't want you to testify, Mr Amster, I want the witness to testify!'

But Amster continued to ask questions to discredit the previous testimonials of the prosecution's witnesses and firearms experts, by asking Mr Lamagna how important it was to 'count the striae on the bullets', knowing full well that the previous experts didn't need to go that far as it was so obvious that the bullets were fired from the same gun.

Amster also pushed regarding the 'two-dimensional microscope' and how it wasn't as good as the three-dimensional ones used nowadays, knowing full well that both kinds of microscope would, and did, determine that the bullet clearly came from the .25 calibre handgun found in Lonnie Franklin's home. Period! It was such a waste of time as we all knew the bullets came from his gun.

On that note, I will end my entry for this day by saying that my main computer crashed this afternoon so I can only hope that Apple can back up my information while they were repairing it (as of 9 p.m. that evening). Fingers crossed they can do it.

★ ★ ★

20 APRIL 2016

On Monday and Tuesday the same 'possible' defence witness was on the stand – David Lamagna. He was the 'potential' witness who had been brought in by Seymour Amster from out of state, at a whopping fee, I might add. For a number of full days this man had been put on the stand, without the jury, just to see if he was qualified enough to then testify in front of the jury when they returned the next week. This is a crazy situation if you ask me.

Mr Lamagna appears in his early sixties and looks as though he has never seen the sun. A self-proclaimed forensic scientist, he has been brought in to testify in this trial for the simple purpose of discrediting all of the prosecution's firearms and toolmark experts.

The six witnesses whom Lamagna has been brought in to discredit all work for top law enforcement agencies, including the LASD and the LAPD. I sincerely doubt these experts ever took part in home study courses – I know these two agencies only hire the best.

In the courtroom yesterday were the same six men from the day before, three of them having already testified on behalf of the prosecution.

So Mr Lamagna was on the stand again and the first part of the day was spent with Mr Amster questioning his witness about his qualifications and experience. The second part of the day was more interesting, when DA Beth Silverman was able to brilliantly cross-examine the witness. Silverman challenged Lamagna's credentials and more so, the lack of them. She also challenged the claims made on his website, which according to him, don't 'pertain' to him directly. He admitted not being qualified in certain areas. Why was it then advertised on his website, Silverman wanted to know. She also challenged the fact that he had deleted certain training from his résumé and wanted to know the reason why. Then she questioned why he had focused for five years on one home study course to gain some qualification. Clearly, she had done her homework.

The day went on with DA Silverman questioning the witness and really making him squirm. She clarified that he doesn't always 'calibrate' his equipment and questioned why he hadn't even brought any documents to court with him so that he could refer to his notes when necessary. She implied that he came very 'unprepared for someone who claims to be so highly qualified'. Silverman even asked if he knew why he was here, to which he responded vaguely.

David Lamagna: 'To hear what my testimony might be regarding the other experts.'

Silverman also asked if Lamagna had 'misled' the defence in leading them to believe that he was more qualified than he might actually be.

Over the course of Silverman's cross-examination it seemed very apparent that this witness was not qualified to be a witness for anyone, let alone the defence in this case. The entire past three days had been to see whether or not David Lamagna could be brought in as a witness in the actual trial. The Judge would determine this, which was why the jury was still not present. When they returned, that was when we would be back in session and until then we were wasting valuable time, it seemed in my humble opinion.

A number of times DA Silverman looked behind her to the six experts sitting there when she asked David Lamagna a strong question that he found difficult to answer. She would give a very confident semi-smile to them all as if to say, 'Really? You claim to be all this and you can't even answer a simple question.' She would also look behind her either for approval or to see if they had any advice to give her in a written note form.

On one occasion Mr Amster actually saw her do this and shouted at her.

Amster: 'Maybe you should look behind you to one of your experts and you'll find out!'

DA: 'I just did!'

But the Judge had had enough and threw her hands in the air, staring down at them both with a glare.

Judge: 'Stop, stop, stop! Stop it, both of you! Stop it!'

Amster immediately apologised although to me the apology seemed somewhat phoney. Beth Silverman sat there silently just shaking her head subtly.

You could tell that Judge Kennedy had reached her limit for the day after the constant bickering, snickering, snide remarks, sighs and rolling of the eyes that went on between the two counsels. However, tomorrow is a new day and she would surely have known that she would have to deal them both all over again.

★ ★ ★

26 APRIL 2016

After a gap of almost a week due to Judge Kennedy giving us and the jury these days off due to scheduling conflicts, we finally were back in session. The defendant, Lonnie Franklin, was wearing the same blue denim shirt, black and silver tie and beige trousers as the previous day. Most of the morning had been spent yet again with the witness David Lamagna on the stand, picking apart the toolmark analysis documentation of the prosecution's witnesses.

Lamagna explained that the 2D microscope is unreliable and he wouldn't use it to examine toolmarks. He said that the 3D mapping microscope is a much more reliable source for this kind of examination. According to him, this is the only method he chooses to use. The older microscope, the 2D version, is what the six previous experts used. This was one of the many areas used by Lamagna to discredit the witnesses from the other side.

The jury were released quite a few minutes before lunch, probably about 11.30 a.m., until 1.30 p.m. after the lunch recess finishes.

I found out (through my law enforcement sources) that juror number ten had been replaced that day. This was confirmed by a reporter, Eric Leonard, who was in the courtroom as well. A man I often listen to on KFI, he's exceptionally good at reporting on all kinds of high-profile cases. He told me that juror number ten had been replaced by juror number five, a Hispanic male, due to illness.

Proceedings were delayed due to an issue with evidence from Lamagna not being turned over to the prosecution. So we waited and waited. In the meantime Mr Atherton made reference to a photograph which was taken on Detective Dupree's mobile phone: it was a picture of a screen shot of Lamagna's work. Atherton said he had not received that picture from the prosecution.

They all started looking for this picture yet no one could

find it. This took almost an hour. DA Silverman even told the clerk that she must have it and she was quick to defend herself with the fact she was 'never even given it'. Meanwhile the Judge kept asking how long until Lamagna would come back, as the jury were still being kept waiting in the hallway. He was apparently done and waiting for a courtesy shuttle from the Omni hotel (where he was staying, at the taxpayer's expense, of course) to bring him back to the court.

At 2.30 p.m. Lonnie Franklin was walked in, wearing the same clothes, and as he sat down, he slipped on a blue and silver tie, which was already tied for him so he just placed the opening around his neck and tightened it.

Lamagna went straight to the stand after handing the flash drive to Dale Atherton.

The Judge then came in at 2.31 p.m. and at 2.36 p.m. the jury walked in, in single file, from the main door we all walked in from.

DA Silverman went over and over Lamagna's résumé with a fine-toothed comb, explaining that he made claims to be an expert in certain things, and she made sure that it was proven to the court that he obviously was not. She alluded to him having to 'pay for his qualifications' and he responded that he was merely 'paying for tuition and membership dues'.

She also challenged his claim of having 'law enforcement training', to which he responded that he had completed several criminal investigative courses. 'Objection! Non-responsive,' she interjected with a roll of her eyes.

She questioned how he had stated that he was a 'constable' and requested him to explain what that meant.

Lamagna: 'A constable is the original police officer here in the United States.'

DA: 'What did you do as a constable?'

Lamagna: 'I investigated the whereabouts of fugitives from justice and I would arrest them and either bring them to a courthouse or a county lock-up.'

DA: 'Were you responsible for investigating crime scenes?'

Lamagna: 'Not during that activity, no.'

DA: 'Were you EVER responsible for investigating crime scenes as a constable?'

Lamagna: 'No.'

There was a lot more back and forth here, questioning Lamagna's integrity, his qualifications and his training. There were many more objections from Amster, and 'Objection! Move to strike. Non-responsive,' from DA Silverman. She eventually established that he had never been out to an active crime scene.

DA Silverman wanted to know exactly how many crime scenes Lamagna had 'reconstructed' (where individuals attempt to reconstruct the crime scene). But he would not give an exact number as he didn't want to guess and then be held accountable if he was found out to be incorrect.

DA: 'How many homicide investigations have you been involved in as a law enforcement officer and not after the fact as a defence investigator?'

Lamagna: 'None!'

Apparently he had listed he was an expert in 'arson investigations'. He didn't state where. DA Silverman challenged him on this and it was only 'after the fact' that he went to these scenes to investigate. The same was asked of his 'alleged blood splatter pattern interpretation', and DA Silverman questioned him heavily on this too, along with him claiming to be a 'DNA' and 'fingerprints' expert.

Most of these questions were objected to by Amster then overruled by the Judge. Lamagna seemed to fail again with his vague answers.

With each answer, Lamagna admitted that he'd only ever been brought to a scene to investigate 'after the fact'. He carried on trying to explain that all the areas on his website and in his résumé where he had stated he was 'an expert in' were basically where he had been trained and not areas he had actually worked in – 'If someone is an expert, then it's someone whom I have hired.'

DA Silverman wanted to know how many autopsies Lamagna had performed, which of course were none. Also, how many cases had he been involved in with 'buried bodies and surface skeletons' and a 'Homeland Security specialist'. These are all quotes and claims on his website where he alludes to being an 'expert'. There were many more quotes she took from his résumé and website but he defended himself by saying that most of them were 'his training' and not actual jobs that he had performed.

DA: 'Did you testify that you are a Certified Medical Investigator? And your answer is that it was correct?'

This was objected to at least eight more times by Seymour Amster and almost all these objections were overruled by the Judge. Amster was not getting what he wanted as the Judge kept overruling everything so he, yet again, requested the sidebar. This time the Judge said no to the side bar and all hell broke loose.

THE TRIAL

Amster: 'That's it! Motion for mistrial!'

Judge: 'Denied!'

Gasps were heard from all over the courtroom.

Amster: 'Your Honour, admonish the audience please.'

Judge: 'Please let's not have any oral reactions to the legal proceedings. The jury will ultimately make their decision based on the evidence. And the jury should disregard any reactions from the audience in terms of how you see the evidence. That will be up to you and not what the audience feels.'

DA: 'Will the court also admonish counsel that those types of remarks in front of the jury, we've said this before, are improper.'

Amster: 'Your Honour…'

Judge: 'STOP, STOP! BOTH OF YOU, JUST STOP!'

Amster: 'Motion for a mistrial!'

Judge (said in a tuneful voice as if talking to an obnoxious child): 'Denied!'

I think we all get the gist here. Ms Silverman had clearly done her homework and she wanted to make it clear to the jury that he was not qualified to make any comment concerning her 'real' toolmark and firearms experts who were still taking time off to sit in the courtroom every day since early the previous week.

DA: 'Have you received any training in firearm and toolmark comparisons?'

Lamagna: 'Specifically in firearms, no.'

DA: 'Were you ever trained to use a comparison microscope to compare toolmarks on firearm components?'

Lamagna: 'No.'

DA: 'Has anyone in the firearm manufacturing industry

ever hired you to do any type of work for them?'

Lamagna: 'The individual I worked with… on the… er… the suppressor project…'

He was rambling on so she repeated the question.

DA: 'Again, my question was: have you ever been hired, paid by any firearm manufacturer as a consultant?'

Lamagna: 'No, I haven't been hired by any major or minor firearm manufacturer.'

DA Silverman repeated the question yet again.

DA (loudly): 'MY QUESTION IS AGAIN, IT'S VERY SIMPLE: HAVE YOU EVER BEEN HIRED, PAID, AS A CONSULTANT BY ANY FIREARMS MANUFACTURER EVER?'

Lamagna: 'Erm, no.'

DA: 'Have you ever worked in a forensic lab that conducts testing, such as the ones you listed on your CV, ever?'

Lamagna: 'No.'

DA: 'Have you ever worked in any government lab?'

Lamagna: 'No.'

DA: 'Any lab that had accreditation?'

Lamagna: 'No.'

This line of questioning went on and on, and became even more specific. Meanwhile Amster kept objecting and the Judge kept overruling.

It was a long day and highly unnecessary to have brought this man to the stand, let alone brought him across the country, put him up in a nice hotel and made him testify simply to try and discredit the very experts that he could only aspire to be.

★ ★ ★

THE TRIAL

Both counsels were fined for misbehaving! The Judge was now $700 wealthier! Well, I'd like to think that she was wealthier due to what she has had to put up with, but the money actually goes to the court.

The morning started quite normally.

The defendant, Lonnie Franklin, was still in the same clothes. I was starting to think he'd spent the last three nights here in the court as he was supposed to change into different clothes daily. This may or may not have an effect on how he was viewed but I don't think the jurors were paying much attention to his dress code.

David Lamagna was back on the stand. The fact that he was being put up in a high-end hotel, the Omni in downtown LA, paid for by the taxpayer, was a total disgrace.

Before I arrived I was told that finally, they did sanction Mr Amster. It was long overdue but he was fined a whopping $500 for delivering a CD or flash drive past the time he was ordered to by the Judge. He had done that so many times before, over the past five and a half years, and I wished he could be fined for all the previous occasions.

DA Beth Silverman was cross-examining the witness in her usual tenacious way. She was continuing to prove that he had very little knowledge at all when it came to being a firearms and toolmark expert. He didn't even have the credentials to make the claims that he does on his own website. She had certainly proved all of this day after day. Her 'real' firearms and toolmark experts had been sitting in the courtroom right behind her since 17 April – ten days minus the weekend. One of her highly qualified witnesses/ experts, Dr James Hamby, was flown in from Indiana. I'm sure Dr Hamby had far more important things to do, at his ripe age of seventy-five and still teaching and working as an expert, than to sit there and listen to Lamagna make false claims, day after day.

In fact Lamagna has been the least qualified witness we have had since this trial began yet for some unknown reason, he's been kept on the stand the longest (at least eight days between the previous week and this one).

DA Silverman: 'Are you violating the code of ethics because you are not validated in being a firearms or toolmark expert?'

Lamagna: 'I'm not in violation, no.'

DA: 'Name me one validated scientific study, anywhere in the world, that supports what you've been saying for use of forensic casework anywhere in this country. Just one, try to name just one.'

Lamagna: 'I can't remember off the top of my head.'

DA: 'That's because none of them exist!'

Amster: 'Objection! Argumentative.'

Judge: 'Overruled.'

There were five more objections made by Amster in less than ten minutes which all resulted in being overruled by the Judge.

Amster: 'Do me a favour, Your Honour, I'm having a headache fast! I need to take a break.'

Judge: 'OK, yes, we'll take a break and you can take an aspirin or whatever you need to take.'

DA: 'He just wants a break so he can properly coach this witness.'

That might be true, Ms Silverman, but this comment won't fly well with the Judge, I thought. She said this rather loudly in front of the jury and the entire courtroom. The jury were now starting to see what craziness there has been between the two counsels for the past five and a half years. I would love to know what they thought.

The Judge had reached her limit.

Judge: 'That's not proper, Ms Silverman.'

Amster: 'Your Honour! Your Honour!'

DA: 'None of what counsel's done is "proper", Your Honour!'

Judge: 'STOP IT!'

Amster: 'YOUR HONOUR! YOUR HONOUR!'

Judge: 'STOP IT! STOP IT! I've told you not to make editorial comments, Ms Silverman, and you continue. I'm going to excuse the jury right now until 11 a.m.'

Turning to the jury, she gave the usual warning: 'Do not discuss this case with anyone or amongst yourselves, etc, etc. Thank you.'

The jury left the courtroom out of the main door, walking in single file as they did every single day, four times a day.

We were left in the courtroom and the Judge continued with Ms Silverman.

Judge: 'I have asked you repeatedly, Ms Silverman, not to make editorial comments in front of the jury…'

DA (butting in): 'That's because the defence does…'

Judge: '…and you are in violation of my order and I'm fining you $200 under code section 177.5. I want you, both of you, to start behaving professionally and we just can't continue to do this.'

DA: 'Are you going to also fine him again too as he's asked multiple times for a mistrial in front of the jury?'

The Judge ignored her question and left the bench.

We all returned at 11 a.m.

DA Silverman pressed the witness, Lamagna, about being in violation and basically being incompetent in the area he claims to be 'expert'. This was met with numerous objections, some of which were sustained. They had been to the sidebar about nine times already before lunch, all because Amster requested it.

After more cross-examination from Ms Silverman, the witness tried to squirm out of answering her very simple questions. He even tried to be combative with her a number of times and was met with her repeating the same question over again, making him look like a complete fool.

We broke for the lunch recess and returned at 1.30 p.m.

The witness, Lamagna, even had the nerve to say that he was more qualified than Dr Hamby, one of the most highly qualified firearms and toolmark experts ever, with decades of experience working with the best law enforcement agencies all over the world! He was one of the 'real' witnesses brought in by the prosecution, who was still there again that day, sitting behind the prosecution. I hoped he would testify.

Lamagna also had the audacity to respond to one of DA Silverman's questions in this way: 'I'm not Arnold Schwarzenegger, I don't have Total Recall!' Also, he would say to DA Silverman, 'You're not explaining yourself!' He criticised all the 'real' experts sitting in the courtroom and how they examined their cases, yet could give no explanation of examining any case the way he said was the correct way.

THE TRIAL

When Ms Silverman said she had nothing further, the Judge let Amster go up for his re-direct.

Amster shuffled to the podium with a sour look on his face and stood there awkwardly with one hand behind his back as he always does. At 2.51 p.m. the defence rested. Finally! We took a short recess and Ms Silverman came back with her rebuttal. At last she was able to put her 'real expert' witness on the stand.

DA Silverman: 'I'd like to call Dr James Hamby to the witness stand.'

This should be good, I thought.

Within a split second, the defence, Amster, called for the sidebar, for the sixteenth time that day. We all looked at each other: what could possibly be the problem now? But it was all a fuss about nothing and Beth Silverman walked back to the podium where she had started off.

DA Silverman: 'Dr Hamby, could you please tell us how you are employed, sir.'

James Hamby: 'Yes, ma'am. I am employed as the director of the Indianapolis International Forensic Firearms Training Centre, which is located in Indianapolis, Indiana.'

DA: 'Could you tell us a little about your education that qualifies you to be in this position.'

James Hamby: 'I have an Associate of Arts in Law Enforcement with a Lifetime Training Certificate in both Sociology and Law Enforcement, a Bachelor of Science degree in Political Studies from the University of the State of New York, a Bachelor of Science degree in Sociology from the University of Maryland, a Master of Arts in Secondary Education from Michigan University and a PhD in Forensic

Science. The title of my thesis was "Forensic Firearms Examination".'

DA: 'Where did you gain your experience with respect to the area of firearms and toolmark comparisons and identification?'

James Hamby: 'This was gained after I returned from Vietnam, where I was a field agent for the US Army Criminal Investigation (CID) – the Army's detectives. I worked at the laboratory over there. I went to the Army lab in August of 1970 and I trained for two years as a firearm and toolmark examiner.'

DA: 'What did that two-year training involve?'

James Hamby: 'I had four training officers who ensured that by the end of that two years I was very well familiar with anything to do with firearms, toolmarks and anything and everything to do with that field.'

He carried on and talked about his thesis, which was published internationally, his years of research, his international training and teachings, the laboratories he was in charge of as a director, and the law enforcement agencies in which he had been employed worldwide. He considered that the diplomas and certificates that David Lamagna received are worthless in the firearms and toolmark industry.

Dr Hamby was such a well-qualified and experienced firearms and toolmark examiner, yet incredibly humble at the same time. Sadly for the defence, his qualifications and experience made Lamagna look more like a used car salesman.

★ ★ ★

THE TRIAL

Lonnie Franklin was walked in by the bailiff and was wearing the same blue denim shirt, beige trousers and blue and silver tie as the previous day. Dr Hamby was on the stand, still under direct examination from the prosecution, DA Beth Silverman. She asked him more about his training, his employment, his experience, his position etc, all relating to him being a firearms and toolmark expert.

After a while it was time for Seymour Amster to cross-examine the witness, whereupon the defence went off in all different directions. He asked why Dr Hamby wasn't qualified in this area or that area, which had nothing to do with firearms or toolmark analysis. None of his line of questioning made any sense as the witness was there as 'an expert on firearm and toolmarks' only. He even brought out a book on firearms and toolmark analysis and started to read from it, trying his very best to discredit the witness. However, he was just discrediting himself, yet again. The Judge looked at him like he was a complete fool.

Judge: 'Are you just reading from a book to the witness? Find the part you want in the book and mark it to show the prosecution. Don't just give them the whole book!'

Amster shuffled back to the lectern, tail between his legs . He then leant back on the partition separating the counsel's area and the gallery. Yes, he leant back on the wooden partition and sat there talking to the witness. If there was a place for him to put his feet up too, he would have done so. Shocking!

Amster continued to grill Dr Hamby as to why he didn't use a 3D microscope and why he only used a 2D microscope.

Dr Hamby explained how by using the 2D microscope along with a certain kind of light that casts shadows, making everything naturally 3D in appearance, and the human eyeball, you have a perfectly valid examination of a bullet and can see with an almost 100 per cent guarantee whether it came from the same gun which would also be examined.

The testimony from Dr Hamby went on for over five hours between the previous day and that one. In summary, it showed that Dr Hamby was beyond qualified in the field of firearms and toolmark analysis and David Lamagna was not. Dr Hamby modestly played down his expertise and lifelong experience and employment, yet David Lamagna embellished all of his limited training and studies yet was never able to back it up with any real employment or credentials. It was interesting to see Lamagna sitting in the gallery throughout Dr Hamby's testimony; I could only wonder what he must have been thinking.

At the end of the day and when the jury had been excused, it was about 4.10 p.m. The Judge brought up the issue of her sanctions from the previous day. It seemed obvious that the defence wanted to apologise for their behaviour in not coming forth with submitting the flash drive on time (which is why they were fined), yet the prosecution, DA Beth Silverman, seemed to stand strong in not wanting to apologise for anything, if I'm not mistaken. She certainly didn't apologise.

The previous day Ms Silverman had been fined for making an honest assessment as to why the defence had called for a break. Her only mistake was that she said it in front of the jury. Well, good for her, I thought.

The Judge pleaded with them both.

THE TRIAL

Judge: 'I just want you to stop it, both of you must stop it! I have resisted countless times during this trial of finding both of you in contempt of court. I don't like sanctioning lawyers, but I finally reached my limit yesterday. I want you both to start acting more professionally from this point forward. Please.'

A few minutes before the end of this exchange, Seymour Amster made a huge somewhat disingenuous apology for the way he had behaved in the courtroom. He said that he was now a 'changed man' and would never act inappropriately and unprofessionally again. He even wanted to focus on 'how good he'd been all day' and how different he'd been from all the times before.

How convenient for him! The defence had just rested and now he wanted to apologise. Clearly, he didn't want to pay a measly $500 out of the enormous sum that he, I was told by my sources, was earning. As far as I was concerned it was a little too late and the apology certainly fell on deaf ears with me. I couldn't help but hope he would be disbarred for life and the Judge and the prosecution win some kind of medal for having had to put up with him!

★ ★ ★

2 MAY 2016 – FIRST DAY OF CLOSING ARGUMENTS

Lonnie Franklin was walked in at 9.10 a.m., wearing black glasses, a light blue shirt, a blue tie and black trousers.

At 9.18 a.m. Judge Kennedy walked in and took the bench.

It was a completely full courtroom – you couldn't even squeeze a mouse in that day. On the left-hand side of the gallery retired detective Paul Coulter and retired detective

Dennis Kilcoyne sat next to each other near the front. There was a lot of media presence and two cameras.

Before the jury came in, the Judge talked about the exhibits she would and wouldn't be allowing into evidence. She ended saying that 'The objection is sustained regarding these items.' Before the jury came in she let the counsels speak and DA Beth Silverman was the first to do so.

DA: 'Your Honour, the defence took the books that were meant for the jury and took them apart and then put them back together and now they are not in the order which we had marked them in. Half of them are upside down and backwards and it hasn't been corrected.'

Amster: 'It's my understanding that it was corrected. May The People let us know exactly what the problem is so we can correct it.'

The jury came in from the proper jury entrance that day at 9.23 a.m. The Judge welcomed the jury as she always did and explained the jury instructions. This took just under forty minutes and later she would say more. She turned it over to DA Beth Silverman to begin her closing arguments.

DA: 'Morning, ladies and gentlemen. Ten young women, all of them brutally murdered by that man – the defendant, Lonnie Franklin – and one woman, Enietra Washington, who barely escaped that tragic fate. Now I told you in opening statements exactly what the evidence would be. And that is exactly what has been presented to you over these past few months. Now, here in closing arguments, I'm going to talk to you about the evidence that was presented, the law that the Judge provided to you just now and how those fit together. It's your job in this case to decide whether the defendant is guilty of the crimes and special allegations charges described in this case regarding the eleven victims who are the subject of this trial. So how do we know who committed these crimes? None of the victims can tell you. They can't tell you themselves because they have no voice. No voices to tell us. The defendant took their voices when he brutally murdered each of them. So who or what can tell us what happened? The evidence in this case. And the evidence in this case speaks very clearly. You just have to listen to what the evidence tells you. The evidence in this case is the voice of the victims who can no longer speak for themselves. So listen to the evidence.

'You have heard an overwhelming amount of evidence over the last few months that connects the defendant to these horrendous crimes and this is my opportunity to take all of that evidence, to piece it together for you, just like pieces of a jigsaw puzzle. You are all familiar with what a jigsaw puzzle looks like, right? You open up a box and you dump out all of the pieces. Then you begin. You begin with that one piece, that first piece. So what's the first piece in this case? How do we begin?

'You heard from Detective Kilcoyne that in June of 2007 a task force was formed at LAPD's Robbery Homicide Division. This took place a few months after the murder of Janecia Peters, who was murdered on January 1st 2007. The task force discovered that this matched a series of murders from the 1980s based on DNA evidence. Those were the murders that occurred between the years of 1985–1988. The task force found another pattern, with respect to these murders: they were all connected to a specific .25 auto firearm that was utilised in the 1980s. Then more pieces were added to complete the puzzle. As you heard, throughout the course of this trial, forensic DNA technology occurred over the twenty-plus years since the murder of Debra Jackson. Law enforcement now have DNA technology at their fingertips to solve cold cases such as these. So the task force went back to those cases, from 1985–1988, and applied the science that existed in 2007 to the killing spree that began in the 1980s. You also heard that from 2007–2010 more and more evidence emerged, all pointing to one person as the killer: this defendant. As you heard, an LAPD surveillance team, including Detective Art Stone and Detective Frank Trujillo, followed the defendant in July of 2010. On July 5th they followed him to John's Pizza in Buena Park and you heard that Detective Stone went into the restaurant, and after speaking to the manager first, they surreptitiously collected items from the defendant. Those items were then transported to LAPD's Crime Lab, where they were analysed by Supria Rosner. She developed four single-source DNA profiles: one was from the defendant's napkin and another was from a piece of his leftover pizza. This DNA profile matched in every location with the DNA profiles developed from the oral swab from Barbara Ware and sperm fraction and the defendant's record sample. The statistical calculation for this match was 1 in 11 quintillion – that's 1 with 18 zeros.

'All but one had cocaine and alcohol in their system except for the youngest, Princess Berthomieux. They were all found with their clothes in disarray, partially clothed usually. They were all found in alleys or in dumpsters surrounded with trash. They were all within three and a half to four miles of the defendant's home.

THE TRIAL

'As you learned throughout the course of this trial, the defendant is a serial killer and hiding in plain sight. He blended in. He lived in the community. He lived at this address where a search warrant was served – 1728 West 81st Street – since 1986. He worked in the South Los Angeles community, driving trash trucks for the Department of Sanitation. Prior to that, he worked at LAPD's garage down in Los Angeles, right under their noses. He dumped his victims like trash in alleys and trash bins. Almost all of the bodies in this case, as you saw, were concealed and hidden under debris, gas tanks, under mattresses, behind bushes, in dumpsters, inside trash bags. Several of the victims, as you saw, were missing their underwear or their bras or their shoes. Some, like Princess Berthomieux, Alicia Alexander and Janecia Peters, were found completely naked! There was no identification on or around any of the bodies at any crime scene. All of them were shot with a .25 automatic firearm or strangled to death. The ones who were shot were shot in the chest, except for Janecia Peters, who was shot in the back. The women who were shot in the chest, the bullet wounds were all with the same trajectory – left to right, front to back and straight down. Eight of them were shot with the same .25 automatic firearm.

'You've heard that Janecia Peters was shot also with a .25 automatic firearm and it was found in the defendant's home during a search warrant, along with boxes and boxes of .25 auto ammunition. Yet no .25 calibre cartridge cases were found at any of the crime scenes, which you would expect.

'All but Princess Berthomieux tested positive for cocaine. Most had consumed alcohol prior to their deaths and we called the testimony of one of the defendant's best friends,

Ray Davis, who testified that the defendant told him that he would always keep alcohol and drugs on hand for "his girls". And, of course, all of these crimes were connected to the defendant by forensic evidences.

'We saw that the defendant concealed and hid his victims' bodies over and over and over and over and over again. Barbara Ware under a gas tank and other debris. Bernita Sparks in a trash dumpster. Mary Lowe behind bushes. Alicia Alexander and Lachrica Jefferson under a mattress. Princess Berthomieux in bushes and Janecia Peters inside a dumpster and a trash bag.'

DA Silverman went on to talk about the difference between first- and second-degree murder. She emphasised about these victims, 'They are not just dead bodies that you've seen throughout this trial who have been depicted in photographs, because we can never do them justice. These victims were all human beings, they suffered from the same frailties, the same imperfections that all humans do. They also had the same hopes and the same dreams for their futures that we all have. Each of them deserves to be treated like human beings. None of them deserved to be murdered and dumped like trash as if their lives had no meaning.'

Ms Silverman went on to talk about 'implied malice' and the fact that these murders were 'deliberately performed'. There's a difference between 'implied malice' and 'expressed malice'. She gave a perfect analogy.

DA: 'Someone who goes to a park with a crowd of people and has no intention to kill anybody but he thinks it would be fun to shoot his gun into the air. This person shoots his gun into the air and a bullet comes down and hits and kills someone. That would be an example of "implied malice". The person didn't intend to kill anybody, the act that he performed was clearly dangerous. There were people in the park and he disregarded those lives. At a minimum, strangulation and/or shooting the victims, in this case in the chest, definitely fits the description of "implied malice", but clearly these acts demonstrate "expressed malice" as well. So let's talk about what that is.'

The DA went on to explain in great detail what 'expressed malice' is. She focused on how the defendant would leave his home every night and prowl the area of South Los Angeles to look for women. He would 'creep' out to find his victims.

DA: 'He got away with murder eight times between 1985 and 1988 – that's eight times in three years!'

It seems science was the only thing to stop this serial killer.

Ms Silverman put each of the victims and the crime scenes up on the ELMO, one by one. It was devastating for the victims' family members and sometimes became too much to bear; a number of them broke down in tears at having to relive, yet again, the brutal murder of their loved ones. She explained that there was sooting and/or stippling found on the clothing of these women, which explains the fact that these murders were all pre-meditated, wilful and deliberate because they were all done at very close range. Some murders and crime scenes were only one block apart yet they were sometimes twenty years apart. They were associated with the same gun and DNA which linked the murders. 'Is that merely another coincidence?' she said with a true sense of confidence in her voice.

THE GRIM SLEEPER

DA: 'This defendant was shooting to kill, he wasn't playing games.'

She talked about the only surviving victim, Enietra Washington, who had lost 20 per cent of all the blood in her body when she became the defendant's victim. However, she lived. Enietra provided the blueprint for all the other murdered women who could not speak for themselves.

DA Silverman explained in great detail how when Lonnie Franklin was interviewed by Detectives Kilcoyne and Coulter on 7 July 2010, the defendant was smug and laughed them off. A few times he would make disrespectful comments, saying one woman was '*fat*' and the other '*butt ugly*'! She pointed out that the same disrespect and disregard was shown 'when he dumped their bodies in filthy alleys, under dirty mattresses or in trash bags and thrown in dumpsters. He also did what nobody who is innocent would do, he laughs! He makes jokes even when there are pictures of ten women in front of him who had been brutally murdered! In the face of that, he laughs! There are ten dead women staring up at him and he's laughing in their faces!

'He demonstrates over and over again in that interview such callous disregard for their lives. When he was asked if he'd seen the billboards around Los Angeles and on Western, near the defendant's home, that his friend Ray Davis talked about, he jokes about the media calling him The Grim Reaper [she meant The Grim Sleeper here], he thinks it's funny. As if being given a monicker of being a serial killer is something that you would laugh at? And he's amused when Detective Kilcoyne refers to him as a "billboard celebrity". Because that is of course what he wants to be, right?

THE TRIAL

'When asked if he owns any guns, he listed several. Such as the .22 rifle, the .38 revolver, the 9mm revolver and a .22 pistol. He said he has no other guns – those are the only guns he has. Yet he conveniently forgets to mention the .25 auto, the gun he used to kill Janecia Peters. When he was asked specifically about the .22 pistol he even joked and played dumb.'

The DA ended her powerful closing arguments and thanked the jury and the courtroom and then sat down. The Judge then called for Mr Amster to start his own closing arguments. This will be interesting, I thought.

Amster: 'Your Honour, ladies and members… Oops, I mean ladies and gentlemen, I want to say that… I want to thank each and every one of you for the commitment you have given this case. It has not been easy. I would also like to apologise on behalf of myself and the defence team but I think mostly on behalf of myself for any drama, maybe improper things that you witnessed. This has not been an easy case. It has been our job to get the evidence that we felt is necessary to present to you. Now it's your job to utilise this evidence as you deem fit. Each of the evidence in this case had a role to play: the defence to present one side of the case and obey the law and the Government to present their side of the case. Many individuals believe that it is the defence team's job to get the defendant off. No, it's our job to question the Government's ethics. Tomorrow we could be legislated right out of existence. There might not have to be defence attorneys in the courtroom but we have chosen as a country to have that. And as long as we, as a community, have chosen to do that, it is up to us as defence attorneys to do our job within the law. It might not always be pretty, but it's what we are obligated to do because we too also have taken an oath to the Constitution. So all that we have done in this case is WE. JUST. WANTED. TO. DO. OUR. JOB!

'As I stated, it is our job to challenge the Government to make sure that they have proved their case, so that you can make a determination on this case: it's only you. It's only you that can make that determination, your interpretation on what matters, it's nobody else's: it is yours.

'No entity or person likes to be criticised. Those who are part of the Government, they don't like to be criticised. You heard the Government make their position on how the evidence should be interpreted. But it's only one interpretation and it really doesn't matter in this case what their interpretation is because this is a case that is based on "circumstantial evidence". Let me start off by explaining to you what "circumstantial evidence" means.'

There was silence, then more silence as Seymour Amster shuffled and paced across the floor back to his seat and then back to the lectern. He was obviously looking for something. So we all waited. Whatever he was looking for, it took a long time to find.

Amster (laughing hysterically): 'I'm sorry, I can't seem to find it.'

Judge: 'Well, why don't you just give them the instructions on whatever number it is? 2.00?'

Amster: '2.00 states… Evidence is either direct or circumstantial evidence. Other than Enietra Washington, the rest is "circumstantial evidence".'

He even made a somewhat ridiculous analogy: 'One example of "circumstantial evidence" is you are in a courtroom and all of a sudden you see a lot of people walk in with umbrellas, which are wet. Wet umbrellas? That's a pretty good idea that it's raining outside. That's "circumstantial evidence". You don't see the rain, but you know from seeing umbrellas and seeing that they are wet, it's probably raining. So the evidence was 'wet umbrellas' which led to the conclusion that it was raining. That is "circumstantial evidence".'

He's off again, I thought.

Amster: 'The defendant's guilt must be proved beyond a "reasonable doubt". Is this Lonnie Franklin's DNA "proved beyond a reasonable doubt"?

'Is this Lonnie Franklin's DNA… "proved beyond a reasonable doubt"? Is this "proved beyond a reasonable doubt"? Each of those factors that are necessary to show the defendant is the actual killer must be proved beyond a "reasonable doubt".

'The Government wants to see patterns: they want to see over a long period of time that this body was found in an alley and that body was found in the alley… You know what? Let me stop here for a moment…

'There is one thing that both the defence and the Government can completely agree on: every single one of the victims in this case's life mattered. There's nothing we will ever say that will persuade you that their life wasn't important or their life didn't matter. Every single one of them had a right to live: they had a life. It makes no difference why they were on those streets or not, that's not the issue in this case as far as what happened. It makes no difference in this case, so, please, if I talk about the circumstances that occurred and I talk about the terrible things that happened, we are not

NOT... TRYING... TO... DIMINISH... THEM... IN... ANY... WAY. THEIR... LIFE... MATTERED! EACH AND EVERY ONE OF THEM.

'But the Government wants to see patterns here, over a long period of time. Saying that because "this body was found in an alley, this body was found".

'You know, there's a story of a rancher that wanted all his neighbours to think that he was a great marksman. He went to his barn and told his neighbours that he was a great marksman. So he fired his gun and he fired several bullets against the barn. There were bullet holes in the barn...'

This went on and on. It was the second day of closing arguments and the bailiff, Tony, threw me out just for holding my mobile phone in my hand. It was 8.40 a.m., long before we began, and other people sitting next to me had their mobile phones out too. Although this might have affected my writing, it didn't, as the lovely Sergeant Westphal let me sit on a chair outside the door. Then I went and sat with my friends in the media on the twelfth floor upstairs to see everything on four television screens.

★ ★ ★

Let me get back to the details of the trial now, and I will bring in once more the defence's first analogy (regarding a rancher) that he used at the end of the previous day of closing arguments.

Amster: 'You know, there's a story of a rancher who wanted all his neighbours to think that he was a great marksman. So he went to his barn and took out his gun and he fired several bullets against the barn. So there were bullet holes in multiple places in his barn. He then went to the bullet holes in his barn to draw the bull's-eyes around those bullet holes.'

Suddenly the defence screamed in a high-pitched voice, 'Maybe he was a good marksman!' Ouch! That really hurt all of our ears, and we all looked at each other (this was the first day of closing arguments so I was sitting in the courtroom that day). 'And maybe he wasn't. But the bullets were there first and then he drew the circles around them. Then he called his neighbours and said, "Look at my barn." He didn't give them all the facts, he didn't tell them what came first. They didn't ask questions, they said, "Wow, he's a great marksman!" And maybe he's a good marksman and maybe he's not, but without the proper inquiries you really don't know. And that is the problem with a pattern: if you don't have all the information, if you don't make all the proper inquiries, then you don't know. Is it a true pattern or is it an illusion? Is The People's case a true pattern or is it an illusion?

'Is there something of deception that is not the science that it should be? That looks like something that it should be, but it is not? That is the inquiry. Those are the questions we would like you to do. Don't be like one of those ranchers. Just because you see the bull's-eyes you must ask the questions: is he truly a good marksman or is this an illusion that is not what we think it is?

'Because...' Amster raised his voice very loudly and went up at least two octaves with this line, for whatever reason, none of us knew. 'Because Lonnie's a... I mean the defendant, works as a sanitation engineer, then he's not... he works... erm... because I mean he works with a garbage truck therefore he knows where all the dumpsters are! But wait a second – he worked from around 1985 to 1989. He knew where all the routes were and the dumpsters were yet he's leaving bodies in alleys? Not in dumpsters for them to be collected by the routes of the sanitation trucks? You can't say you've got a pattern but exclude parts of the pattern!'

Amster had reached a vocal peak now, squawking like an angry bird, hands flailing as he shouted this at such an elevated level. He continued…

'…So if you're working as a sanitation engineer and you know the routes and you want to get rid of the bodies, well, it's easy to just put that body in a dumpster and then put it in the garbage truck and take it to the dump, then that's the end of it. Noooo! This is an illusion. Doesn't mean he didn't do it…'

Again, two octaves higher with this one word: 'Noooo!'

Finally, back to his normal level of speaking: 'But it doesn't mean he did it either. It's just a part of a pattern that really doesn't exist. And then they say it's a "body dump". So what? All that tells us is that this crime occurred someplace else, it doesn't really tell us who did it. Then there are differences in the crime scenes – some are under mattresses, some are not. But it really doesn't make a difference because it could be just sufficient evidence for culpability or lack of culpability. The issue is not that it was a "body dump", the issue is what do we have to show who did the crime?

'A "body dump" doesn't matter, because the Government has chosen to try this case under the theory that the defendant is the actual killer. That means to find him culpable, to find him guilty of first- or second-degree murder, you have to prove that he's the actual killer. So you have to abide by their decision and find him guilty of the actual murder.'

He went on to talk about the defendant's DNA being found on some of the bodies, but there was also DNA from other people found on those same bodies. He talked, or rather shouted, about the fact that 'So what if the defendant is obsessed with sex and a lot of women made it easy for him to have sex? He wanted to take pictures of various women in states of undress but it doesn't make him a murderer,' alluding to the fact that this had nothing to do with the fact a lot of them were found to be murdered and/or shot and survived the attack just like Enietra Washington. Amster mentioned the defendant's friend Ray Davis, who was put on the stand the previous month: he had said that he saw Franklin with lots of women. He didn't call the police because he never saw anything wrong with what was going on.

Amster: 'These were Lonnie's girls. Lonnie would give clothes to girls.

'How can you determine that malice aforethought existed in each of the cases when you do not have an eyewitness? If multiple people were present, you have to determine who... pulled... the... trigger... in... this... case?'

Now I don't know of any time in history when there was an 'eyewitness' who saw a serial killer kill his victims – it just doesn't happen, it is always based on all the evidence collected, but Amster was trying to dismiss this. He went on to emphasise to the jury that they must base their decision on all the evidence in this case, they must make sure it was beyond a reasonable doubt. When he started to shuffle around, for no reason, the Judge asked if it was a good time to end the day.

So we ended a few minutes before 4 p.m. before returning at 9 a.m. the following day.

★ ★ ★

3 MAY 2016 – SECOND DAY OF CLOSING ARGUMENTS

This was the day I was thrown out by the bailiff as I was holding my phone, as explained earlier.

Taking notes from right outside the door, I could hear Seymour Amster was going on and on about Enietra Washington, who had described the suspect as being approximately twenty years of age (Franklin was in his thirties at the time). He said this case was merely one of 'circumstantial evidence'. He spoke of there being a phantom nephew who picked up Enietra Washington and drove to her to his 'uncle's house' to get something. It seemed Amster had made up an imaginary person who drove to the defendant's home and that it really wasn't Franklin at all. How far-fetched could that possibly be?

Amster brought up yet again about the neighbours of the rancher in his marksman analogy, asking the jury, 'Are you going to be the neighbours of the rancher and make your decision based on illusion and deception?' He even added, 'The Government didn't use proper science.'

The defence went on and on about this 'mystery man' and also referred to 'the nephew'. He said the picture of Enietra Washington, which was found behind a wall in Lonnie Franklin's garage, was probably 'accidentally' dropped there. He even said because so many items were seized from Franklin's home over those three days in July 2010, maybe the picture was placed there or perhaps it wasn't even found in the garage at all! He added that in the case of Enietra Washington the DNA of nine different individuals had been found but none from Lonnie Franklin.

Then Amster suddenly started screaming again, in a high-pitched wail, while trying to discredit the nine law enforcement officers and investigators from the Coroner's Office in the Janecia Peters case.

Amster: 'HOW MANY LAW ENFORCEMENT OFFICERS DO WE HAVE THERE? ONE... TWO... THREE... FOUR... FIVE... SIX... SEVEN... EIGHT... NINE! DID ANY ONE OF THEM EVER THINK, FOR ONE SECOND, WHY WOULD WE PUT THIS GARBAGE BAG THAT MS PETERS WAS IN, WRAPPED AROUND WITH A LARGER BAG? WHY DON'T WE DO THAT BEFORE TRANSPORTATION? WHY DON'T WE PRESERVE THE EVIDENCE? WHY DON'T WE MAKE SURE THAT BEFORE WE FLIP THIS AND HAVE IT TOUCH ALL OF THIS OTHER GARBAGE, FOR POTENTIAL TRANSFER OF DNA, WHY DON'T WE MAINTAIN THE INTEGRITY OF THE ITEM? AHHHH! IS THAT A REACH? YEAH, IT PROBABLY IS A REACH, I'LL GIVE YOU THAT! BUT I'LL TELL YOU THIS MUCH: WHY NOT? THAT... IS... THE... PROBLEM... IN... THIS... CASE... THERE'S NO CONCERN TO MAINTAIN THE EVIDENCE...'

Amster continued to yell and scream, flap his arms around, pace and shuffle around the courtroom floor, saliva shooting from his mouth and going red in the face. His yelling just started to blend in after a while.

THE GRIM SLEEPER

We went for lunch recess and on my return I was told by the sergeant that my situation had just got worse. Apparently I had been seen talking to a juror and now I was not allowed back on any day of the trial. What?! When did I talk to a juror? So many people asked me why I was standing outside and I responded to each of them in the same way: 'I was thrown out by the bailiff.' No one was wearing a juror's badge. There were so many people in that courtroom, especially on important days, that people just blended into one unless I knew them. Apparently one of those who asked me why I wasn't inside was a juror. Now I wouldn't even know if it was a male or female juror who spoke to me, as I don't remember because so many people asked me why I wasn't inside the courtroom as I had been for the past four months.

Apparently my name was brought up so it was all 'on the record'. How would any of the jurors even know my name? I never spoke to any of them, at least not to my knowledge, except to explain I had been thrown out. In fact, because I don't have the transcript and also wasn't in the courtroom, I really don't know who stated my full name but I'd like to find out. I bet this made the bailiff's day.

Anyway, to go back to the hearing… Amster went on and on about the 'reasonable doubt' there should be in all of the evidence which The People brought in. He even had the audacity to say yet again that the scientific evidence was 'inferior and not up to standard'. He then recapped with the following:

Amster: 'One, we have stated the DNA evidence in this case leads to reasonable doubt. Furthermore, we have stated the reason why Enietra Washington's testimony leads to reasonable doubt. Furthermore, we have given you our reasons why ballistic evidence leads to reasonable doubt.

'It is our position that the scientific analysis done by the Government in this case is based on inferior technology in science and we've given our reasons concerning the ballistics and the DNA evidence. Furthermore, it is our position that mistakes made during the search of Lonnie Franklin's home do not cause the evidence seized there to be absolutely viable. That is for YOU to use your inquiring minds to ask the questions as to how much weight you put on the evidence that was gathered during that search.'

And he went on…

'This is a "circumstantial evidence" case; you must consider all these interpretations of the evidence. It is the Government's job to eliminate all these interpretations that point to Mr Franklin's innocence. This they cannot do. Why? Because the mystery man, with the mystery DNA and the mystery gun… Your job as stated so many times is to follow the law. It's not easy. Do your job by analysing evidence and the testimony you heard and following the instructions you have been given. Make your decisions based on the law. You have been a dedicated jury and I thank you for taking the time out of your lives.'

Although this was the day I was thrown out, I have stated earlier how many people were trying to get me back in the courtroom, but to no avail. However, I did have friends in high places – much higher than the ninth floor where we were at the time. The courtroom is on the ninth floor and the media are often on the twelfth floor if they're not in the courtroom. A few of those reporters suggested I go up there to watch the trial with them. On days when the media had been there over the past few months I had been able to watch the proceedings on a number of live streaming newsfeeds.

On this final day of closing arguments, I really needed to observe. There was nothing that would have stopped me from hearing DA Beth Silverman blow away the defence for one last time and give her final performance of this phase of the trial. So I decided to join my media friends up on the twelfth floor and watch Ms Silverman blast away on about four live feed monitors.

The Judge turned to her at just after 2 p.m. and said, 'Ms Silverman.' She walked slowly and deliberately up to the lectern.

DA Silverman: 'Good afternoon, ladies and gentlemen. The only deception that has been perpetrated in this case is by the defence. The entire defence from the beginning of this case through closing arguments where we heard for the first time that there was some "mystery man" with a "mystery gun" with "mystery DNA" is now, at the end of the case, with no evidence to support it! What the defence wants you to do in this case is to engage in speculation and what you heard from the instructions that were given to you by the court is that that's something you can't do: you have to base your decision on the evidence. That doesn't mean imaginary evidence. That doesn't mean evidence that could be based on speculation. The theory of the defence is basically equivalent to the skies opening up, a spaceship descending and murdering all of these women. We have the same evidence of that that we do of some "mystery nephew" who we've never heard of going to nobody that exists.

THE TRIAL

'Don't you think if there was evidence of a "mystery nephew", his words himself, don't you think we would have heard about this at some point before now? Do you think that if someone says something over and over for four and a half hours that somehow that makes it true? Or that if you raise your voice enough times that suddenly that's going to lend it some credibility?

'What the defence has told you today is that some nephew picked up Enietra Washington and said he wanted to go to his uncle's house, which we presume is Lonnie Franklin's house. So is the defence saying that the person who's a murderer wouldn't also lie? The fact that the defendant said to Enietra Washington, "I want to stop off at my uncle's house to pick up some money." What's the logical reason that the defendant would do that that day? He was coming out of a store, he sees Enietra walk by and paying attention to his customised Pinto.

'When he sees that he'd caught her attention, he tries to ask her if she wanted a ride and she rejected his offer numerous times. After about the third time and him saying a rude comment like, 'That's what wrong with you black women, no one can be nice to you,' she started to feel sorry for him and then reluctantly got in his car with him, finally accepting his offer of a ride.

'Why then would he say he had to stop at his home, which he referred to as his uncle's home? Because he didn't have his gun! He had to go back to his house to get the gun! He didn't know he'd run into a lady that he was interested in and he's angry. Why is he angry? For the same reason he told us. Because initially she refuses his ride. She didn't want to get into the car with him but he makes her feel guilty. The power of manipulation, that's what we heard from the defence throughout this case. Then the defence told us that the police were brought to the area and that "they could have taken DNA samples from everybody". What year is this? This was 1988! There was no DNA! AGAIN… THEY… ARE… JUST… MAKING… THINGS… UP! But of course, what do you expect? They don't have anything! But what else are they going to do? They have to make things up because the evidence in this case is so substantial.

'So now, we have a "mystery man"! Let's look at what we had throughout this trial: a red herring. You know what a red herring is? A red herring is a smoked fish and back in the days in Europe, specifically in London, England, they would drag a smoked fish across the trail to throw off hunting dogs to attempt to distort, distract and manipulate. That's what the defence did this morning and all day yesterday. They're just trying to distract you. Not only do they do that in arguments but they've done this throughout the case.

'Let's take a look: the DNA statistics, that's not real science. Even though even his own scientists use it and he admitted it's used throughout the country and the world but suddenly "it doesn't work". But it doesn't work if it points to the defendant's guilt yet it does work if it points to some "unknown male". The firearms analysis in the case was based on faulty science even though it's used across the country and across the world and has been for 100 years. Remember the very beginning of this case? Just to give you a pattern that went on with the defence throughout the entirety of this case. Remember the testimony of Dr

THE TRIAL

Fajardo, with question after question after question from the defence saying, "Well, maybe the bodies in this case, maybe they were misidentified? Maybe they were switched at the Coroner's Office? How do you know the toe tie was labelled correctly?" What did we hear about that? We heard from Dr Fajardo that identification of decedents is one of the main functions at the Coroner's Office.'

DA Silverman continued by explaining in great detail how the defence had tried to mislead the jury from the start. Even near the end of the case when the family members of the victims went on the stand and identified their loved ones by saying, 'Yes, that was my mother,' or 'That was my sister,' or 'That was my daughter.' So although the defence was happy to mislead the jury initially, it went on and got worse from there. We then heard about gang members. Silverman then quoted how the defence had wanted to sway the jury.

DA: 'Let's divert attention away from this case yet again and let's look at the gang graffiti!

'We heard from Detective Dupree that gangs don't care about that kind of stuff. Another attempt to mislead.'

DA Silverman then spoke about the defence persisting in the line that it was probably the murderer/s of these women. That didn't work so then Amster even brought up the transients – 'Now he says that the transients are responsible.' She continued with how he focused on orange peel found underneath a body, trying to divert attention again to the peel. Even the detective testifying had to laugh at how that could possibly be related – all this to divert attention away from the evidence in this case.

Silverman continued with even more damning truths.

DA: 'Now, as of today, we have this grand conspiracy theory that happened in this case. The sheriffs, the LAPD, the DA's office... everybody conspired against this defendant. Even his own nephew! That's what you're not allowed to do, what he did. That's the opposite of following the law in this case, which is basing your decision on what's presented in this courtroom. How many times did we hear Judge Kennedy talk about [how] you're not allowed to listen to anything outside of this courtroom? "Don't listen to the radio, or television. Don't read the newspaper because you must only listen and go on the evidence you hear in court."

'Now today, they come in and say there's a "mystery man", a "mystery gun" and "mystery DNA". How long did he take to come up with that story? And now he has an imaginary nephew! On top of all of this he manipulated and distorted the evidence.'

Ms Silverman went on to repeat all the areas in which Amster would try to discredit the testimony of the only living eyewitness.

DA: 'When the defence said to you over and over that "if you don't have enough evidence then you can't convict", my question would be: what more evidence could you possibly have when you have DNA, firearms evidence, circumstantial evidence of all the evidence that was found in his home, an identification, the murder weapon? What more is there? What other type of evidence could exist in the universe that would be sufficient? Because certainly if you had that, he would be telling you that that wasn't believable or credible or reliable evidence either!'

THE TRIAL

The previous day Amster had told the court that it was 'his job to prosecute bad Government'. DA Silverman was firm in stating that was completely false.

DA: 'There's no "bad Government" here. There's evidence and we present it! A selected jury makes a decision. And he's not a prosecutor! He's a defence attorney and it's his job to represent his client. That doesn't mean that his job is to mislead the jury. He repeatedly took evidence out of context throughout this entire trial. According to him now, all the evidence amounts to nothing. The DNA evidence is irrelevant. The firearms evidence isn't good enough. The patterns that are obvious are meaningless. In fact, he even said, "The Government wants to see patterns." The Government isn't a person, the "Government" doesn't want to see anything!

'The patterns are obvious to all of you, and Detective Kilcoyne testified to this at the beginning. Showing the patterns of the evidence that had the same DNA profiles over and over and over again between these cases. This is not something "the Government wanted to find"! It is something that existed. The bodies were killed and dumped in the same manner. The victims were all of the same type, African-American young women. The murder weapon was the same .25 calibre firearm. We didn't create this, the defendant created it! We just presented it!'

At this she smiled and said that the defence wanted to tell the jury that all those patterns were 'meaningless'. Even Franklin's best friend's testimony was meaningless.

DA: 'And you didn't hear from one DNA expert, not one, between all the laboratories, that ever said, "You know this

DNA profile was similar to the defendant's but it wasn't him. It must be someone who is related to him." That's not what you heard. You heard it was a match! And that's the point of the statistics that it is so rare.

'Again, you didn't come into this courtroom from under some dark hole. DNA is used to exonerate the innocent and it's used to convict the guilty.

'You also heard from counsel when he made a lot of comments about the "randomness of nature" that can cause two strands to be the same. That's not the way DNA evidence works. If it was someone related to the defendant it would have showed that and they wouldn't have been "matches". They were all "matched" to the defendant!'

DA Silverman again brilliantly picked apart the defence's one star witness, David Lamagna, saying that he had 'no training, no experience, he's not qualified in offering expert opinions and not an expert in firearm and toolmark comparisons. Yet he explains how he knows how it should be done although that's not how he does it himself as he says he can't afford it!'

Apparently, Lamagna really makes his money by travelling around and criticising the real firearm and toolmark examiners with unsubstantiated claims. He thinks he's smarter than everybody else and also more experienced. His opinions are complete garbage, DA Silverman went on to say, and when you hear what he says, 'It's garbage in and garbage out.' She clarified this with the following statement: 'That's the only way he can make a living as nobody would hire him!' Ms Silverman wasn't bashful in saying how dishonest a witness David Lamagna had been. It was a battle when she had to ask him multiple times and repeat the same question over and over just to get him to answer directly.

DA: 'One of the most embarrassing moments for him was when I'm showing him photographs of his microscope set up in the jury room, with his hands. His microscope, by the way, which he purchased off the internet. Then he ermed and ah'd as to whether that was actually a photograph of his hands and also, if it was even his microscope. We all know how that went down. It went from bad to worse.

'If there's a witness who is clearly and wilfully false and is only there to mislead you, then you must throw out the entire testimony as you would with a piece of mouldy bread. You're not going to pick around the mould and eat the rest of it, you throw out the whole thing!'

Ms Silverman then explained to the jury how the intent to kill was very clear. All these women were shot at close range and the stippling and sooting proved this. They were all shot in the heart. There was a very deliberate intent to kill and not an intent to just scare as if you were simply waving a gun around then shot someone in the leg.

Most times, there are no witnesses to crimes, especially the ones the defendant committed. He silenced the only witnesses there could have been by killing these women. There is no law in the jury instructions where there has to be a witness to a crime or there would be a lot of criminals walking among us.

DA Silverman then explained what reasonable doubt is and how there was 'NO reasonable doubt in this case'. She told the jury to base their decisions on the evidence and their own common sense.

DA: 'The evidence in this case couldn't be any clearer. What the defence wants you to do in this case is go on a fishing expedition. They want you to believe that the evidence in this case is really only a bunch of coincidences. Well, what he [Amster] gave you, and what he wants to hang his hat on, are way too many coincidences to even be in the same sentence as the word reasonable!'

She added that the defence wants the jury to believe that the defendant was just the object of some grand conspiracy. Therefore they would have to believe that the defendant must be the unluckiest man on the face of this planet because the entire universe was conspiring against him – 'That is just not reasonable! Don't buy into the defence's absurd excuses as the evidence in this case is staggering.'

DA: 'It's your responsibility to hold the defendant accountable for his choices. For his deliberate and pre-meditated actions of his vicious killings of ten women and the attempted murder of the eleventh victim. It's your responsibility, based on the evidence and based on the law, to tell this defendant that he is guilty of first-degree murder with a special circumstance. It's time, ladies and gentlemen, to bring justice to these women. It's time.'

And on that strong finish, DA Beth Silverman closed her notes and gracefully left the lectern.

The Judge continued to read the rest of the jury instructions.

★ ★ ★

At 1.36 p.m. on 5 May 2016, Lonnie David Franklin Jr was found guilty of ten counts of murder in the first degree and one count of attempted murder. Justice had finally been served and I hoped this would help in giving some kind of closure to the most important people in this trial – the family members of these victims. However, just when you think that this is the end to a terrible ordeal and that the monster will never be heard from again, so we begin the next phase. It is a very short phase called 'the penalty phase'. This happens in all death penalty cases. In essence the prosecution can bring in more evidence to reinforce the defendant's guilt, if they so wish. Both sides can also bring in witnesses to testify as to why the defendant should be put to death, and for the defence, witnesses who believe he should not.

★ ★ ★

12 MAY 2016 – START OF THE PENALTY PHASE

The penalty phase went as follows: all of the regular people, those who had attended the main trial (the guilt phase), were now seated to begin the first day of the penalty phase. This included the jury, the prosecution, the defence, family members of the victims and spectators and reporters in the gallery.

Some of the same witnesses from the guilt phase were brought to the stand day after day to re-testify. These included firearms experts, criminalists and law enforcement officers. I felt that it wasn't necessary to bring them back again as we had heard it all before the first time in the previous guilt phase of the trial. However, new detectives also testified, who were involved in the cases of the five new victims, whom the prosecution added to this phase of the trial.

Sherry Costa came to the stand to talk about her late niece, Barbara Ware, whom she loved dearly. After her, Treva Anderson was called. She was the sister of Barbara Ware, who again spoke fondly of her sibling and how they grew up. All this was heart-wrenching to say the least.

Soon afterwards, the daughter of Debra Jackson – Anyata Jackson – took the stand. Her story was extremely powerful. As a young girl and in temporary foster care, Anyata was excited to learn that she was to be reunited with her mother, Debra, within a few weeks. Anyata had maintained a strong loving bond with her mother throughout her time in foster care; she spoke to her daily and saw her every weekend. She was really looking forward to being reunited again, but sadly Debra was murdered only days before she would have had her daughter home with her permanently.

More family members took the stand, including the granddaughter, Myah Green, of Debra Jackson. Also, Debra's son – Jermaine – testified about losing his beloved mother.

There were four new victims whom the prosecution decided to bring in as more evidence against Franklin. These victims were never mentioned in the guilt phase of the trial so as not to delay it any further. Family members also came to the stand to give their own heartfelt testimony.

Sharon Dismuke was found on 15 January 1984.

Inez Warren was found on 15 August 1988.

Georgia Mae Thomas was found on 28 December 2000.

Rolenia Morris went missing on 20 September 2005 and her body was never found. However, her driver's licence and two photos of her were found on a shelf in Lonnie Franklin's garage.

Ayellah Marshall went missing on 11 January 2006 and her body was never found. However, her high school ID card was found in the mini fridge of Lonnie Franklin's garage, along with photos of the other known victims who were found.

★ ★ ★

The penalty phase is always the most emotional part of any trial, and this one happened to be just as emotional as all of the penalty phases I've attended before. Detective Darren Dupree was brought to the stand. This time he testified and went over the newly mentioned victims in this case and also where they were dumped. Eerily these victims were dumped so near to the previously known victims, it was uncanny.

Amster was accused by the Judge of being 'threatening' towards the jurors: he was clearly making them uncomfortable with the delivery of his questions, which were supposed to be directed to the witness on the stand, yet the jurors felt they were being aggressively directed at them. After Amster had apologised and that was all cleared up, he was not forthcoming as to whether or not he would be bringing back his 'Sorenson witnesses'. In fact, the DNA analysis lab was not called upon again.

On one of the penalty phase days, no sooner had Judge Kennedy taken her position at her bench than Amster spoke up in a sudden burst. He wanted to make sure that he was allowed to talk to the witness Ingrid W., who would be brought in from Germany to testify. The prosecution had subpoenaed a woman in Germany who had been gang-raped by a number of men, and Lonnie Franklin had been charged and prosecuted for this crime in 1974. It is unknown whether or not Amster spoke to this witness, however I presume he did not.

This story was very interesting to me as Franklin had told me in great detail, years earlier, how he had 'had sex with a white German woman'. He said he'd met her with some of his Army buddies and they all had sex with her as she 'was loose'. He told me that they all had sex with her at the same time but he had made sure he 'went in first'. I obviously had to disguise my absolute horror and disgust when he told me this story. Later, I found out that Ingrid was brutally raped by three men at knife point and Franklin was the last to do so. This was not consensual sex but a brutal rape.

★ ★ ★

12 MAY 2016

The prosecution presented their final witness, Ingrid W. from Germany, who in 1974 was kidnapped from a train station in Stuttgart by three black men, one of whom was identified as Lonnie Franklin. These men gang-raped her in a field and throughout the ordeal, the innocent 17-year-old was convinced she was going to die.

A JAG officer also testified, along with an army records supervisor. Both validated that Franklin was the perpetrator and had served time in a German prison. He was convicted and sentenced to three years and four months in prison. In the end, he served less than a year for this crime and then discharged from the army immediately afterwards on 24 July 1975.

The sister of Lachrica Jefferson testified very emotionally about the loss of her sibling, who was also her best friend. Then Billy Ware testified about the loss of his sister Barbara ,and Diana Ware, stepmother to Barbara, testified too. It was absolutely heartbreaking to hear the testimonies of these innocent family members having to hear about how and why this monster chose to take their lives.

16 MAY 2016

Closing arguments for the prosecution were strong and powerful and were delivered by DA Beth Silverman. After showing a number of horrific images of deceased women on the autopsy table, she then told the jurors that they should show Franklin 'the exact same mercy as he showed to his victims, because that's what he deserves'. She went over each crime in great detail, reminding the jury that throughout this phase the defence hadn't put a single family member or friend of Franklin's on the stand to spare his life. Whether they were called upon or not, no one knows. Not even Franklin's wife, Sylvia, or his daughters, or son, or any of his friends came to court to speak on his behalf. None of them even came to say if he had any redeeming qualities to possibly try and save him from receiving the death penalty. That told me a lot.

Silverman also re-clarified to the jury who this monster really was and reminded them of the numerous unknown victims who were still out there and had met the same fate at Franklin's hands. At the time of writing police believe the list of victims exceeds twenty-five. DA Silverman explained how 'life' in prison is still 'life', which is something that his victims never had. 'They will never take another breath,' she added in a chilling tone. She talked of the never-ending pain that the family members of these innocent souls would continue to feel and how their lives would never be the same. At the end of the trial they would go home and still have to bear the pain from their loss.

3 JUNE 2016

Surprisingly, Dale Atherton spoke for the defence's closing arguments and not Seymour Amster, who had been the main defence attorney for the defendant. Atherton tried to mitigate the prosecution's DNA evidence by saying there were other men's DNA found on the bodies besides Mr Franklin's. He spoke of there still being the 'mystery gun' out there (the gun used in eight murders which was never found). Of course the court had heard all this before so it was a moot point. Too many other factors proved Franklin's guilt and hence the jury had unanimously convicted him less than a month before.

Atherton then went on to speak passionately about giving Franklin mercy and sparing him the death penalty.

Dale Atherton: 'The ripples of mercy will extend deeper and farther than the ripples of revenge.'

Throughout this plea he was genuinely emotional. He was almost in tears and his eyes welled up a number of times. He even read an excerpt from Shakespeare's *The Merchant of Venice* on 'mercy' and quoted a few other well-known extracts, which were very appropriate although I didn't have the chance to write them down.

These closing arguments ended mid-morning on 3 June. Judge Kennedy read the jury their instructions before they were sent to the jury room to deliberate. By mid-afternoon the jury still had not reached a verdict, so Judge Kennedy decided to let them all go home for the weekend. They were told to return on the Monday at 9 a.m., making sure to not watch the news or talk to anyone regarding this case, to continue their deliberations.

6 JUNE 2016

Just before twelve noon the bell rang and we were told that the jurors had reached a verdict, which would be read at 12.30 p.m. It had taken just over five hours of deliberation for them to come to their decision, much of it on the previous Friday.

'DEATH! DEATH! DEATH!' was all you could hear outside the courthouse from the bystanders.

Family members were crying and consoling each other. Dear Mary Alexander, the mother of Alicia Alexander, was shaking with emotion. Her son, Donnell, mouthed to an alternate juror the words 'Thank you.' She responded with a slight smile acknowledging how hard this must have been for all of them.

Judge Kennedy thanked the jurors profusely and said that they were the best set of jurors she had had in her twenty-eight years on the bench and that she would miss them greatly.

The Judge would give her final sentencing on 10 August 2016.

THE GRIM SLEEPER

In most death penalty cases, in fact in about 99.9 per cent of the time, a judge agrees with the jury. Hopefully this Judge would agree that the death penalty would be agreed upon on that day.

10 AUGUST 2016 – THE GRIM SLEEPER SENTENCED TO DEATH BY JUDGE KATHLEEN KENNEDY

At 8.30 a.m. on 10 August 2016 we all gathered on the ninth floor outside Dept 109. I arrived very early as I knew there would be a lot of people there, including the victims' family members.

The first people I went up to were the loving and close-knit Alexander family. I shook their hands and gave Donnell a hug. I had grown to know them over the past six years and had had a number of conversations with Donnell. Porter and his wife Mary Alexander lost their daughter of barely eighteen years old, Alicia 'Monique' Alexander. Donnell was her older brother and there were other family members there too. The whole family had been coming to court for every pre-trial arraignment and had had to live through the details of their precious Monique's death, and also to sit in the same room as the monster that brutally murdered her on 11 September 1988. At times they had also had to suffer the antics and delays of the defence. This day was their day, a day they knew justice would finally be served.

The next person I approached was the woman I had wanted to talk to since 2010 when I first started attending the pre-trial arraignments, Ms Diana Ware. Over the years I had watched her make every effort to attend every court appearance of her daughter's suspected killer. On the rare occasion she didn't attend on a day, over the years, it was only because her health was bad. Now in her late seventies, she would diligently take the bus for every pre-trial arraignment. Ms Ware was wearing a beautiful blue and white floaty top and her hair was done to perfection. This was her day to get justice for her daughter and she had a different air about her today, almost one of complete satisfaction as if she somehow knew in her heart the Judge would agree with the jury and sentence Franklin to death.

Barbara Ware had only just turned twenty-three when she was brutally killed at the hands of Lonnie David Franklin Jr.

From 8.40 a.m. when the doors to Dept 109 opened, DA Beth Silverman was hugging the family members and they were chatting and hugging her in return. She looked as elegant as always, wearing a black jacket over a black and white spotted dress.

By 9.15 a.m. only five of the jurors had come through the door, but they didn't come in together as they weren't summoned. It was their choice if they wanted to be there for the final sentencing. Wearing black-rimmed glasses, Lonnie David Franklin Jr was walked in soon after, handcuffed and in his orange jumpsuit. He looked as though he was chewing something as he sat down and throughout some of the proceedings. He faced forward with the same blank stare he had had throughout the trial.

At 9.21 a.m. Judge Kennedy took the bench. She began by stating that the defence had made complaints about 'prosecution misconduct'. Everyone had been sitting and waiting for the verdict, and then Seymour Amster spoke first to complain that the prosecution shouldn't have brought in four new murder cases in the penalty phase of the trial, which he claimed was 'prosecution misconduct'.

The 'penalty phase' of a trial is usually focused on the defendant and whether he/she should live or die.

Ranging from one octave to another in just one sentence, Amster implied that 'bringing up these new murders tainted the mind of the jury'. He even stated that it wasn't fair that 'serial murderers should automatically be given the death penalty'! He then brought up the case of another serial killer (one I've interviewed a number of times): Chester Turner. Turner was given the death penalty on 10 July 2007, then sent to Death Row for a few years, then brought back to be tried again for four additional murders. He then received the death penalty for the second time and was sentenced to death again on 19 June 2014. No one, including the Judge, really understood why the defence were bringing this up. However, Amster was of course was going for another mistrial, so when he had finished the Judge turned to the prosecution.

Judge: 'Ms Silverman.'

DA Silverman stated that she was one of the prosecutors on the Chester Turner case of 2007, and the first jury convicted him of multiple murders and he was therefore sentenced to death. Then, finding there were a number of other murders, he was brought back from Death Row to be tried again in front of another jury in 2014 to give some sense of justice and closure for the families of those additional victims.

DA Silverman: 'It seems that the argument that the defence counsel is making today is that somehow he thinks that serial killers are a "special class" and that they should be given special treatment and should be treated differently from any other capital case.'

She called the argument 'disingenuous at best' and then proceeded to let the court know how everyone had been impacted by the evidence shown in the courtroom. She said how conscientious, diligent and professional the jury had been the entire six months of the trial – she herself could never have imagined a better jury. She stated that there was no real sense of closure for the victims' family members yet she felt they would now have a sense of peace that justice had been served.

After Ms Silverman finished speaking it went back to Amster, who raised his voice so much that he was shouting, just as he had done since the trial began and throughout the pre-trial hearings.

The Judge chose to ignore these rantings and instead turned to commend the jury on how great they were in every way. She also stated that no evidence in favour of the defendant was presented by the defence – there was nothing they brought in to the penalty phase that could show that he had had a tragedy in his childhood. Judge Kennedy stated there is no 'automatic death penalty for serial killers' and that the evidence spoke for itself. She explained that after she had also independently reviewed all the evidence, along with what was presented in trial, she firmly believed that the aggravating factors far outweighed the mitigating ones.

We had a short recess and then returned, and Judge Kennedy asked the defence if the defendant would like to speak. Amster responded that he did not wish to speak. Then

THE GRIM SLEEPER

Ms Silverman invited seventeen members of the families of the victims to speak. One after another stood up to speak in such heartfelt and emotional words it brought tears to my eyes and I'm sure I was not the only one.

Ms Laverne Peters walked to the lectern to make her statement. She was the mother of Janecia Peters, who was found murdered on 1 January 2007 at the tender age of twenty-five. She said that the defendant who had killed and discarded her daughter in a trash bag would now be living his life in a jail cell that would become *his* trash bag.

Jovana Peters then stood up and with a shaky voice she spoke through her tears about how her sister Janecia was taken in such a tragic way. Growing up, they had been best friends.

Then Barbara Ware's step-sister, Larina Corlew, stood up and spoke. Barbara died on 10 January 1987 at the young age of twenty-three. Her sister spoke of the love she had for her late sister and how they would run through the rain to their father's house before the clock struck twelve midnight on New Year's Eve. It was the first time she had ever seen her father cry. He never knew his daughter was murdered by a serial killer as he died before Franklin was arrested. Barbara was a mother, a daughter, a sister and a niece. Her sister ended very strongly with, 'It's now your turn, Lonnie David Franklin. You're out!'

Henrietta Wright's daughter, Rochell Johnson, spoke next. She said that she has finally found peace. She said that what Franklin did to the community was 'butt ugly' and that the crimes he committed over and over had made his life 'butt ugly'. She brought up these words because when Franklin was being interrogated, he saw a picture of Henrietta and declared she was 'butt ugly'.

Another family member of Henrietta's got up to speak but it was hard to hear as she spoke quietly, obviously filled with emotion. I believe it could have been her sister or a cousin.

The woman who grew up with Princess Berthomieux like an older sister, Samara Herard, stood up next to speak of her love for Princess: 'I can't even begin to explain. You wait so long and you don't think it will come. You knew in your heart it would be this, but it's surreal, she deserved to live a full life. I'm here for her.'

More family members stood up to speak about her.

The uncle of Alicia 'Monique' Alexander, who had stayed with the Alexander family throughout college, stood up to give a heartfelt statement. He called Franklin a 'monster' and said his actions had deeply changed who he was. He explained that he is a Christian and a spiritual person and has been taught to forgive. However, he cannot forgive Franklin for taking the life of such a sweet and innocent person as 'Monique'.

Then a woman by the name of Carmela stood up to speak of her sister, Alicia 'Monique'Alexander. She had no family of her own, so they were sisters but not by blood. Mary and Porter Alexander were her godparents and therefore 'Monique' became her sister. She recalled how they sang together in church and at home and how they shared a life together. Through the tears she spoke as best she could of how this tragedy has made her godparents suddenly get old and their health deteriorate rapidly over the years. She thanked God, the jury, the Judge, Beth Silverman and Darren Dupree. She told Franklin that he has a daughter, nieces and a granddaughter of his own and how would he have liked this to happen to them? She added she will never have closure, she is just trying to have peace.

Then the only living survivor, Enietra Washington, stood up to speak. As always she was wearing a very glamorous outfit. Today she wore a long bright blue summer two-piece. She said Franklin was so evil and that he was 'right up there with [Charles] Manson' and that he had destroyed her trust in men as he took all of that trust away.

Enietra went on to say in a stern voice that because Franklin had no remorse there was no way that any of us could grant him forgiveness. She explained how she was so hurt by what he did to her and she has no closure because every day she is fearful.

Another woman, Laura Moore, got up and said she was shot six times by Franklin in 1984, but thankfully she had lived. She explained her painful story to the court. She was never called upon during the trial, however she was allowed to speak at the very end.

Donnell Alexander stood up, dressed immaculately in a tan suit, tie and brown shirt – the whole family had always dressed so well every single day in court for the past six years. He spoke of his beautiful baby sister Alicia 'Monique' Alexander. He explained that being in the trial was the hardest thing he'd ever done and yet he believes in the system. 'This is the last time that Franklin will take another life,' he said, staring coldly at the back of the defendant's head.

Porter Alexander then stood up to speak of his beloved daughter Alicia 'Monique' Alexander. He said to listen to the pain spoken by all the family members, and that for someone to take the life of so many people was 'mind-boggling'. Franklin was 'atrocious' and the 'day of reckoning is here'. He added that he hoped they really 'take him out', meaning he really faces the execution that he deserves.

Mary Alexander slowly stood up to speak of her daughter Alicia 'Monique' Alexander and how their lives had changed since the tragedy. She spoke of how Franklin has no conscience whatsoever and how much she misses and loves her daughter and how she wakes up in the night and cries. She was glad she lived long enough to see this day come. Then, in the most powerful way, she made Franklin turn around and look into her eyes. She asked how he could have taken the life of such an innocent person who had never done any harm to him. He mouthed the words 'I don't know why,' or 'It wasn't me.' It was very hard to tell as his mouth didn't open much when he spoke those words.

Ms Diana Ware had been to nearly every court appearance over the past six years when her health would allow it. She then rose to a standing position and walked slowly to the lectern to speak of her beloved stepdaughter, Barbara, who was taken from this world on 10 January 1987, two days after her twenty-third birthday – 'When Mr Franklin killed her, he extinguished the promise of the potential life of a 23-year-old single mother who had begun to turn her life around. He brutally murdered her. A hole has been left in our family that has never been filled.'

Barbara's father, and Diana's late husband, had passed away in 2002, never knowing their daughter was a victim of a serial killer. Barbara looked over at Franklin and asked him why he did what he did. 'What was in your mind?' she asked, with a stern look in her eyes, although he continued to face forward. She said she forgives Franklin because the Lord says she must. However, she cannot forget.

She called Franklin 'a wolf in sheep's clothing'. He stole all of her tomorrows. There will be no wedding, no other children. There will be no family reunions, no cookouts, no birthday parties, no more memories to be made. She thanked the prosecution, the Judge and everyone in the courtroom for their support. She even said she prays for Franklin's soul and reminded him that he too would have to answer to the Lord, our Saviour, one day.

Seventeen of the victims' family members, as well as surviving victims, stood up to speak, and I will recount a few of their testimonies here:

Lachrica Jefferson's sister Romy Lampkin said: 'You took my only sibling from me. You destroyed a lot of lives and now today is your fear day. You sit there with a blank face with no remorse and today is our day.'

Alicia 'Monique' Alexander's brothers – Darin and Donnell. Her mother and father – Porter and Mary. Mary even made Franklin look at her but before she did this, she said: 'Thank God for this day.' Then she made him turn around and look at her, which he did, then she went on to say: 'I would like to know why?' as he looked in to her eyes. 'I know she didn't do anything to hurt you. I know that.' Franklin slowly nodded.

'I know I am supposed to forgive and love everyone,' Mary Alexander continued on. 'I have forgiven you but it is hard. You did so much wrong, not just to my daughter, but to all of the others.'

THE TRIAL

There were also family members who weren't able to be present and therefore wrote a letter to be read by DA Beth Silverman to the court. Billy Ware, the sister of Barbara Ware, wrote one such letter as he resides in another state. He said that he would never forgive the 'little arrogant man' who killed his sister so brutally and left her in an alleyway. He also wrote that he hoped Franklin doesn't die of old age as he wants to watch him die. Also, the son of Henrietta Wright wrote a letter and Beth Silverman read his heartfelt words to the court.

The last woman to stand up and speak was another family member. She was soft spoken so her name was hard to hear. She was very Christian and she said she forgave Franklin for killing these young women, and that she prays he asks God to forgive him as that's what he needs to do. She told him he'd caused so much pain to so many people, although we feel sorry for him, and beneath his hard, cruel exterior probably deep down he is also hurting and broken just like he has made all of these family members.

'You really need to be delivered,' she pronounced before walking slowly back to her seat.

When each of the female family members went up to the lectern to say their statements, DA Beth Silverman gently stroked their backs, giving them the strength to be able to speak and clearly showing how much compassion she had for all of them.

The Judge then told the court that the last family member had spoken, and then turned to Franklin and said, 'Now the time has come…' She went on to say that the eleven women were all defenceless and not a threat to him in any way. How there was no justification for what he had done as it was not justifiable under the laws of God nor the laws of man.

After saying the names of each and every victim, Judge Kennedy then said these words, 'It is the judgment and sentence of this court, you shall suffer the death penalty.' She said that the total restitution that Franklin owed was $22,478.22 and he agreed to this amount (restitution is for funeral and burial costs). She stated, as is always said at the sentencing of a death penalty case, the defendant would be taken to San Quentin State Prison within ten days of that date. Franklin sat there with the same blank look on his face as he has done throughout the trial. I was relieved for the family members that justice was finally served.

This concluded the final day of a highly emotional six-month trial, decades of pain experienced by all family members, and frustration and time wasted by all law enforcement who knew from the start this man was guilty but had taken over six years to prove it. Everyone was in the courtroom at this time including the prosecution and the defence.

It was all over. First, I shook the hands of both prosecutors, Beth Silverman and Marguerite Rizzo, and told them what a fantastic job they had done. I gave a big hug to Detective Dupree, who is not only a great detective but also an outstanding human being. Then I shook hands with and gave a hug to so many of the family members who must have been so relieved that justice had finally been served. Following this I went downstairs and said my goodbyes to all of the sheriff deputies I had got to know for the past five months and others over the past six years. It's sad when you see people every day that you may never see again.

THE TRIAL

It was the culmination of another incredible experience in my life where I worked so very hard in trying my best to document all the testimonies, the emotions and the physical attributes of certain people tried and really just to put the reader in the courtroom with me.

EPILOGUE

ANITA LIMBRICK

Along with a large and very loving family, few people know that Alicia 'Monique' Alexander had a big sister who is currently an LA County Sheriff deputy. Anita Limbrick has been with the LA County Sheriff's Department for twenty-eight years and was in the Sheriff Academy when the tragic news of her sister's passing happened. Anita was twenty-six and Alicia barely eighteen years old when the tragedy occurred. She left home when Alicia was nine years old as she was headed for UC Berkeley, so she wasn't living in the family home at the time. However, she would talk to her family daily.

Anita applied, a year before her sister's death, to the Sheriff Academy. She wanted to be a cop because she was very athletic and preferred to apply for the Sheriff's Department than LAPD. A lot of her family is in the Sheriff's Department and LAPD and also in law enforcement in other areas of California. A sergeant pulled her out of her class in the academy when he found out the sad news about her sister, and asked if she'd prefer to go to the academy later, but Anita wanted to continue as she knew this was what her sister would have wanted her to do.

With fond memories Anita looked back on the bond she had with her younger sister and with a smile she said:

'Alicia loved people – no one was ever a stranger to her. She loved pleasing people all the time and loved living her life to the fullest. She was a really fun-loving happy girl and everyone around her couldn't help but to love her too. In fact she would often enter competitions and even wanted to grow up to be a singer. She just loved to sing.'

The Alexander family was, and still is, a very open and inviting family. So much so that they would let various people live with them over the years. Many were kids who just needed a place to stay for a while as they weren't being treated right at home and some were adults. When Alicia was about fifteen or sixteen Anita knew that she did experiment with smoking marijuana as she would smell it when she came home. This progressed after a while to crack cocaine. To her family's dismay, she hung out with other girls who did crack as well, so they knew about her drug use and didn't like it at all. They even tried to get her into a rehab but she assured her parents that she could stop on her own. On the day she was killed, Anita had assured her family that she wasn't doing crack cocaine at the time.

Crack is one of the hardest drugs to give up, some say it takes a hold of you even more than heroin, but Alicia was an honest girl and they believed that she truly wasn't doing cocaine. There was no doubt she was trying to quit and her whole family were behind her all the way. In fact her parents, Mary and Porter, were watching her constantly at the house to make sure she didn't leave to take any drugs and that she'd always come home safely every night – which she always did.

In fact Alicia never needed money as her generous brothers and parents would give her money regularly. We know there was never any money exchanged with the monster who took her life out, in fact it was quite the opposite. Both Anita and her brother Donnell believe that she knew Lonnie Franklin from the neighbourhood. 'There's no way she would ever get in a car with someone she didn't know, or know of. She wasn't like that. Maybe she was just too trusting,' they both stressed to me in their own ways. However, on that fateful night in September 1988 she innocently did get in the orange Pinto with Franklin for whatever reason. It might be because he offered her drugs, or perhaps because 'no one was a stranger to sweet Alicia'. Sadly we will never know.

Anita wants to see the death penalty carried out on Lonnie Franklin – and soon. She feels her sister would want the same fate for him too.

★ ★ ★

DONNELL ALEXANDER

Anita's younger brother and Alicia's older brother, Donnell Alexander, is a man whom I had got to know since late 2010. I had seen Donnell, his mother Mary, his father Porter and his younger brother Darren in the courtroom over the years of countess pre-trial hearings.

Along with the rest of his family, Donnell always dressed as if they were going to church. Always wearing a well-tailored suit, he would nod to me every time we shared the same bench in Department 109 on the ninth floor of the Criminal Courts Building. Over the years the nods would turn into a pleasant exchange and sometimes often a mutual heavy sigh of frustration, with a shake of our heads in disgust at the tactics that Seymour Amster would play in delaying the trial date even further. I would try to put myself in their shoes and wondered what they were thinking about why I was there.

When Donnell and I talked, he spoke with tears in his eyes of all of the great memories he has of his baby sister. Some from sadness at her loss, but most were of the loving memories he has which he holds so dear to his heart. Donnell was seven years old when this beautiful baby girl entered the world. She was christened 'Alicia Monique Alexander'. The whole family loved both names, and as Donnell says, 'Some days she was "Alicia" and we would call her that and on other days they would call her "Monique". She was just so cute. She learned to walk earlier than any other kid and even almost potty-trained herself at a much younger age than any other toddler.'

It was a great surprise for Donnell and the rest of the family that this little girl knew so much and she was still only a toddler. Her eagerness to learn amazed them every day. She even learned some Spanish when she was in nursery school. Donnell said, 'What a bundle of joy she was and always full of such excitement.'

EPILOGUE

The Alexander family all went to church every Sunday after breakfast all together and Alicia would happily come along, looking as pretty as she always did. They did this throughout her childhood and with all the family into adulthood. Alicia was a good girl and loved her family deeply.

I asked Donnell about the pain he felt at that tragic time in September of 1988, and being a very emotional man, it devastated him and still does to this day. But he's strong and sees everything in life as positive and moving forward. When I asked him about that day, he said of his baby sister, 'Alicia was like Little Red Riding Hood. She was on her way to Grandma's house and then the big bad wolf came.'
He then went on to say this short analogy for other parents, 'When you send your little girl out, you must make sure she doesn't lose her direction.'

Donnell was twenty-five years old when his eighteen-year-old sister's life was cut way too short. However, this positive family only sees good and moves forward with love in their hearts. To this day Donnell feels like his life is like being in a playing field and his baby sister 'Monique' is up in heaven watching him from the sky like a guardian angel – this is what keeps him going every day. He also feels, 'If "Monique" was alive today, she would be most likely be counselling kids, ice-skating, doing sports. She would most definitely be in the field helping people and she'd probably have three kids at least by now.' He chuckled at the vision of how grown-up Alicia would be today.

Donnell stood firm when he said that if his sister had a voice right now, she would forgive Franklin for what he did to her.

'She would forgive him and wash her hands of him,' he said with a loving smile. 'Because she was a good Christian, she would forgive him for he knew not what he was doing. He was under a demonic power or control. He's [referring to Franklin] been used as a tool to take out good people.'

On a personal level Donnell just wants Franklin 'to go back to wherever he came from'. The Alexander family are not a judgemental family in any way so I took that to mean 'the earth'. He should go back to the dust, the earth he came from – just no longer exist in the world as a human form.

I wanted to know what Donnell and his family thought of the defence lawyer, Seymour Amster, and still he refuses to say a cruel word about anyone.

'Well, that was a test for our whole family.' This was of course regarding having to deal with such a seemingly unbalanced and unprofessional person for all those years and the games he played during the trial and leading up to it. He continued with, 'and I'm glad we all passed that test.' Oh, they passed the test all right – they passed with flying colours!

The Alexander family have never been the same since that tragic day. When it first happened and for years after, their mother Mary could barely eat. Porter and Mary were just two people existing in the same home and barely functioning. Now, decades later, still as close-knit a family as you could ever imagine, they live their lives day to day and get through. The memory of Alicia 'Monique' is with each of them every day. I know with their positive attitudes they think of all the good times they had. They hold no hate in their hearts, which amazes me.

EPILOGUE

If we could all take a leaf out of the Alexander family's book, we would learn how to be better people. I hope I can. I'm so appreciative of them all for giving me the chance to get to know them and Alicia, before she went to heaven, and for them to share with me such a deep and personal experience.

★ ★ ★

DETECTIVE DARREN DUPREE

Growing up as a young child in South Central Los Angeles and being a black male, Detective Darren Dupree knew the very same streets Franklin trawled. Little Darren Dupree would walk really fast down those very same dirty alleyways when he'd take the shortcuts on his way to 95th Elementary School to get to the bus stop on time. Those were the very same alleyways where Lonnie Franklin Jr so callously dumped the bodies of unsuspecting young black women he had used for whatever he could get from them. Oftentimes Dupree would see dead bodies littering the alleys back in the eighties when he was just an innocent child walking to school. Little did he know that a few decades later he was to be in charge of one of the most prolific serial killer cases in Los Angeles history. Nothing was out of the ordinary to see the bodies of those who had most likely died of a crack overdose or been killed by a pimp, because there was a crack epidemic at the time Dupree was growing up. Sadly, law enforcement just didn't have enough manpower to close every one of those cases.

Detective Dupree is a very sophisticated, good-looking and highly personable man. When he has time, he has time for everyone no matter who you are – he's the least judgemental person you could ever wish to meet. Dupree was Homicide Detective Greg Kading's right hand man on the task force of this case, and the two had previously worked together closely to uncover more into the lives of American rappers Tupac Shakur and Biggie Smalls after they were killed in 1996 and 1997 respectively. The Biggie Smalls case had only just been disbanded when Dupree joined the Grim Sleeper case a week before Franklin's arrest in July of 2010.

The Grim Sleeper task force aka '.25 Calibre Auto' was formed in 2007. Dupree took part in screening over 400 cases of dead and missing person females from 1976 when Franklin came home from Germany until 2010 when he was caught. These were all cases from South Central Los Angeles. They even had a number of suspects who were being looked at, but there was never a clear-cut suspect in any of those cases. Until the day when an undercover detective pretended to be a busboy in a restaurant in Buena Park called John's Incredible Pizza, and Franklin's DNA was taken from various items including a small piece of uneaten pizza. That was when they found their man.

When I asked what he thought about the period of time when Franklin apparently didn't kill, Dupree quickly said that he never thought The Grim Sleeper ever 'slept' in those thirteen years: 'However, I do think that he might've stopped killing for a temporary period after the Enietra Washington attack on 11.20.1988. The reason being was because he knew she had survived as it was talked about in the media. The following case that I worked on after that was in 2002, with Princess Berthomieux.'

Detective Dupree feels that one of the reasons why Lonnie

EPILOGUE

Franklin murdered these women in South Central LA, his own community, was because of an event in Germany. Franklin was stationed in Germany while in the Army and he'd told me all about his romantic escapades with women over there. However, I now realise just how fabricated these stories were. A rape is not a 'romantic encounter', which is how he described it to me. Hence I will continue.

Franklin told me in one of my interviews about him and his buddies going out on the town in Germany and meeting up with a girl who they all had sex with because 'she was so loose'. Foolishly, I actually believed him.

The truth of the matter was he raped this poor young woman. He raped her brutally with his two buddies, who held a knife to her face. Thankfully, not long after, he was caught and convicted of rape. The victim, Ingrid W., was able to lure him back the next day with the promise of a 'date' and Franklin fell for the bait only to find the cops were there laying in, waiting to take him down.

After spending just under a year in jail for this crime, although he had been sentenced to one year and four months, the way it all went down stuck in Franklin's head forever. He then had a vendetta out for any feisty and clever females who would cross his path. Detective Dupree felt that this is one of the reasons he would be nice to some females he knew who would work in the street, yet others he would kill and discard as if they were trash if they gave him any kind of a problem.

Strangely enough, Franklin was never known to be a sexual deviant in his school years, Dupree explained. He was never in trouble for fighting or being aggressive so when the rape in Germany happened, Ingrid led Dupree to believe that Franklin was the least aggressive of the three men. In fact, the other two were brutal, she told him. Dupree said: 'Franklin is smart and calculating and became streetwise by hanging on with people on the streets. That's when he started to show aggression. But he was a little man, with a "little man's complex", so he had to use a gun.'

I asked if there was any kind of a relationship that Detective Dupree had with Franklin, but he was quick to say, 'Not at all because he lawyered up the moment he gave the initial interview with Detective Kilcoyne and Detective Coulter. That was the day he was arrested,' and there was no talking to him past that point. However, Franklin would always nod to Dupree in court every day. Well, they were only sitting three seats away from each other.

When I asked this seasoned detective whether he thought Franklin was a sociopath or a psychopath, he immediately fired back with 'He's a lot of both of those! He's a rejected small little man that would brag and boast. All he does is talk, talk, talk from one subject to the next to make himself look bigger than he is. He would brag about the photos he took of all the women and the prostitutes. He had to have the most women, the most photos. He had a little man's complex and was a know-it-all.'

Franklin's older brother, Christopher, caused a lot of damage to Franklin's childhood (according to Franklin himself) in making him feel inferior by continuously dismissing him when his little brother needed him most. According to Detective Dupree, 'Franklin had no redeeming qualities at all! He was clever, he stopped killing for a few years because he thought he was going to get caught – he thought his wife would find out about it so he had to keep her at bay. She didn't go in that garage; she didn't bother with anything outside of that back door. Had she set foot in that garage or that camper, she would've seen all the nudie photos and known. But it was a dirty grimy mess back there so she never went back there.'

When I pressed him further about why nobody showed up at the penalty phase of the trial to support Franklin, Dupree continued on: 'They [his family] knew he did it, but in the black community you respect your dad and stand by the ones that stand around. This was why they didn't show up – they couldn't face the situation.'

What he was telling me was that in the black community, the fathers who don't take off and leave the mother to raise the child by herself are very hard to come by. So a father who still stays with the family, as Franklin Jr did, is a father to be respected no matter what. Most men will leave the child with the mother, who then has to take on the added responsibility of playing both parental roles.

Detective Dupree firmly believes that the total number of murders that Lonnie Franklin most likely committed was between twenty and twenty-five, but those cases were never closed for various reasons.

★★★

From the day of Franklin's sentencing, it was mandatory that within ten days of the Judge's decision, Lonnie Franklin must be released from the Men's Central Jail and immediately taken into the custody of the San Quentin State Prison, where

Death Row is located. From there he would spend a number of months being graded and housed in the Adjustment Centre (the AC), which is a section of the prison. He would either be graded A or B and then be moved to East Block, which is the main part of Death Row.

An 'A' grade means that a condemned inmate is trusted enough to have some kind of leniency in his lifestyle. This means that he will most likely be put on a yard with inmates similar to himself. He will be allowed a television, a radio and various packages to be sent to him by his family if they wish to do so. He will also be allowed contact visits with his visitor(s) in a cage for up to five hours each time.

If he were to be graded 'B', he would not be allowed any of the privileges I've described above and would only be allowed one-hour visits from behind glass.

We all know that Lonnie Franklin deserves none of this because of the heinous crimes he committed and the families he ruined in his wake. However, this is the justice system here in California, and while we have such a weak Governor in office, it is unlikely he will ever get close to the death chamber: he will die of old age before his time is up.

This concludes the end of a very sad chapter in the lives of so many innocent family members. These innocent families are the main victims here. Our justice system is broken. It shouldn't have taken over five and a half years to come to trial, especially when this was a slam-dunk case of 100 per cent guilt! Seymour Amster should not have been allowed to continue with his craziness and utter disrespect of the Judge and the prosecution and many of the witnesses who testified. A lot needs to change in the American justice

EPILOGUE

system today, and I hope and pray I will see it happen within the next decade. When I look back on my interviews with Franklin, I find myself thinking about how different he was to the other serial killers I've met and questioned. I didn't find him to be controlling, nor did he seem to take pride in his crimes (not all serial killers take pride in their crimes, but some do). In fact, he never spoke about them. He always had boundless energy, and his mind and eyes would be all over the place, causing me to have to constantly reel him in. I found Franklin to be a total gossip and a bit of a busybody. If anything, this made talking to him even more unnerving. As for myself, I haven't heard from Franklin since he arrived on Death Row and have now moved on from writing books on such depraved killers to a completely different, yet very exciting and fulfilling, career.

My book is dedicated to all of the innocent souls who are no longer with us here on earth, but will forever remain in our hearts:

Debra Jackson (1956–1985), aged twenty-nine;
Henrietta Wright (1951–1986), aged thirty-five;
Barbara Ware (1964–1987), aged twenty-three;
Bernita Sparks (1964–1987), aged twenty-three;
Mary Lowe (1961–1987), aged twenty-six;
Lachrica Jefferson (1966–1988), aged twenty-two;
Alicia 'Monique' Alexander (1970–1988), aged eighteen;
Princess Berthomieux (1987–2002), aged fifteen;
Valerie McCorvey (1968 –2003), aged thirty-five;
Janecia Peters (1983–2008), aged twenty-five.

THE GRIM SLEEPER

It is also dedicated to to the victims whom Franklin is suspected of killing, including Sharon Dismuke, Rolenia Morris, Georgia Mae Thomas, Ayellah Marshall, Inez Warren and to the gutsy Enietra Washington whose life was spared. May God bless you all and may you rest in peace knowing that justice has finally been served.

ABOUT THE AUTHOR

Victoria Redstall is a British author, investigative journalist and true crime expert. Working closely with US law enforcement over the years, Redstall has interviewed many of America's most feared serial killers in prison and appeared on television as a consultant and correspondent on American homicides. She is also the author of *Serial Killers: Up Close and Very Personal* and lives in Los Angeles.